Acknowledgments

During the writing of this second edition I have become aware that thanks are due not only to those who have helped with this edition but also to those who gave me so much help with the first. It is appropriate therefore to record the continuing assistance provided, without their knowledge, by John Blackmore, Howard Levenson and Gail Williams. Jeremy Cooper, Joan Fletcher, Gerry Horwood and Jeremy Roche, all of whom helped me with the first edition, and were prepared to do so again for the second edition; many thanks are due to them for their time, their ideas and their corrections.

The London Borough of Richmond upon Thames again allowed me to discuss my work with one of their senior social workers, Trisha Comley. Her enthusiasm for the project has been unstinting and on countless occasions she has provided information and comment about the practice of social work and the relationship between the law and that practice. Her contribution has been invaluable.

Interest and encouragement has again been provided by Caroline Ball and Gwyneth Roberts, fellow members of the Social Work and Law Research Group.

I am delighted to acknowledge the help given to me by all these people. Errors in the text are my sole responsibility.

Acknowledgment is made to the Child Poverty Action Group and the Welfare Rights Bulletin for permission to reproduce the social security benefit rates at the end of Chapter 11. The Children Act forms, which are reproduced at the end of Chapter 3, and the Mental Health Act forms, which are reproduced at the end of Chapter 8 are Crown copyright and are reproduced with the permission of the Controller of Her Majesty's Stationery Office.

Koblers Bakery, St. Margarets, again sustained me during the writing of this edition and has this time been joined by the Turks Head. The now ageing Amstrad word processor has performed faultlessly, though a strange buzzing sound is beginning to make itself heard as I make this acknowledgment to the 'green screen'.

My family have always supported and encouraged me during the writing of this second edition. For this, and for many other things, I dedicate this to Sue, Kate and Laura with many thanks and much love.

St. Margarets.
April 1993.

Stop Press

Two particular aspects of the Criminal Justice Act 1991, the operation of the unit fine system and the limited ability of courts to take previous offences into account when sentencing, have been subject to considerable public criticism and media comment since the implementation of the Act in October 1992. On 13 May 1993 the Home Secretary, Kenneth Clarke, announced significant reforms to the Act.

The unit fine system is to be abolished, though courts will still be required to take an offender's ability to pay into account when fixing the level of a fine. Sentencing courts will again be allowed to consider all offences before the court and an offender's previous criminal record when deciding on an appropriate sentence.

It is expected that the necessary amendments to the Act will become law in June 1993.

References to the unit fine system and to sentencing decisions in chapter 6, on the criminal justice system, particularly sections 2.5, 2.6.1 and 2.6.3, and in chapter 7, on youth justice, particularly sections 2.6, 2.7.1 and 2.7.3, should be read as subject to these changes.

Stuart Vernon.
15 May 1993.

Contents

Chapter 4   The breakdown of domestic relationships   85

Table of Statutes

Using the book

This book is written as a basic text for the Diploma in Social Work; the qualifying course taken by social work students. It is also expected that it will be of use to those in practice, particularly in the years immediately after qualification, and to a wider audience within the legal profession and those working within the general field of social welfare .

The subject matter included ranges from the law that is relevant to the major areas of practice, such as child care, child protection, youth justice and work with people who have a physical disability or learning difficulty, to areas of law which are relevant across the full spectrum of practice and client groups such as social security benefits, housing rights and race. Every attempt has been made to place the discussion of law within the context of practice and to identify the dynamics of the relationship between law and social work practice.

Since the publication of the first edition of this book the statutory framework of social work has undergone a number of significant changes. The Children Act 1989 was implemented in October 1991, the Criminal Justice Act 1991 in October 1992 and the National Health Service and Community Care Act 1990 in April 1993. The speed and complexity of changes in practice required by these pieces of legislation is considerable; discussion of the impact of this new statutory framework must therefore remain relatively speculative until a few years of experience allows firm conclusions to be drawn.

An attempt has been made to make each chapter self-contained in the sense that each provides a discussion which can stand on its own without the need for frequent cross references to other chapters. This allows readers to dip in and out of the book when this is necessary. This has meant that there are some inevitable repetitions particularly in the chapters on the criminal justice system and the youth justice system; similar overlaps will be found in the chapters on the Children Act 1989 and the breakdown of domestic relationships.

THE STRUCTURE OF THE BOOK

Each chapter of the book, except for the chapters on the legal system and on social workers, lawyers and the courts, follows the same format. It is hoped that once readers become familiar with the structure they will be able to use those parts of each chapter which are appropriate to their course or to their particular needs.

An INTRODUCTION seeks to set the scene by establishing the relationship between the particular aspect of the law considered in the chapter and social work practice. Some information on chapter content may also be provided.

The section on THE LAW provides information on the relevant law and legal processes, placing such information in the context of practice wherever possible.

The third section of each chapter, SOCIAL WORK LAW AND PRACTICE: issues for discussion, is more discursive, dealing with issues concerning the relationship between law and practice that are of significance or contemporary interest. Often this section will look at the debate or agenda for reform.

As part of a desire to allow the book to be used within a model of interactive teaching and learning each chapter provides a number of CASE STUDIES which can be used as a basis for consolidating an understanding of the area of law, for discussing how the law relates to practice and for identifying models of legally competent practice. There are no right answers to these case studies, they are merely vehicles for teaching and learning to be used where they might be of some benefit.

The ACTIVITIES section is included to encourage an active participation in learning which goes beyond the classroom and the agency placement. Some of the suggested activities can be used to consolidate work done in college or on placement, others are specifically designed to enable students to build up collections of materials and to keep up to date with contemporary developments in both the law and practice.

A selection of ADDRESSES and telephone numbers are included to enable students to contact pressure groups, publishers and other interests. Again this information is included as part of the objective of making the book participative and of studying law in the context of social work practice.

No attempt has been made to provide a definitive list of relevant groups and addresses. The more use is made of the ACTIVITIES and ADDRESSES sections the more names and addresses will be identified. There is an enormous amount of good quality materials available to those who are interested and a surprising amount is available free of charge.

Suggested MATERIALS for 'ordinary practice' have been identified in the final section of each chapter. Again, this is not intended to be definitive but merely to give some indication of materials which will be useful in practice. An attempt has been made to keep references to 'textbooks' to the further reading section.

STUDYING SOCIAL WORK LAW

The need continually to up date information and build up a set of materials on the law as it relates to social work practice complements the desire to make the teaching and learning of law on social work courses a participative exercise. There are, of course, a number of ways of achieving this objective and examples are to be found in the activities section of each chapter. Students can also be encouraged to keep a 'scrap book' of newspaper cuttings; the quality press coverage of relevant issues is considerable and is a good source of comment and information. Video collections can be established by groups of students and small study groups can share information and materials collected whilst on placement. Bulletin boards can be created and continually up dated to the benefit of the whole course group. Involvement in creating course materials and using such materials to extend the basis for discussion can only enhance the quality of a course and of student commitment to it.

Teachers will have developed their own individual courses and methods over a period of time and there is no intention to supplant tried and successful methods and materials. This book is intended to be used as a vehicle for teaching and learning and it can be used in a number of different ways. Nonetheless it is hoped that it will be found useful and help in consolidating 'social work and the law', or 'social work law', as a major element of social work training courses and an enjoyable and stimulating discourse within social work.

Introduction

The first edition of this book, which was published in the summer of 1990, made frequent reference to the rapid pace of change in the law as it relates to the professional practice of social work. Such comments envisaged the need to update the information contained in the first edition; 3 years later that need is such that this second edition includes substantial changes in a number of areas.

The implementation of the Children Act in October 1991 has changed the legal structure within which social work practice with children and families takes place and has substantially altered the work of the courts dealing with such a jurisdiction. The Criminal Justice Act 1991 was implemented on 1 October 1992 and has already had a considerable impact on the sentencing practice of the criminal courts. The Act also created the Youth Court which now deals with 17 year old defendants in addition to the 10-16 year old defendants dealt with by the old Juvenile Court. The National Health Service and Community Care Act 1990 was implemented in April 1993 and the legislation is, in its turn, having a significant impact on the provision of care and other services for large numbers of vulnerable people.

Though the frequency and speed of change in the law relating to social work will again feature as a context for this second edition it is to be hoped that a period of 'legal stability' is now established in which social workers can develop the knowledge, skills and values appropriate to professional practice within this radically changed legal structure.

This edition has taken account of helpful comment by reviewers of the first edition. There is now a table of statutes, diagrammatic representations of the courts and an extended discussion of social workers, lawyers and the courts. The opportunity has been taken to add a new chapter on Education and the Law.

The law that is described and discussed is that which is in force in England and Wales.

SOCIAL WORK AND THE LAW

The law sets the statutory framework for social work in a number of settings and with particular client groups. This aspect of the relationship between law and social work practice is sometimes identified by the phrase 'the professional law of social work'. The areas of practice so designated include child care, mental health, work with people who are elderly, have a chronic illness, a physical disability or learning difficulty, youth justice and probation work. Within these areas of work the statutory framework is marked out by a number of powers and duties enacted by Parliament. Examples include the power of a local authority to take care proceedings under section 31 of the Children Act 1989 and the duty of a local authority under section 47 of the same Act to investigate any situation where they have information suggesting that there may be grounds for bringing care proceedings in respect of a child or young person in their area. Other powers and duties are attached to individual social workers rather than local authorities; an example is the power of an approved social worker to apply for the admission of a patient to psychiatric hospital under the provisions of the Mental Health Act 1983.

An explanation of the concepts of a 'power' and a 'duty' is necessary. A 'power' allows a local authority or social worker to decide whether to do something; it is a 'may' concept. A 'duty' imposes a requirement on an authority or social worker to do something; it is a 'shall' concept. Powers and duties are important concepts in the professional law of social work and it is necessary to understand when a power is provided by Parliament and when a duty is imposed.

'Powers' and 'duties' are often joined with the concept of a 'right'. This concept is less easy to define and it is usually used to describe an entitlement to something as in 'a client's rights'. The notion of a right should be widely understood and can encompass eg housing and welfare rights and the right of social workers and clients not to be discriminated against on the basis of race or gender. These are legal rights in the sense that they may be enforced through the law. Other rights are more nebulous eg the right of an elderly person to be treated with dignity and the right of patients to self determination.

It is clear therefore that the relationship between law and social work extends beyond the statutory framework of powers and duties covered by the professional law of social work to encompass areas of law where clients have legal 'rights'. Equally important is the ability to enforce entitlement to these rights so that an understanding of the legal system and of legal services is also necessary to enable clients to gain access to the law.

Any book on social work and the law must cover the statutory framework of the professional law of social work as a minimum. But practitioners and clients will confront the law in other ways, many of which do not fit within the clients group structure of the professional law. It is necessary therefore to acknowledge this feature of social work practice and to consider, in addition to the professional law of the client groups, the other issues of housing, welfare rights, race and relationship breakdown. The result is that this book takes a wide definition of the law that is relevant for social work. No apology is made for this though one is no doubt necessary for those areas which have been omitted and which particular readers think should have been included.

PUBLIC CONCERN OVER SOCIAL WORK AND THE LAW

That the law is these days publicly acknowledged as one of the principal contexts of social work practice is due to a number of factors. The published reports of a number of child abuse inquiries in the late 1980s received enormous media comment; these, in turn, have been superseded by reports in the last 18 months on the experience of children whilst in the care of local authorities in different parts of the country.[1]

The high profile implementation of the Children Act 1989 took place at the same time as the public debate concerning policies associated with community care provisions of the National Health Service and Community Care Act. Publicity surrounding the new sentencing provisions of the Criminal Justice Act 1991

---

[1] Eg the Staffordshire 'pin down' inquiry and the successful prosecution of Frank Beck for indecent assaults on children in local authority care.

has also been significant. The result is that issues concerning the legal context surrounding social work now 'enjoy' a high public profile at the same time as professional interest is centred on developing practice within the Children Act and the new Criminal Justice Act, and with the implementation of community care legislation.

THE POSITION OF LAW IN SOCIAL WORK TRAINING

In social work education the importance of the legal context has been recognised for some considerable time. In 1974 the Central Council for Education and Training in Social Work (CCETSW) published Paper 4 'Legal Studies in Social Work Education'. The group concerned in preparing the report had received a number of criticisms about the state of social workers' knowledge of law. These criticisms centred on a perceived lack of knowledge and understanding of the specific law relating to the professional practice of social work and of the administration of the law and the legal system. Concern was also expressed that social workers lacked knowledge of their clients' general legal rights. The report advocated an increased recognition of the importance of law teaching in social work education and offered a quite detailed framework for the necessary development.

However, new research undertaken in 1987, and published by CCETSW in 1988 as Paper 4.1 'The Law Report, Teaching and Assessment of Law in Social Work Education', found that on many courses law teaching was still very much a marginal activity and that there were huge variations in the quality of law teaching, the content of law courses and of commitment to it as a major area of study for social work students. In the more than 10 years since Paper 4 had been published it seemed that little had changed.

The publication of the Law Report came in the same era as the publication of the reports of a number of major child abuse inquiries. They drew specific attention to the legal aspects of child care practice and of child protection work. Indeed Louis Blom-Cooper in 'A Child in Trust: The Report of the Panel of Inquiry into the Circumstances Surrounding the Death of Jasmine Beckford' paid particular attention to social work training and to the place of law teaching in it. Dissatisfaction with the situation exposed by the inquiry is reflected in the report's comment that 'Training in legal studies must not be allowed to remain any longer the Cinderella of social work training.'

The Social Work and Law Group which undertook the research that formed the basis of the Law Report continued their work after its publication and with a research grant from CCETSW undertook a further investigation in 1989 which was able to identify an increased interest in, and commitment to, law teaching and assessment on social work courses.[2] The increasing status of law in social work training may owe something to the Law Report but the importance of the abuse inquiries should not be underestimated, not least in their impact in the construction of a demand for legal knowledge from social work students, practitioners and employers.

THE SEARCH FOR 'LEGAL COMPETENCY'

Other factors are also at work. Moves toward the universal adoption of a new social work qualification — the Diploma in Social Work — to be awarded after 'a minimum of two years study and supervised practice at higher education level' are now almost complete.[3] One of the principles of the Diploma in Social Work is a definition of practice competency based on the three elements of knowledge, skills and values. The notion of 'legally competent social work' has been considered by the Law and Social Work Research Group in their report, published as Paper 4.2 (see above). Arguing from the principle that all law teaching on social work courses should be 'vocational' in the sense of informing and being informed by practice, the report concludes that placement is central to the 'legal education' of social work students. Concentrating on the elements of knowledge and skills, the report rejects an educational structure which allots knowledge teaching to the colleges and skills teaching to placement, and argues for the development of a 'social work law' which would form the basis of teaching and learning in college and on placement.

[2] 'Towards Social Work Law: Legally Competent Social Work Practice'. Published by CCETSW in 1990 as Paper 4.2.
[3] See: 'Requirements and Regulations for the Diploma in Social Work'. CCETSW Paper 30. 1989.

TOWARDS 'SOCIAL WORK LAW'

Taking the constituents of competence as knowledge, skills and values 'social work law' may be seen to encompass:

* substantive legal knowledge pertinent to specific client groups;

* substantive legal knowledge transcending client groups and relating to social work conceptualisations as a whole;

* the development of conceptualisations which help in understanding the relationship and interaction between social work, its practice and the law;

* an understanding of relevant legal processes and procedures;

* an identification and development of relevant skills for 'legal competence';

* an identification and development of social work legal roles and of the values that underpin them.

Together these elements might form the basis for the establishment of 'social work law' as not only an area of legitimate enquiry but an 'applied subject' in its own right.

THE LAW IMPROVEMENTS PROJECT

In 1990 CCETSW initiated a Law Improvements Project to inform the law elements of the new Diploma. The aims of the project were:

> to improve the quality and effectiveness of the teaching and learning of law and of the assessment of legal competence on social work qualifying courses.

More particularly the project was charged with identifying the core competencies (knowledge, skills and values) in law required of all social workers; with working towards the effective integration of college and placement based teaching and learning; and in developing teaching methods and models of good practice for achieving these. Additionally CCETSW asked the project to distinguish what law teaching and learning is 'core' for all social workers, what can be left to new areas of particular practice which all students will develop as part of their qualifying training, and what has to be left to post qualifying training.[4]

The project was completed in 1991 and its report was published by CCETSW in October of that year under the title 'Teaching, Learning and Assessing Social Work Law'.

The report provides a model social work core law curriculum for Diploma students which acknowledges the elements of knowledge, skills and values.

In many respects the report can be seen as providing a curriculum checklist or specification for law teaching on Diploma in Social Work courses; as such the opportunity is taken here to quote at length from Chapter 3 — 'The Aims of Law Teaching on DipSW Courses'.

3.4.1 Knowledge: Students need to understand:

a) that the law gives social workers their licence to practice:

    i) as employees of statutory bodies (when, for example, employed as a local authority social worker), or as officers of the court (when employed, for example as a probation officer);

    ii) by defining the various client groups towards whom social workers have responsibility;

    iii) by defining a social worker's legal functions in relation to each client group;

b) that the law is a tool which, when correctly used, promotes and encourages good social work practice: eg by emphasising prevention and rehabilitation, by setting out the conditions upon which compulsory powers to set aside a client's rights accord with proper legal safeguards, such as due process of law;

c) that social and legal institutions and processes, such as the court system, to which social workers' practice most often relate, are frequently identified as discriminatory and racist in operation and practice.

---

[4] As part of their qualification trainee social workers will be expected to acquire 'competence in working with individuals and families and groups over a sustained period in a particular area of practice within the relevant legal and organisational frameworks'. CCETSW Paper 30.

Students need to know:

a) the substantive law relevant to social work practice, its nature and sources;

b) the relationship between local authority policy and the law;

c) the structures and processes of the relevant court and tribunal systems.

3.4.2 Values: Students need to have:

a) a commitment to social justice and the concept of equal opportunities: eg the right of individuals to receive care/treatment and control in the context of:

— the least restrictive alternative;

— normalisation/non-stigmatisation;

— anti-discriminatory, anti-racist practice;

— ethnic/cultural/language needs;

with access to appeal and choice, as far as it is possible;

b) a commitment to social order: eg the right of society to protection from significant risk, danger of harm; recognition of the rights of significant others eg victims.

Issues of discrimination and civil rights are intrinsic to these values/ aims, and social work law courses will need to consider them regularly and routinely as they affect social work practice and social services provision.

3.4.3 Skills: should include:

a) cognitive, interpersonal, decision-making and administrative skills eg ability to assess, to plan, to communicate, to provide support for clients, families and carers;

b) ability to work in an anti-discriminatory, anti-racist mode; to use correct and appropriate knowledge and values in the interest of the client, the agency, the courts and society;

c) ability to conduct him/herself appropriately in adult and youth criminal courts; in family proceedings courts in England and Wales; .... Ability to prepare and present evidence.

d) development of appropriate report-writing techniques;

e) ability to work in a multi-disciplinary setting eg with lawyers, police, doctors and health visitors;

f) ability to use emergency procedures appropriately in relation to all client groups.

From this 'prospectus' for the legal aspect of social work teaching it is clear that this area of teaching and learning is both considerable and complex in its inter-relationship between the knowledge, skills and values of social work law. Nonetheless it is now recognised as having an identity which marks it out as an essential element of training courses and of competent qualifying social workers. Those who teach, study and practise within this aspect of social work are themselves part of the development of 'social work law' and of a legally competent social worker profession properly qualified to practise their profession within the legal framework laid down by Parliament and to the benefit of their clients and of society.

CHAPTER 1

Social workers, lawyers and the courts

1 INTRODUCTION

The courts are often perceived by social workers as a frightening and even hostile environment. Lawyers are seen as coming from a distinct professional position which may not be sympathetic to the concerns and interests of social work and its clients; magistrates and judges wield considerable decision making powers, the exercise of which may support the aims and values of social work, but equally may frustrate them. Important aspects of social work are subject to the control and scrutiny of statutory provisions and judicial decision making; indeed this external legal reference is crucial to the place of social work in our society and is one of the mediums through which the profession is accountable for its actions.

Social workers who are frequent players in the courts or who work closely with the law, have a professional understanding and even familiarity with its provisions and practice. A professional 'ease' with the law becomes part of their competency as a social worker. Though other social workers may never attain this position, an understanding of the circumstances in which a social worker must deal with courts of law and with lawyers may help to reduce the anxiety and unease which often accompanies this aspect of practice.

Lawyers in England and Wales are common lawyers; they have been educated and socialised into a particular way of thinking about the problems that clients bring to them. The common law has historically been developed through case law in the sense that disputes have come before the courts for resolution and the judges have developed legal rules to decide the cases before them. In this sense the common law has often had a very practical basis, a pragmatic character that distinguishes it from systems of law which derive their rules from general principles set out in codes of law as is most often the case in continental Europe.

The influence of this historical legacy still has an impact on the way in which lawyers go about their work. Cases are about 'solving problems', 'finding a way out of this' or 'how do we achieve this?'. Being a lawyer is often about working creatively with the law, using the rules where possible to promote the interests and wishes of a client.

Principles that underpin the law in England and Wales are frequently stated in very general terms, be they expressed in an Act of Parliament or in a precedent decision of the House of Lords or the Court of Appeal. This generality facilitates creative work by judges and lawyers and should also encourage social workers not to view the law as a rigid set of rules that control or frustrate their practice. Section 1 of the Children Act 1989, which identifies the welfare of the child as the paramount consideration for the court when it is considering the upbringing of the child, is an example of a general principle within which constructive social work practice can take place. The principle of the Criminal Justice Act 1991 which requires a community sentence to reflect the seriousness of the offence and to be appropriate for the offender in the sense that it addresses his or her offending behaviour and reduces the risk of further offending by the offender, can be understood as another example of a principle which facilitates creative thinking by the social worker or probation officer preparing a pre-sentence report and planning for work with the offender. The flexibility of legal principle as a sight for constructive practice is a feature of English law which applies to the practice of both law and social work.

The relationship between lawyer and client and that between social worker and client are often characterised as being very different. It is possible to argue that because lawyers take instructions from clients their relationship is characterised by the autonomy or self determination of the client. The relationship between social worker and client might be characterised as being different at least to the extent that social work clients do not give 'instructions' and that, in some situations, social workers can trigger the use of compulsory powers in the best interests of their clients eg a compulsory admission to hospital of a person suffering from a mental disorder. Closer analysis of the two relationships suggests that the differences are often much less than this comment suggests.

The ability of a client to instruct his or her lawyer is mediated through a number of factors of which the professional expertise of the lawyer is one and the relative intellectual and material resources of the client is another. Any observer of proceedings in the magistrates' court will be able to provide evidence that the majority of people who appear there do what their lawyers tell them. The essence of the lawyer/client relationship is the request for professional advice; in reality that advice is accepted.

The relationship between social worker and client is subject to a number of principles that underpin social work practice. The self esteem, independence, dignity, individuality and self determination of the client are important objectives for practice.

Differences between the two relationships are most obviously identified in the breadth and depth of the relationship. Clients see lawyers in respect of fairly narrowly defined concerns; for example, when defending a criminal prosecution, or applying for a contact order under the Children Act. The lawyer's interest starts and ends, and is restricted in its scope, by the specific task. The relationship between a social worker and his or her client is far broader and often encompasses much more than the issue which triggered the relationship. This distinction can be seen in the detachment which characterises the relationship between lawyer and client. This detachment is often valued in the sense that it facilitates the taking of an objective view of the circumstances of a client. There are circumstances in which detachment and objectivity are necessary in social work practice but there are also many situations where a practitioner must become involved with the experience of a client and respect a clients subjective definitions of that experience.

When the two professions work together both must be prepared to respect the professional expertise of the other. When a local authority decides to seek a care order local authority lawyers will take instructions from social workers. In such circumstances the need is for objective legal advice on the prospects for such an action. It is not the lawyers' task to advise on whether the care order is necessary for the welfare of the child; but it is their task to advise on whether the local authority has sufficient evidence to satisfy the family proceedings court that the child in question is, for example, suffering significant harm. If the evidence is not there then the application is futile notwithstanding the view of social workers involved in the case that a care order is necessary.

Understanding the work of lawyers and the skills that they bring to their professional task is important for social workers so that they are better able to work with lawyers when called upon to do so.

2   COURT BASED SOCIAL WORK

Social workers are not just observers of the legal system; many are important participants; some occasionally, others on a regular basis. Some indication of the variety of circumstances in which a social work practitioner will be involved in court based work is given below:

i) the probation service has statutory responsibilities within both the criminal justice system and as the court welfare service in family proceedings. Currently social work provides the educational and value base of probation work.

ii) guardians ad litem are charged by the legal system with representing and safeguarding the interests of children involved in a variety of family proceedings. The panels from which courts make appointments are comprised of experienced social workers.

iii) local authority social workers and probation officers are often asked by the youth court to provide pre-sentence reports under the Criminal Justice Act 1991 so that youth offenders can be appropriately sentenced. If a supervision order is made by the court either the social services department, or the probation service for older offenders, will be required to supervise the order. The probation service provides the same service in the Crown Court and adult magistrates' court.

iv) in a hearing to decide on an application for a care order under the Children Act 1989 the court will require a number of welfare reports to assist in the proceedings. It is likely that most will be written by a social worker.

v) social workers apply to the family proceedings court for an emergency protection order under the Children Act 1989 and for warrants so that police officers can enter and search premises for children who need protection.

vi) social workers can apply to the magistrates' court for an order to compulsorily remove an elderly person and others who are unable to care for themselves from their own home under the provisions of the National Assistance Act 1948.

vii) an education welfare officer may apply to the family proceedings panel for an education supervision order under section 36 of the Children Act 1989.

In all these circumstances, and in others, social workers are participants in court based work. They are required by the law and by the nature of particular legal proceedings to undertake a number of roles and functions and it is important for an individual social worker to understand the nature of their involvement in such legal proceedings. There are times when it is difficult to identify the particular role and there may also be conflicts and tensions between different roles.

Three particular roles are considered as examples of this feature of social work practice; the preparation of pre-sentence reports for sentencing in criminal courts; the application for a care order in the family proceedings court and the work of guardians ad litem in the family proceedings court.

2.1 PREPARING PRE-SENTENCE REPORTS

Pre-sentence reports (PSRs) are written by probation officers or social workers to assist sentencers in determining the appropriate sentence for a criminal offender. The sentencers may be judges in the Crown Court or JPs in the adult magistrates' court or in the youth courts. There is little doubt that well prepared written reports are extremely influential in determining the sentence imposed by a criminal court and conversely that an ill prepared and presented report is ineffective and sometimes counter productive in the sense that sentencers reject proposals and choose a different, and possibly, less appropriate sentence.

The preparation of PSRs is now subject to the requirements of the National Standards for the Supervision of Offenders in the Community published by the Home Office in 1992. These standards are detailed and determine that a PSR should address the current offence, provide relevant information about the offender and present a conclusion which may include a proposal for the most suitable community sentence where appropriate.[1] The role of the report writer is identified by the National Standards in the following terms:

> It is essential that advice and information in a PSR is provided *impartially* by the report writer. Thus the PSR must present a balanced picture, drawing fairly on both aggravating and mitigating factors in a case. This does not, however, preclude the report writer from presenting facts or advice relevant to a particular sentence (for example, in supporting a programme of community supervision and drawing attention to the likely negative consequences of custody for the offender or his or her family, or in the case of a violent or sexual offence, including evidence of risk to the public or serious harm from the offender, as a result of which the sentencer may impose custody) *provided* the distinct role of the sentencer is respected.

To the requirement of impartiality in the preparation of PSRs other characteristics and skills need to be added:

— a requirement to work to agency policy and practice;

— an understanding of the policy and practice of the sentencing court;

— good literacy and communication skills;

— an ability to write concisely (National Standards recommend that where possible a PSR should be no longer than two pages);

— sufficient experience to appreciate when it is appropriate to be in court when the PSR is presented and the sentencing decision is made;

— good presentational skills: how to address the sentencing court;

[1] Pre-sentence reports are required by the Criminal Justice Act 1991 where the court is considering a custodial sentence or one of the more serious community sentences, ie a community service order, a combination order, or a probation order or supervision order with additional specified requirements. Sentencing policy and practice under the Criminal Justice Act 1991 is considered in the chapters on the Criminal Justice System and Youth Justice.

— to develop appropriate professional relationships with lawyers mitigating on behalf of offenders who are the subject of a PSR so that the same message is given to the court;

— to develop good working relationships with court officials.

This list can of course be extended; however it should give some idea of the range of skills, knowledge and experience necessary for effective court based work in the preparation and presentation of PSRs.

Should the court decide to impose a supervision order or a probation order then the author of the report may become the supervising officer. If this is the case the role to be adopted, for example, by a probation officer supervising an offender sentenced to a probation order changes to:

a professional relationship, in which to advise, assist and befriend the offender with the aim of:

* securing the offender's co-operation and compliance with the probation order and enforcing its terms;

* challenging the offender to accept responsibility for his or her crime and its consequences;

* helping the offender to resolve personal difficulties linked with offending and to acquire new skills; and

* motivating and assisting the offender to become a responsible and lawabiding member of the community.[2]

2.2   APPLYING FOR A CARE ORDER

Applications for a care order under the Children Act 1989 offer an example of a particular difficulty facing social workers in the family proceedings court. Where proceedings are brought by a local authority, on the basis that a child is suffering, or is likely to suffer significant harm and that this is due to the care being given to the child by the parents, a local authority social worker who has been working with the family may be required to give evidence for the authority. Such evidence may

[2] National Standards, page 32.

be needed to substantiate the allegation of the authority that the child is, or is likely to, suffer significant harm. It may seem initially that the social worker is required to take sides. The nature of the evidence is such that an allegation is being made against the parents though the outcome of the proceedings is that the child may be taken into care. This interpretation of the role of the social worker is mistaken. Though evidence must be presented to establish the grounds for the application, and must in turn be accepted by the court for the order to be made, the purpose of the application is to safeguard and promote the welfare of the child. As such the social worker is giving evidence to facilitate this objective; in a very real sense the social worker is working on behalf of the child who is the subject of the proceedings rather than against the interests of the parents of the child.

Understanding this focus ensures that the court, and all those involved in the hearing, can overcome any tendency to adopt an adversarial approach to such proceedings. Indeed Parliament intended that such family proceedings should not be understood or run as adversarial proceedings and the statutory requirement that the court should take the child's welfare as the paramount consideration confirms this intention.

Inevitably though, when an application for a care order is opposed by the child's parents there are bound to be tensions in the role of a social worker who has worked with the family to try to prevent the necessity for bringing such proceedings, and who may continue to work with the family and the child after a care order is made. The partnership principle, under which social services departments are expected to work in partnership with families of children in need to obviate the necessity to bring care proceedings, suggests that this tension is inevitable. It is to be expected that the experienced social work practitioner is able to negotiate this tension and prevent it spilling over into conflict in either day to day dealings with the family or in court proceedings.

2.3 THE ROLE OF THE GUARDIAN AD LITEM

A guardian ad litem is a qualified, experienced and independent social worker appointed from a panel established in a particular area to represent the child's interests to a court hearing 'specified' family proceedings. These proceedings are:

a) applications for care or supervision orders;

b) cases where a local authority has been ordered by the court to investigate a child's circumstances and the court has made or is thinking of making an interim care order;

c) applications to discharge or vary a supervision order, or discharge a care order;

d) proceedings in which there is an application for a residence order or contact order in respect of a child in care;

e) applications for emergency protection orders and child assessment orders;

f) appeals concerning care and supervision orders and child assessment orders.

It is clear from this lengthy list that guardians will be appointed in a substantial nunber of cases and that their work is crucial to promoting the philosophy of the Children Act, namely that when a court is making a decision concerning the upbringing of a child that the child's welfare shall be the court's paramount consideration.

The Family Proceedings Rules 1991 specify the tasks of a guardian:

— to appoint a solicitor to represent the child;

— advise the child as is appropriate to their age and understanding;

— advise the court on the wishes of the child;

— advise on the appropriate court level for the hearing of the proceedings;

— advise on what order should be made to secure the welfare of the child.[3]

The guardian will instruct the solicitor appointed to represent the child. Difficulties arise when the child's wishes conflict with the guardian's instructions and the solicitor considers the child to be competent to give instructions. In such circumstances the solicitor should take the child's instructions and the court may be faced with conflicting arguments concerning the outcome of the proceedings. The solicitor will be representing the wishes of the child as articulated in the instructions given by the child and the guardian will be articulating their understanding of the interests and welfare of the child. The court is, of course, bound by the section 1 principles of the Children Act: the child's welfare is the paramount consideration, the principle that delay is likely to prejudice the welfare of the child and the requirement that the court should make no order under the Act unless it considers that doing so is better for the child than making no order at all.

There has been some concern over the independence of guardians arising from the fact that guardians are paid by the local authority in their area, so that the guardian will often be paid by the local authority that is bringing the proceedings in which the guardian is representing the interests of the child. The possible difficulties associated with this have been highlighted in a recent case where the Director of Social Services for Cornwall sought to control expenditure on the fees of guardians by limiting the hours for which they would be paid to 65 hours per case. The Divisional Court quashed the Director's decision on an application for judicial review and confirmed the independence of guardians ad litem and the importance of this independence for the confidence of the courts and the public.

These three examples illustrate the variety of court based work for social work practitioners. They highlight some of the skills necessary for effective practice in the area and the necessity for social workers to take account of a number of factors including the role of other professionals, particularly lawyers and court officials and those who hold the power of decision makers in the courts, namely judges and magistrates.

[3] Volume 7 of 'Guidance and Regulations under the Children Act 1989' provides guidance on the content of guardian's reports.

CHAPTER 2

The legal system

1 INTRODUCTION

Social work courses cannot, nor should they, attempt to turn out professional social workers who are also quasi-lawyers or para-legals. Nonetheless it is important for social workers to have an understanding of the legal system and of the nature of English law. A number of social work practitioners, particularly local authority field workers, approved social workers and probation officers, have an established statutory role in relation to particular aspects of the law and the legal system and other social workers may come into contact with the law through their professional practice with clients. An understanding of the legal system should therefore be an essential element of professional competency within social work and the needs of many clients will include the need for preliminary informed advice about the law and the legal system that can only be provided by a social worker who is familiar with the nature of English law and the operation of the legal system.

1.2 CONTENT

The chapter will begin by identifying how legal principles and rules are made and developed by Parliament and the courts. This will allow some brief discussion of the nature of English law and of the power and influence of the judges.

A distinction will be made between the criminal law and the civil law; this will be followed by a brief description of the court system, the character of which owes something to this distinction.

Some time will be spent on identifying the availability of legal services in the belief that such information is important for clients and social workers. The enforcement of a client's legal rights is often only possible through the courts and tribunals of the legal system. For many social work clients access to the legal system will only be possible through the legal aid system.

2   THE LAW AND THE LEGAL SYSTEM

2.1   WHERE DOES LAW COME FROM AND HOW DOES IT CHANGE?

2.1.1   Parliament's legislative procedures

Within the framework of the British constitution Parliament is the supreme law making body. The majority of legislative proposals are introduced into Parliament as a Bill by the government of the day. Bills go through a complicated procedure in the Commons and the Lords which includes debates in both houses and more detailed scrutiny by committee; if they successfully complete this stage they go to the monarch for the royal assent, at which stage they become an Act of Parliament (otherwise known as a statute).

The link between politics, policy and law is often lost and it is important to understand that many statutes have a considerable political or policy history. For example, the Children Act 1989 is the culmination of a child care law reform process which included the inter departmental report 'Review of Child Care Law' published by the DHSS, a review by the Law Commission, the child abuse inquiries of the late 80s and the government's White Paper 'The Law in Child Care and Family Services'. An understanding of the policy background to statute which concerns social work practice helps to make more sense of an Act when it becomes law.

Though all Acts go onto the statute book the date of implementation may be delayed until some time after the royal assent. Such was the case with the National Health Service and Community Care Act 1990 which was not implemented (in the main) until April 1993. Similarly the Criminal Justice Act 1991 was not implemented until October 1992. Sections 1,2,3 and 7 of the Disabled Persons (Services, Consultation and Representation) Act 1986 have never been implemented. The practice of implementing Acts in stages, or even of non implementation, can cause considerable confusion and it is important for social workers to know what sections of relevant statutes are in force and from what date.

2.1.2 Secondary legislation

Acts of Parliament often contain provisions which allow Ministers to make law themselves; the power to make 'delegated legislation'. This power, which is increasingly important, is most frequently used by the making of regulations which are contained in statutory instruments. As an example the Social Security Act 1986 introduced the broad principles of income support and family credit and gave the Secretary of State the power to make regulations which detail both benefits. A number of regulations have been made under the Children Act 1989, eg the Children's Homes Regulations which provide, among other things, detailed legal provisions concerning the conduct and administration of children's homes and issues of control and discipline within them. Social workers must therefore take account of both primary legislation (Acts of Parliament) and secondary legislation (regulations in statutory instruments); both constitute the law.

2.1.3 Codes of Guidance and Circulars

Some Acts are supported by Codes of Guidance or Practice which provide detailed advice from government departments on how statutory provisions should be interpreted and acted upon. The homelessness provisions of the Housing Act 1985 are supported by a Code of Guidance which is very detailed in its interpretation of the relevant sections of the Act. The Children Act 1989 is itself supported by substantial guidance described in the volume concerning residential care in the following terms:

> The guidance in this volume is issued under section 7 of the Local Authority Social Services Act 1970 which requires local authorities in the exercise of their social services functions to act under the general guidance of the Secretary of State. It is the fourth volume in a series designed to bring managers and practitioners an understanding of the principles of the Children Act and associated regulations, to identify areas of change and to assist discussion of the implications for policies, procedures and practice.[1]

[1] Preface to *The Children Act 1989 Guidance and Regulations* 'Residential Care' (1991) Volume 4 HMSO.

As a general rule these Codes are not legally binding, nonetheless their content is very important and must be considered by social workers working within statutory provisions.

Government departments also issue a large number of circulars which detail how statutory provisions should be implemented and administered. These may be extremely influential within social work as statements of officially defined good practice. An example is the guidance concerning client access to manually kept social work records. The circular, identified as LAC(89)2, provides guidance to local authorities concerning their position under the Access to Personal Files Act 1987 and the Access to Personal Files (Social Services) Regulations 1989.

2.1.4   Judicial law making

Statutes (Acts of Parliament) provide the majority of legal rules by which the courts determine criminal prosecutions and civil disputes which come before them. This task often requires the judges to interpret the meaning of specific provisions contained in Acts of Parliament. Authoritative interpretations of statute by the senior appeal courts constitute legal rules in themselves. In addition a number of areas of law have been developed by the judges and are not subject to statutory provision. In such areas judicial rulings constitute the law and may influence or control social work practice. An example is the judgment of the House of Lords in the case of *F v West Berkshire Health Authority* [1989] 2 All ER 545 which deals with the difficult issue of the sterilisation of adult women who are incapable of themselves consenting to the operation because of their learning difficulty. The judgments of the House of Lords judges set out the circumstances in which such operations can take place and provide a procedure through which the doctors involved in such cases can apply to the courts for a declaration that such an operation would not be unlawful.

2.1.5   The influence of the judiciary

The English legal system accords considerable importance and influence to its judges and in particular to the senior judiciary who sit in the House of Lords and the Court of Appeal. This characteristic of the legal system is firmly located in legal history and is derived from the development of legal rules by judges in the everyday hearing of disputes. As a result the English 'common law' is said to be characterised by a pragmatism and detail which distinguishes it from the 'civil law' of continental Europe which is based on legal codes containing statements of principle from which detailed legal rules can be derived. Such distinctions are of course simplifications but the position and power of the judiciary in the English legal system, and consequently of their decisions, should not be underestimated.

Though Parliament is the source of virtually all new law the judges retain their law making power through their ability to interpret the meaning of statutes and to develop legal rules through the doctrine of precedent.

The system of binding precedent is based on a hierarchy of courts and on the rule that the decisions of the superior courts constitute precedents which are binding on inferior courts. The House of Lords is the senior court of the hierarchy and together with the Court of Appeal they formulate the legal rules which must be followed by the other courts in the system ie the High Court, the Crown Courts, the county courts, and the magistrates' courts.

Because precedents are made by the senior courts in their everyday work of hearing appeals new rules of law can be made very quickly and what may be lawful one day can be rendered unlawful the next. Whilst such radical changes in the law are rarely made by the judges the character of judicial law making requires those who are affected by particular laws to keep abreast of their development. Legal rules in the English legal system are not static, rather they are subject to development, interpretation and change by the senior judiciary. This feature provides the flexibility and dynamism of the legal system.

2.1.6 How does social work deal with the law and official guidance?

It should be understood that the law comes to social work agencies and to individual social workers in a number of ways. Acts and regulations constitute law, while Codes of Guidance and Circulars contain advice and recommendations which may well constitute an official definition of good practice. Agencies and individual workers should ideally be aware of each of these sources of law and official advice.

For many individual social workers their knowledge and understanding of the law that circumscribes their practice is received, not through the law, but through agency statements of practice and procedure. As an example, the law on 'child protection' is contained in Part V of the Children Act. The sections in this part of the Act contain a number of powers and duties which are to be exercised largely by local authority social workers. However, in practice social workers in child protection teams will be working to a very closely defined procedure which has been worked out and prescribed by reference to the Act and to the detailed guidance in 'Working Together', a guide to arrangements for inter-agency co-operation for the protection of children from abuse, published jointly by the Home Office, the Department of Health, the Department of Education and Science and the Welsh Office in 1991. Child protection work will also have to take into account the perceived meaning and impact of court decisions and of the working relationship established by a particular social services department with other agencies working in the same field and area. It is of course important that in such a sensitive and difficult area of practice individual social workers should be clear about what is good and necessary practice, however, an understanding of the statutory responsibilities should not be completely lost within the detail of practice procedures.

2.2   CRIMINAL LAW

2.2.1   Crime and the criminal justice system[2]

The criminal law is concerned to protect the social order. Through history the state, primarily by statute but also by judicial law making, has defined behaviour which is seen as threatening the social order, as a crime.

2.2.2   The language and the actors of the criminal justice system

The police are responsible for ensuring that the everyday social order is upheld, for investigating breaches of the criminal law

---

[2] A more detailed discussion of the criminal justice system is provided in Chapter 7. A similarly more detailed discussion of the youth justice system is provided in Chapter 8.

and for the apprehension of those who are alleged to have committed a crime. Criminal prosecutions are brought by the Crown Prosecution Service in the magistrates' courts and the Crown Courts. Defendants plead guilty or not guilty to specific charges and the prosecution is required, in a criminal trial, to prove the allegation contained in the charge beyond a reasonable doubt. Defendants who plead guilty, or are found guilty after a criminal trial, become offenders and are subject to sentence.

It may be useful to see the criminal justice system as being administered by and through a number of agencies and key actors. These include the police, the Crown Prosecution Service, the magistracy, the judges, the criminal courts service (court clerks etc), juries and the Probation Service.

Most criminal offences are defined by Act of Parliament and for the majority of offences a successful prosecution will need to establish that the criminal act was committed (the actus reus) and that the defendant had the necessary criminal intent (the mens rea).

2.2.3 The criminal courts

Criminal prosecutions are brought in the magistrates' courts and the Crown Courts. The Crown Courts hear the more serious charges where defendants are tried by a jury and the magistrates' courts deal with the less serious charges. Cases in the magistrates' courts are heard by benches of lay magistrates or by a single stipendiary magistrate. (See diagram on p 18.)

The maximum sentencing powers of the criminal courts are set out in statute by Parliament but both judges and magistrates have considerable discretion in fixing sentences.

2.3 THE CIVIL LAW

2.3.1 Civil disputes

Disputes involving individuals, companies, public bodies and local and central government may have to be resolved by the civil courts. Examples of such disputes include alleged breaches

CRIMINAL PROSECUTIONS/ADULTS -COURT STRUCTURE

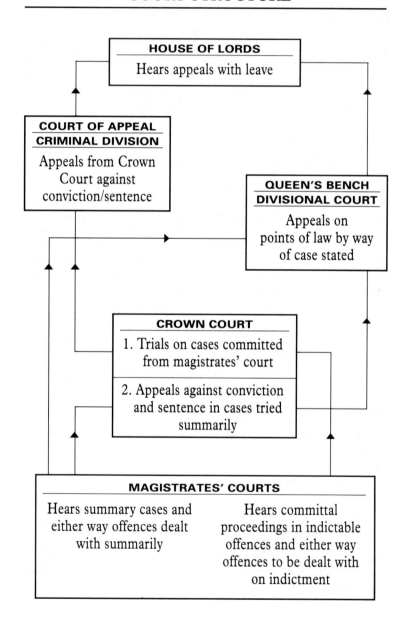

HOUSE OF LORDS

Hears appeals with leave

COURT OF APPEAL CRIMINAL DIVISION

Appeals from Crown Court against conviction/sentence

QUEEN'S BENCH DIVISIONAL COURT

Appeals on points of law by way of case stated

CROWN COURT

1. Trials on cases committed from magistrates' court

2. Appeals against conviction and sentence in cases tried summarily

MAGISTRATES' COURTS

Hears summary cases and either way offences dealt with summarily

Hears committal proceedings in indictable offences and either way offences to be dealt with on indictment of contract, actions for damages arising from negligence, divorce actions, landlord and tenant disputes and family proceedings under the Children Act 1989. Such disputes do not generally constitute a threat to the social order and therefore do not involve breaches of the criminal law. The interest of the state is therefore limited to defining, by statute and judicial precedent, legal principles to govern the multitude of everyday relationships involving the individuals and other bodies identified above, and to determine the disputes that arise when such relationships break down. The state also provides the courts and tribunals which are available to hear and determine these disputes.

2.3.2   The language of the civil justice system

The parties in civil disputes are generally known as plaintiffs and defendants though in divorce proceedings they are petitioners and respondents. Civil actions are taken to secure appropriate remedies or orders. These include awards of damages as compensation for loss suffered, injunctions designed to prevent or stop unlawful activities and possession orders in landlord and tenant disputes. The number of orders available in civil actions is considerable and each is designed to provide the relief or order appropriate to the dispute.

The burden of proof in civil actions is on the plaintiff who is required to establish their case on the balance of probabilities.

2.3.3   The civil courts

Major civil disputes are heard in the High Court by a High Court judge. There are three divisions of the High Court, the Queen's Bench Division, the Family Division and the Chancery Division; each has its own specialist jurisdiction.

Less serious civil disputes are heard in the county courts by a circuit judge or by a district judge. The jurisdiction of the county courts is defined and limited by statute though recent reforms to the civil justice system, introduced by the Courts and Legal Services Act 1990, have significantly increased their jurisdiction.

CIVIL PROCEEDINGS -COURT STRUCTURE

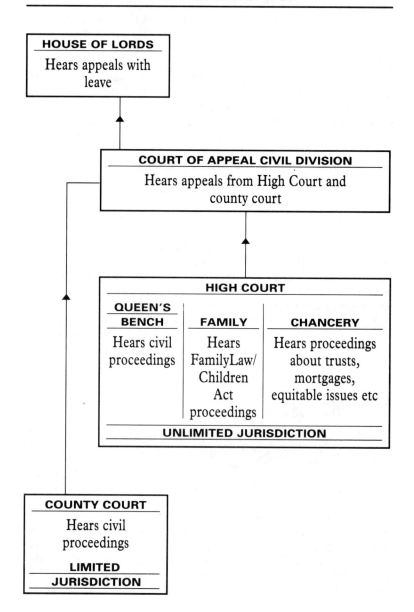

HOUSE OF LORDS

Hears appeals with leave

COURT OF APPEAL CIVIL DIVISION

Hears appeals from High Court and county court

HIGH COURT

QUEEN'S BENCH	**FAMILY**	**CHANCERY**
Hears civil proceedings	Hears FamilyLaw/ Children Act proceedings	Hears proceedings about trusts, mortgages, equitable issues etc

UNLIMITED JURISDICTION

COUNTY COURT

Hears civil proceedings

LIMITED JURISDICTION

2.4   THE HOUSE OF LORDS AND THE COURT OF APPEAL

The House of Lords is the senior appeal court of the legal system and hears both civil and criminal appeals. Its decisions set precedents which bind all other courts in the system.

The Court of Appeal has a criminal division and a civil division. Whilst it is bound by the precedent decisions of the House of Lords the large number of cases heard by the Court of Appeal means that its influence is considerable; its decisions are binding on all other courts below it in the hierarchy. The Master of the Rolls heads the civil division and is said to be responsible for the development of the civil law whilst the Lord Chief Justice, who heads the criminal division, is, in the same way, responsible for the development of the criminal law.

2.5   TRIBUNALS

A large number of disputes, mainly concerning the operation of some state benefit or public service, are not heard in courts but are dealt with by one of the many tribunals that are a feature of the legal system. Tribunals are an important and distinct system for adjudication which is largely separate from the court system. Individual tribunals, such as social security appeal tribunals and mental health review tribunals, are of particular interest to social work and its customers.

2.6   LEGAL SERVICES AND LEGAL AID

The vast majority of legal services are provided by a private legal profession on a fee paying basis and court costs in the civil justice system, though subsidised by the state, are also charged to the users of the system. Access to the legal system is therefore dependent on the ability to pay and many people would not be able to take or defend a civil action or defend a criminal prosecution without some form of financial help. Such help is provided through the legal aid scheme which has four main elements: legal advice and assistance, assistance by way of representation (ABWOR), civil legal aid and criminal legal aid. The scheme is administered under the provisions of the Legal Aid Act 1988.

The Legal Aid Board now administers those parts of the scheme which were previously administered by the Law Society, ie legal advice and assistance, ABWOR and civil legal aid. Eventually it is envisaged that the Board will take over the administration of criminal legal aid, which is currently the responsibility of the criminal courts, so that in time the Legal Aid Board will administer the whole of the legal aid scheme.

2.6.1 Legal advice and assistance (the green form scheme)

The green form scheme provides preliminary advice and assistance on any matter of English law but its availability to individuals is dependent on a means test and the possibility of a contribution. Green form advice and assistance from a solicitor can cover almost any legal matter including writing letters and negotiating. The amount of advice and assistance that can be given under the green form scheme is a maximum of two hours' worth of work or three hours' work in matrimonial cases. A solicitor's work under the scheme may only be preliminary to an application for the grant of full civil or criminal legal aid.

2.6.2 Assistance by way of representation (ABWOR)

Assistance by way of representation (ABWOR) provides for the cost of a solicitor to prepare a case and represent the client before the family proceedings panel in the magistrates' courts. Such cases include separation, maintenance matters, applications under the Children Act for residence and contact orders and matters concerning paternity. ABWOR is also available to patients appearing before a Mental Health Review Tribunal and to prisoners facing disciplinary charges before a prison Board of Visitors.

2.6.3 Civil legal aid

Civil legal aid is available for representation and the other costs of a civil action subject to the applicant satisfying a means test and a 'merits' test. The means test is based on disposable income and capital and the applicant is often required to make a contribution to the costs of the action. The 'merits' test requires anyone applying for civil legal aid to show that they have reasonable grounds for taking or defending the court action and that it is reasonable to grant legal aid in the circumstances of the applicant's case. The proceeds of a successful legally aided civil action are available to reimburse the legal aid fund for its expenditure on the case.

2.6.4   Criminal legal aid

Representation and the other legal costs of the defence in criminal proceedings can be paid for by the criminal legal aid scheme. Applications are made to the criminal courts, almost always to the magistrates' court where they are decided by the Clerk to the Justices. Applicants must satisfy a means test and, subject to their resources, may be required to pay a contribution. The award of criminal legal aid is subject to the criterion that its grant is required in the interests of justice. The Legal Aid Act 1988 sets out the criteria for deciding whether this test is met:

— the charge is a grave one in the sense that the accused is in real jeopardy of loosing their liberty, livelihood or suffering serious damage to their reputation;

— the charge raises a substantial question of law;

— the accused is unable to follow the proceedings and state their own case because of their inadequate knowledge of English, mental illness or other mental or physical disability;

— the nature of the defence involves the tracing and interviewing of witnesses or expert cross examination of a prosecution witness;

— legal representation is desirable in the interests of someone other than the accused.

2.6.5   Duty solicitor schemes

Those who are questioned by the police are entitled to free legal advice available through a duty solicitor scheme. A similar scheme will provide free advice or representation for those appearing at the magistrates' courts for the first time.

2.6.6 Law centres

The law centre movement, which began in Britain in the late 1960s and early 70s, is an important initiative in the provision of legal services to those who might otherwise suffer an 'unmet legal need'. Law centres provide expert and usually free legal services in those areas of law which have a particular impact on the poor and disadvantaged sections of the community. In many respects they serve the same categories of the population as social work by providing legal skills and knowledge to those with housing and social security problems, people who are elderly and vulnerable, people from the ethnic communities, and in the fields of youth justice and domestic violence.

Law centres use different models of legal practice ranging from individual case work to community work but all adopt a deliberately partisan approach to their work. This has often led individual centres into conflict with local authorities over, for example, housing standards and repairs on council estates. Such conflicts can be particularly difficult where the local authority is also funding the law centre. Financing the law centre movement is a continuing problem and the provision of funds by local authorities and the Lord Chancellors's Department has never been sufficient or permanent enough to establish the movement in the mainstream of legal services provision.

3 THE LAW, THE LEGAL SYSTEM AND SOCIAL WORK PRACTICE: some issues for discussion

3.1 LEGAL SERVICES FOR SOCIAL WORK CUSTOMERS

Many social work clients will need the services of a lawyer either to enforce a right or to defend their property, person or other interests. For many clients their only access to the legal system will be through legal aid; equally their ability to adequately defend a criminal prosecution will depend on legal representation. In such circumstances it is incumbent upon social workers to have an adequate knowledge of the structure of legal services and some 'local knowledge' so that clients can be directed to appropriate help.

The Law Society publishes a series of Solicitors' Regional

Directories which list solicitors who do legal aid work and also include the particular areas of work that individual firms will undertake. Unfortunately this list is no real guarantee of a particular expertise so that social work clients referred to a firm of solicitors on the basis of the Directory may not receive the expert help they need. Social workers who are able to refer a client to a lawyer who has specialist skills and knowledge are performing an important professional service for their client. Understanding who can provide appropriate legal services in a particular locality is a valuable skill and such knowledge should also extend to the availability of other advice and support agencies, eg. money advice centres, community relations councils, welfare rights advice centres and housing aid centres.

Legal services under the legal aid scheme may, however, not be available to support the interests of a social work client. For example, the legal aid scheme will not pay for someone to be legally represented before a social security appeal tribunal. An appeal to such a tribunal from the decision of an adjudication officer can often involve difficult points of law and many appellants, including those who are also social work clients, will encounter the greatest difficulty in making their appeal adequately. Social workers with clients in such a position may be able to refer them to a law centre, a tribunal representation unit or other advice agency which can represent their interests. In the absence of representation a client who has access to expert advice is in a better position than one who does not, and referral to an advice agency may help the chances of a successful appeal.

A variety of legal and quasi-legal services are available and social work clients are frequently in positions where they require such services. An important aspect of social work practice is the ability to put the client in touch with the appropriate legal service. This is likely to be more difficult if plans to reduce legal aid expenditure in 1993/94 announced by the Lord Chancellor are implemented. The Lord Chancellor claims that the cost of legal aid has increased by 130% in the last four years and that its budget must meet agreed expenditure figures. It is planned to reduce the legal aid financial eligibility limits thereby excluding a significant proportion from the scheme altogether and requiring many more to contribute to the costs of their legal aid. The plans have incurred the anger of the legal profession and many of the senior judges; the Lord Chief Justice, Lord Taylor, has suggested that the plans constitute 'an abdication of responsibility to a large section of those for whom the legal aid scheme was devised'. Lord Donaldson, the former Master of the Rolls, has responded to the Lord Chancellor by claiming that 'Justice is not an optional extra in a society based on the rule of law.'

If access to legal services is to be denied to many who are now able to get legal aid, including many social work clients, then it is possible that social workers and others may face increased pressure to offer advice and assistance to clients who previously would have had access to a lawyer through the legal aid scheme.

4 ACTIVITIES

1.   There is no substitute for seeing a court at work. Access to the youth court may be possible through placements with social services departments or the probation service. Those who cannot secure access to the youth court will nonetheless benefit from observing the adult magistrates' court.

2.   Get hold of available leaflets about the legal aid system. These should be available from citizens' advice bureaux, the magistrates' courts, the Crown Courts and possibly also from the county courts.

3.   Construct a directory of advice agencies in your area which are able to provide legal and quasi-legal advice and assistance for social work clients. Which agency would be able to represent a client before a social security appeal tribunal?; before other tribunals?

4.   Which solicitors will do work under the legal aid scheme in your area? What are their areas of expertise? Are they sensitive to the problems faced by social work clients?

5.   Do clients have access to a law centre in your area? What sort of work does the centre do?

6.   Generally become familiar with the agencies of the legal system in your area. Where are the courts (magistrates', county, Crown), the police stations? Where are the providers of legal services: the law centre, legal aid solicitors, advice centres, CABx,

tribunal representation units? It is particularly useful to know someone you can contact or refer a client to.

7. There are a number of journals which provide information and comment on some of the issues covered in this chapter. Have a look at any of the following:

Adviser;
Childright;
Community Care;
Journal of Social Welfare Law;
Law and Practice;
Legal Action;
New Law Journal;
Social Work Today.

5 ADDRESSES

Children's Legal Centre,
20 Compton Terrace,
London N1 2UN.
Phone 071 359 6251. Advice
Line. 2–5pm weekdays.
071 359 9392. Administration
and sales.
Fax 071 354 9963.

Law Centres Federation,
Duchess House,
18–19 Warren Street,
London W1P 5DB.
Phone 071 387 8570.

Legal Aid Board,
5th and 6th Floors,
29–37 Red Lion Street,
London WC1R 4PP.
Phone 071 831 4209.

Liberty,
21 Tabard Street,
London SE1 4LA.
Phone 071 403 3888.
Fax 071 407 5354.

National Association for the
Care and Resettlement of
Offenders (NACRO),
169 Clapham Road,
London SW9 0PU.
Phone 071 582 6500.

6   MATERIALS

6.1   BASIC MATERIALS FOR PRACTICE

Going to Court. (Information sheet.) Published by the Children's Legal Centre.

Legal aid leaflets:

— *How to get Free or Low Cost Help.*

— *A Practical Guide to Legal Aid.*

Published by the Legal Aid Board. 1992.

Know Your Rights. Published by Liberty. 1990.

NACRO Factsheets: (National Association for the Care and Resettlement of Offenders):

— *Courts and Sentencing.*

— *The Probation Service.*

6.2   FURTHER READING

White, R. *The Administration of Justice* (2nd edition 1991) Blackwell.

Dyer, M. *The Law Machine* (1989) Penguin.

CHAPTER 3

The Children Act 1989

1 INTRODUCTION

Child care work is one of the areas of practice that today dominates public discussion of social work. This level of concern reflects the considerable publicity surrounding child abuse inquiries in the late 1980s, the inquiries concerning children in care in the early years of this decade such as the Staffordshire 'pin down' inquiry and the impact of the Children Act 1989. The Act, which was implemented in October 1991, extends beyond child care law to encompass private legal proceedings arising from the breakdown of domestic relationships involving children.

1.1 CHILD CARE PRACTICE

Child care work involves social work intervention into family life. Such intervention encapsulates a tension that exists between the autonomy and privacy of the family and the paternalistic responsibility of the state to protect and control the lives of children when and where necessary. Within the dynamics of this tension lie some of the important dilemmas of social work practice. Social work intervention into the private domain of family life is frequently seen and experienced as a form of state control of that family though the motivation for such intervention is essentially supportive of families with children in need; an expression of the principle of partnership in which local authority services are made available to help parents care for their children within the family. Despite the motivation for intervention and the principle of partnership which should inform any such intervention, the involvement of social work within the family may carry with it class and racial definitions of good and appropriate parenting and it may ultimately lead to the compulsory removal of children into care.

Failure to intervene in family life to protect children can have, literally, fatal consequences and the social work profession has been the subject of considerable criticism when it gets such decisions or their timing wrong. The child abuse inquiries of the late 1980s have exposed the enormous difficulties inherent in this aspect of child care practice and in many ways they have provided conflicting messages for the profession. The Jasmine Beckford Inquiry carried the message that social work intervention was needed at an earlier stage to protect children in the face of abuse; in contrast the Cleveland Inquiry was critical of the social workers involved on the grounds that the removal of a number of children from their families was precipitate and unwarranted. The removals evidenced a failure to make a wider assessment before taking action, and a failure among the social workers involved to reappraise their practice and consider their priorities.

Concern about the response of social work to the abuse of children within their own families has more recently been joined by concern about the treatment of children already in the care of local authorities. The Staffordshire 'pin down' inquiry identified a grossly restrictive and harsh environment for some children in the authorities' care and the conviction of Frank Beck on charges involving the indecent assault of children in local authority care have raised concerns about the quality and accountability of residential care for children.

The dilemmas of child care work provide evidence of the tension that exists between the state, whose power is exercised by and through social work, and the relative autonomy or privacy of family life. This tension is itself overlaid with another: that between parents' rights and children's rights. The 1980s has seen an increased understanding of the nature of children's rights and a willingness of the courts to recognise specific examples of such rights. The *Gillick* case[1], in which the House of Lords upheld the legality of providing contraceptive advice to children under 16 without parental consent, was brought by a mother who argued that her rights as a parent over her children extended to the ability to consent to or forbid the provision of such advice. The Children Act reflects an increased recognition of the rights and interests of children and is itself often referred to as a child centred piece of legislation. Section 1 of the Act endorses this principle:

[1] *Gillick v West Norfolk and Wisbech Area Health Authority* [1986] AC 112.

When a court determines any question with respect to the upbringing of a child or the administration of a child's property or the application of any income arising from it, the child's welfare shall be the court's paramount consideration.

Section 22 sets out the general duties of local authorities to children being looked after by them:

(3) It shall be the duty of a local authority looking after any child —

a) to safeguard and promote his welfare; . . . .

1.2   CHILD PROTECTION

The child abuse inquiries provided a focus for legal discussion on issues of child abuse and child protection and they highlighted deficiencies in child protection law which, it was argued, should provide an appropriate balance between the interests of the child, which must be the predominant criteria, the parents and the state. The Children Act 1989 includes provisions which increase the power of the state, largely through the agency of social work, to intervene in order to protect children in an emergency, but also reduces the maximum periods of such emergency intervention and provides increased safeguards for parents in such proceedings.

1.3   REFORM OF CHILD CARE LAW

Concern about the legal framework of child care was expressed in a number of official reports in the 1980s including the second report of the Social Services Committee 'Children in Care' (March 1984), the inter-departmental working party report 'Review of Child Care Law' published by the DHSS in September 1985, and the review of child law by the Law Commission. In January 1987 the government published its White Paper 'The Law on Child Care and Family Services'. Concern in these reports and in the White Paper centred on the complexity of child care law, the number of overlapping jurisdictions exercised in respect of children and the use of wardship by local authorities as a backup jurisdiction to provide powers not available under the existing statutory provisions. The continuing debate about the possibility of a 'family court' was also part of the context of reform of child care law. These, and a number of other concerns raised by the child abuse inquiries, have been addressed by the Children Act 1989 which was implemented in October 1991.

'The Introduction to The Children Act 1989', published by HMSO, describes the Act in the following terms:

> . . . the most comprehensive piece of legislation which Parliament has ever enacted about children. It draws together and simplifies existing legislation to produce a more practical and consistent code. It integrates the law relating to private individuals with the responsibilities of public authorities, in particular local authority social services departments, towards children. In so doing the Act strikes a new balance between family autonomy and the protection of children.[2]

Given this description and even a cursory glance at the statute itself, there is no doubt that the provisions of the Act provide a legislative framework for a substantial part of social work practice with families and children, and for much else of concern to social work.

1.4   THE ACT

1.4.1   Structure of the Act

The Act is arranged into 12 parts and 15 schedules. *Part I* provides a number of general principles which underpin the operation of the Act and the work of those who have statutory powers and duties under it. *Part II* specifies a number of orders which can be made in 'family proceedings' including the 'section 8' orders; financial orders for children and the family assistance order. *Part III* is entitled 'Local Authority Support for Children and Families' and provides for the work of local authorities in respect of children 'in need'. *Part IV* provides for care and supervision orders and identifies the functions and work of guardians ad litem. *Part V* deals with the protection of children at risk including emergency protection orders and child assessment orders. *Parts VI to X* deal with the welfare of children living away from home. *Part XI* details the position of the

---

[2]   Foreword to 'An Introduction to the Children Act 1989'. HMSO.

Secretary of State and *Part XII* includes a number of miscellaneous provisions.

1.4.2   Youth justice

The Act does not substantially affect the youth justice system though it does provide for the inclusion of a residence requirement in a supervision order made by the youth court in criminal proceedings against a child or young person. Criminal prosecutions are taken in the youth court established by the Criminal Justice Act 1991 which was implemented in October 1992.

1.4.3   Adoption

The government has established a review of adoption law with the prospect of new legislation in 1993. In the meantime the Children Act makes some changes to adoption law and procedure. Proceedings under the Adoption Act 1976 are family proceedings so that a 'section 8 order' under the Children Act may be made in such proceedings.

Under the Children Act the Registrar General is required to establish an Adoption Contact Register to enable adopted people to contact their birth parents and other relatives.

1.4.4   Guidance and regulations

A significant amount of secondary legislation has been made under the Children Act. These regulations, which are contained in statutory instruments, are published by the Department of Health and other departments involved in a series of volumes. The regulations cover a number of areas concerning child care law and practice including residential care, private fostering and child protection.

The same series of volumes contain detailed guidance from the Department of Health, and other departments, on the exercise of powers and duties under the Act. Such guidance, though not legally binding, is issued under section 7 of the Local Authority Social Services Act 1970. This section requires local authorities, in the exercise of social services functions, to act under the general guidance of the Secretary of State.

The preface to one of the volumes, 'Residential Care', Volume 4, sets out the rationale behind the publication of such guidance:

> It is the fourth volume in a series designed to bring to managers and practitioners an understanding of the principles of the Children Act and associated regulations, to identify areas of change and to assist discussion of the implications for policies, procedures and practice.

The Act, its regulations and guidance are overlaid by individual local authority policy and procedures so that practice with children and families takes place within a complex relationship between law and policy.

2   THE LAW

This section is necessarily detailed but an attempt has been made where possible to structure information within contexts that are familiar to social workers.

The principles of the Act will be identified first and then consideration will be given to the duties of local authorities to children and families. Discussion of the orders that are available in relation to children in 'family proceedings' will be followed by a look at the provisions concerning care and supervision orders. The framework for protection of children at risk will conclude this analysis of the Act.

The Act is a complex piece of legislation and this chapter cannot provide a comprehensive review of its provisions. The emphasis will be on the impact of the law for social work practice and it seeks only to provide an introduction for qualifying social workers. More detailed discussion of the law is provided in 'An Introduction to The Children Act 1989', by the volumes of guidance and regulations, both published by HMSO, and by any one of the detailed texts available as guides to the law.

2.1 THE PRINCIPLES OF THE NEW ACT

The Introduction identifies a belief that underpins the Act:

> . . . that children are generally best looked after within the family
> with both parents playing a full part and without resort to legal
> proceedings.

The principle of *'parental responsibility'* is used throughout the
Act to describe the duties, rights and authority which a parent
has in respect of a child. Under the Act parental responsibility
is a continuing concept and can generally only be restricted by
court order.

Local authorities have a general duty under section 17(1):

a) to safeguard and promote the welfare of children within their
area who are in need; and

b) so far as is consistent with that duty, to promote the upbringing
of such children by their families.

Implicit within these principles and general duties is the notion
of *partnership* between social services departments and families.
This partnership extends to situations where children in need
are living with their families and also when such children are
being looked after by the local authority.

2.1.1 Section 1 principles

1(1) When a court determines any question with respect to —

a) the upbringing of a child; or

b) the administration of a child's property or the application of
any income arising from it,

The child's welfare shall be the court's paramount consideration.

Section 1(3) provides a checklist for the court to consider when
it is dealing with the making, variation and discharge of contested
orders under Part IV of the Act, ie care and supervision orders,
and education supervision orders. This checklist includes the
wishes of the child where appropriate, the child's needs, the child's

background, age and characteristics and the capability of others to meet these needs as factors to be considered by the court.

Section 1(2) identifies the general principle that *delay in proceedings to determine the upbringing of a child is likely to prejudice the welfare of the child.*

Section 1(5) tells the court that in deciding whether to make an order under the Act '*it shall not make the order or any of the orders unless it considers that doing so would be better for the child than making no order at all.*'

These general principles, which the court is required to consider, will also clearly have an impact on the preparation of welfare reports for the court. Any recommendations contained in such reports should obviously address the welfare principle, the checklist, where appropriate, and the principle of no order unless the welfare of the child requires the court to make one.

2.2   THE COURT(S)

Child care jurisdictions have always reflected the division between what are known as private law proceedings between parents and partners and public law proceedings brought by local authorities. The Act moves beyond such a distinction by establishing what are called '*family proceedings*' which encompass both private law and public law applications under Parts I, II, IV and V of the Act and therefore include applications for care and supervision orders and applications for 'section 8 orders'. The Act also brings a number of other 'private law' matters, such as divorce, domestic violence, occupation of the matrimonial home, and applications for financial relief between spouses, within the definition of family proceedings . The consequence of making such matters family proceedings is that the orders provided in Part II of the Act, ie section 8 orders, financial orders and family assistance orders, can be made in respect of the children of the parties involved in the proceedings. The High Court, county courts and magistrates' courts have concurrent jurisdiction to hear family proceedings.

In the magistrates' courts jurisdiction under the Act is exercised by family panels. There are provisions for transferring family proceedings between courts.

2.3 LOCAL AUTHORITY SERVICES FOR CHILDREN AND FAMILIES

Part III of the Act, together with Schedule 2, provides a framework for the support of children in need and their families. The emphasis is on voluntary support based on a partnership between parent(s) and the local authority. Detailed guidance to local authorities concerning Part III of the Act is contained in 'Family Support, Day Care and Educational Provision for Young Children' published as Volume 2 'The Children Act 1989, Guidance and Regulations'.

Section 17(1) establishes the general duty of local authorities to promote the welfare of children in need within the family where possible by providing a range of services appropriate to those children's needs.

Section 17(10) defines a child in need:

> . . . a child shall be taken to be in need if —
>
> a) he is unlikely to achieve or maintain, or to have the opportunity of achieving or maintaining, a reasonable standard of health or development without the provision for him of services by a local authority under this Part;
>
> b) his health or development is likely to be significantly impaired, or further impaired, without the provision for him of such services; or
>
> c) he is disabled.

From the social work point of view it is important to note that the duty extends to children who are disabled, mentally or physically, and includes the blind, deaf and dumb.

Services may be provided by local authorities, or arranged by them, for children and/or families so long as they are directed to safeguarding and promoting the welfare of the child. Section 17(6) defines services to include 'assistance in kind or, in exceptional circumstances, in cash'.

Part I of Schedule 2 identifies specific duties for local authorities in relation to the services established in section 17. They include:

— the identification of children in need and the provision of information;

— the maintenance of a register of disabled children;

— the assessment of children's needs;

— the prevention of abuse and neglect;

— the provision of accommodation in order to protect a child;

— provision for disabled children;

— provision to reduce the need for care proceedings;

— provision for children living with their families (family support);

— the provision of family centres.

Section 18 imposes duties on local authorities to provide day care for pre-school children and after hours care for school age children.

The Guidance contained in Volume 2 gives an indication of the rationale behind these provisions:

2.1 Section 17 of Part III gives local authorities a general duty to safeguard and promote the welfare of children in need and to promote the upbringing of such children by their families, so far as this is consistent with their welfare duty to the child, by providing an appropriate range and level of services. Schedule 2 contains further provisions designed to help children in need continue to live with their families and generally to prevent the breakdown of family relationships. Partnership with parents and consultation with children on the basis of careful joint planning and agreement is the guiding principle for the provision of services within the family home and where children are provided with accommodation under voluntary arrangements. Such arrangements are intended to assist the parent and enhance, not undermine, the parent's authority and control. This new approach should also be developed when a child is in care, provided that it does not jeopardise his welfare.

Clearly therefore, service provision should be directed to supporting children in need and to achieving their upbringing within their own family wherever possible. These principles are central to the philosophy of the Act and should constitute a powerful influence on the allocation of resources and the development of practice.

2.4 ACCOMMODATION PROVIDED BY THE LOCAL AUTHORITY

As part of the Part III package of services to families with children in need, local authorities are able to provide accommodation for children on a voluntary basis. In the circumstances of section 20(1) they must do so.

20(1) Every local authority shall provide accommodation for any child in need within their area who appears to them to require accommodation as a result of —

a) there being no person who has parental responsibility for him;

b) his being lost or having been abandoned; or

c) the person who has been caring for him being prevented (whether or not permanently, and for whatever reason) from providing him with suitable accommodation or care.

In addition subsections 20(4) and (5) enable local authorities to provide accommodation for children under 16 and for young persons under 21 on the basis that to do so would safeguard or promote their welfare.

The Act requires local authorities to consult with the child it is proposing to accommodate so far as this is reasonably practicable and consistent with the child's welfare (section 20(6)).

When a child is being accommodated by a local authority under the Act parental responsibility does not, in law, pass to the authority. The concept of delegation best expresses the situation in which those with parental rights in respect of a child delegate those powers necessary for the upbringing of a child to a local authority. The philosophy of the Act seeks to encourage agreements between those with parental rights and local authorities who do the 'accommodating' so that there is a shared responsibility for the child based on partnership and agreement wherever possible.

2.4.1   Objections to and removal from local authority accommodation

The voluntary basis of accommodation by a local authority is emphasised by section 20(7) which prevents local authorities from accommodating children in the face of an objection from a person who has parental responsibility for the child and is willing and able to provide or arrange accommodation for the child.

Section 20(8) provides that any person with parental responsibility for the child may remove the child from accommodation provided by the local authority at any time. This right is subject to section 20(9) which specifies that sections 20(7) and (8) do not apply while anyone in whose favour a residence order is in force agrees to the child being looked after by the local authority.

2.4.2   Duties owed by local authorities in respect of children being looked after by them

Within the langauge of the Act children who are being accommodated by the local authority and children who are in the care of the local authority are being *looked after* by the authority. Section 22 imposes a number of duties on authorities in respect of all children being looked after by them.

(3)   It shall be the duty of a local authority looking after any child —

a)   to safeguard and promote his welfare; and

b)   to make such use of services available for children cared for by their own parents as appears to the authority reasonable in his case.

The principles of partnership and consultation are underlined by section 22(4) which requires a local authority before making any decision in respect of a child they are looking after, to consult the child, the parents, those with parental responsibility and others if appropriate, and to give due and appropriate consideration to the child's wishes and to those of others consulted.

In addition section 22(5) requires that decisons concerning

children being looked after take into account the child's religion, racial origin and their cultural and linguistic background.

Children being looked after by a local authority, whether in care or not, may, by section 23(2), be placed in a variety of forms of accommodation and in accordance with regulations made under section 23(5) there are limited powers to allow a child in care to live at home.

2.4.3   Contact and rehabilitation between children and their families

Section 34(1) requires local authorities to facilitate reasonable contact between a child in their care and the parents, relatives, friends and others connected with the child so long as this is reasonably practicable and consistent with the child's welfare.

Schedule 2, paragraph 15, requires local authorities to endeavour to promote contact between children they are looking after and their families so long as this is consistent with the child's welfare. Section 23(6) requires that where a child is being looked after by a local authority arrangements are made for the child to live with his or her family unless this is not reasonably practicable or consistent with the child's welfare.

When read together with the principle in section 17(1) to promote the upbringing of children by their families these provisions constitute a substantial principle of rehabilitation which should have an important influence on social work practice with children and their families.

2.5   SECURE ACCOMMODATION

Section 25 deals with the issue of secure accommodation. Subsection (1) sets out the limited circumstances in which accommodation may be used for restricting a child's liberty.

> 25(1)   Subject to the following provisions of this section, a child who is being looked after by a local authority may not be placed, and, if placed, may not be kept in accommodation provided for the purpose of restricting liberty ('secure accommodation') unless it appears —

a)   that:

    i)   he has a history of absconding and is likely to abscond from any other description of accommodation; and

    ii)   if he absconds, he is likely to suffer significant harm; or

b)   that if he is kept in any other description of accommodation he is likely to injure himself or other persons.

The Secretary of State has power to make regulations to specify the maximum period of time that a child may be kept in secure accommodation before court authorisation is needed. This period is currently 72 hours.

Where a child who is being accommodated by a local authority is placed in secure accommodation, a person with parental responsibility for the child may remove the child from the accommodation whenever they wish and without notice.

2.6   THE ORDERS THAT CAN BE MADE IN FAMILY PROCEEDINGS

2.6.1   Parental responsibility

The Act uses the phrase 'parental responsibility' to sum up the collection of duties, rights and authority which a parent has in respect of his child.[3]

Parental responsibility originates in married parenthood. An unmarried mother has parental responsibility for her child though the child's father may acquire parental responsibility by formal agreement with the mother or by court order. Parental responsibility may also be vested in others in addition to natural parents.

Others may acquire parental responsibility by court order or by their appointment as a guardian. Under the Act parental responsibility may be acquired by an order under section 4(1)(a), by a care order, a residence order or an emergency protection order (see below).

[3] 'An Introduction to the Children Act 1989'. HMSO. Chapter 2 provides a detailed discussion of the concept.

Parental responsibility is a continuing responsibility so it is unaffected for example, by divorce, but it may be limited by court order and cannot be exercised in conflict with a court order. It is shared by parents and it can be shared by parents with others so that when a child is in care parental responsibility is shared between parents and the local authority.

2.6.2   Section 8 orders

These orders can be made by the court in family proceedings upon application or on its own motion; they allow the court to resolve disputes about the upbringing of children.

Contact order

Such an order requires a person with whom a child is living to allow a child to have contact with or visit or stay with a named person. Orders can be as wide or narrow as appropriate.

Residence order

This is an order which determines with whom a child is to live. If a residence order is made in favour of a non-parent then by section 12(2) that person will also have parental responsibility in respect of the child whilst the order remains in force.

The concepts of residence and parental responsibility are different so that where, upon divorce, residence is ordered for one parent both parents will nonetheless retain parental responsibility.

It is possible under the provisions of section 11(4) for a residence order made in favour of people who do not live together to specify periods of residence in different households.

A prohibited steps order

This order prevents a person with parental responsibility from taking a step specified in the order without the consent of the court. This order is by nature a 'single issues' order and is used where contact and residence orders cannot provide for the necessary control over a child's upbringing.

A specific issue order

The order provides directions for settling an issue concerning the upbringing of a child. Again such an order can only be used where the main orders concerning contact and residence are not sufficient.

2.6.3   The availability of section 8 orders

Section 8 orders are available in family proceedings which include:

— wardship;

— proceedings under Parts I, II and IV of the Act;

— divorce and judicial separation;

— domestic violence;

— magistrates' courts' matrimonial jurisdiction;

— adoption.

The orders, together with parental responsibility orders, can be made in any family proceedings so, for example, they are available, subject to specific statutory restrictions, to courts dealing with cases involving domestic violence and in applications by local authorities for care orders.

Some people are able to apply for a section 8 order as of right and they therefore do not require the leave (permission) of the court; other applicants require the leave of the court. Generally parents, guardians and those in whose favour a residence order has been made may apply without leave. The list is extended when the application is for a residence or contact order only and includes step-parents.

It is intended that anyone with an interest in the child should be able to get access to the courts to seek a section 8 order, so this is provided for in the Act subject to leave being granted by the court. Children under 16 may apply for leave to seek a section 8 order in respect of themselves. Where a child has reached 16 the court may not make a section 8 order other than to discharge or vary an existing order.

Where a child is legally in the care of a local authority no order, other than a residence order, may be made. If a residence order is made in respect of a child in care it has the effect of discharging the care order.

Local authorities are not allowed to apply for a residence or contact order in respect of any child.

The Act does not set any specific criteria for the grant, variation or discharge of these orders. As a consequence courts hearing such applications are required to consider them in the light of the principles set out in section 1 and to apply the welfare checklist set out in section 1(3) of the Act. The child's welfare is therefore the paramount consideration for the court and there is a presumption that no order will be made unless the court considers that it would be better for the child to make an order than not to do so. The general principle that delay in determining the application is likely to prejudice the child must be taken into account. The court must also take into account those matters specified in the welfare checklist:

— the ascertainable wishes and feelings of the child concerned (considered in the light of the child's age and understanding);

— the child's physical, emotional and educational needs;

— the likely effect on the child of any change in circumstances;

— the child's age, sex, background and any characteristics that the court considers relevant;

— any harm the child has suffered, or is at risk of suffering;

— how capable each of the child's parents, and any other person in relation to whom the court considers the question to be relevant, is of meeting the child's needs;

— the range of powers available to the court under this Act in the proceedings in question.

2.6.4   Financial orders for children

Section 15 of the Act refers to Schedule 1 which establishes a comprehensive system of financial provisions in respect of children. This important provision is now itself overlaid by the provisions of the Child Support Act 1991 within which the Child Support Agency will seek to enforce the liability of parents to maintain their children.

2.6.5   Family assistance orders

These orders, available under section 16, can be made in family proceedings and under them a probation officer or local authority social worker will advise, assist and befriend the person(s) named in the order. The persons in whose favour an order may be made are parents, the child, or any person with whom the child is living or anyone in whose favour a contact order is made. The child is not required to consent to the order being made though the consent of others named in the order is necessary. The order may be made for a maximum of six months.

The idea behind the order is to provide short term assistance, on a consensual basis, to families or individuals going through or coming to terms with the breakdown of their relationship. As such it is different from a supervision order but its availability supplements the powers of the courts where it is thought that the more powerful supervision order is not necessary.

2.7   CARE AND SUPERVISION ORDERS

Part IV of the Act deals with care and supervision orders and as such it is of primary importance for social work practice. Care orders can now only be made under the Children Act. Supervision orders are available under the Act and 'criminal' supervision orders will continue to be available under the Children and Young Persons Act 1969 in the youth court.

2.7.1   Who may apply?

Only local authorities and authorised persons, currently the NSPCC, may apply for a care or supervision order. The Secretary of State has the power to authorise other applicants. The two orders may also be made in the course of other family proceedings.

2.7.2 The grounds

These are set out in section 31(2):

> (2) A court may only make a care order or supervision order if it is satisfied —
>
> a) that the child concerned is suffering, or is likely to suffer, significant harm; and
>
> b) that the harm, or likelihood of harm, is attributable to —
>
>> i) the care given to the child, or likely to be given to him if the order were not made, not being what it would be reasonable to expect a parent to give to him; or
>>
>> ii) the child's being beyond parental control.

The grounds in section 31(2) are the only grounds on which a care order or supervision order can be made in all the different 'varieties' of family proceedings. The court to whom the application is made is bound by the welfare principle and must take account of the welfare checklist.

Section 31(9) defines 'harm' as ill-treatment or the impairment of health or development. These concepts are further defined:

— 'development': means physical, intellectual, emotional, social or behavioural development;

— 'health': means physical or mental health;

— 'ill-treatment': includes sexual abuse and forms of ill-treatment which are not physical.

Section 31(10) gives a definition of 'significant':

> Where the question of whether harm suffered by a child is significant turns on the child's health or development, his health or development shall be compared with that which could reasonably be expected of a similar child.

2.7.3   Interim orders

Interim care and supervision orders may be made under section 38(1) and because applications for the full orders are 'family proceedings' the court may make a section 8 order in addition or as an alternative to an interim order. Interim orders may be made on the basis that the court is satisfied that there are reasonable grounds for believing that the circumstances of the child fall within the conditions in section 31(2) — the grounds for the full orders.

Directions may be attached to an interim order by the court to allow assessment and examination of the child. A minor with appropriate maturity and capacity may refuse to be examined or assessed.

Time limits on interim orders are imposed by section 38(4). The initial order may be for up to eight weeks with further orders of up to four weeks. There is no statutory limit on the number of interim orders the court can make but section 1 sets out the general principle that delay is likely to prejudice the welfare of the child concerned.

2.7.4   What is the legal effect of a care order?

Section 33(3) details the legal significance of a care order:

> While a care order is in force with respect to a child, the local authority designated by the order shall —
>
> a)   have parental responsibility for the child; and
>
> b)   have the power (subject to the following provisions of this section) to determine the extent to which a parent or guardian of the child may meet his parental responsibilty for him.

It should be noted that though the local authority has parental responsibility in respect of the child in its care so also do the parents or guardian. Parental responsibility is thus shared so that parents have a voice in the upbringing of their child even though s/he is in the care of the local authority. However, the authority has the power to limit the exercise of parental responsibility by parents or guardian but such a power must not be used unless the authority is satisfied that to do so is necessary to safeguard or promote the interests of the child.

2.7.5   Contact for the child in care

Section 34 includes a requirement that the local authority allows reasonable contact between a child in its care and the child's parents or guardian and any person in whose favour a residence order was in force or who had the care of a ward of court prior to the making of the care order.

If the authority wishes to deny contact then it must get authorisation from the court. The authority has a short term power (maximum of seven days) to deny contact under section 34(6).

The court has power to make a contact order where disputes arise concerning the fulfilment of the presumption of reasonable contact contained in section 34(1).

The court is also required, on making a care order, to consider the arrangements which the authority has made or is proposing to make concerning contact for the child and to invite comment on them from the parties. The court has the power to make a contact order when it makes a care order and this power is to be used if no satisfactory arrangements have been made or agreement reached. The emphasis is on voluntary agreement between the authority and parents over the issue of contact.

2.7.6   The supervision order

The grounds for making a supervision order are the same as those for a care order. Supervision orders are to be made for one year initially and this may be extended by the court for a period of up to three years.

By section 35(1) the supervisor is under a statutory duty to advise, assist and befriend the child who is the subject of the order and additionally to take the necessary steps to give effect to the order and to consider whether to apply to have the order varied or discharged. The additional duties are directed toward making sure that supervision orders are kept under review and are not left to 'drift'.

Other details concerning the administration of supervision orders are contained in Parts I and II of Schedule 3 to the Act. Included in these provisions is the power of the supervisor to give directions to the supervised child including where to live and the requirement to participate in specified activities. The supervisor may also impose obligations on any 'responsible person', such as the person with parental responsibility for the child, who must consent to this. The objective is to encourage participation by parents in, for example, mother and baby groups and child care classes. Supervision orders under the Act may include, with the consent of the 'competent' child, requirements in relation to medical and psychiatric examination and treatment.

2.7.7 The discharge of care and supervision orders

Care and supervision orders expire when the child reaches the age of 18.

Under section 39 both orders may be discharged by the court on the application of the person with parental responsibility for the child, the child or the local authority in whose favour the order was made.

No grounds for the discharge of the orders are specified by section 39 so that the court is bound by the principles set out in section 1, principally that 'the child's welfare shall be the court's paramount consideration'.

2.7.8 Education supervision orders

Section 36 provides for a new education supervision order. Such orders may be made by the court on the application of the local education authority on the grounds that the child is of compulsory school age and is not being properly educated.

Being properly educated is defined by section 36(4) as:

> receiving efficient full time education suitable to his age, ability and aptitude and any special educational needs he may have.

If a child is not being properly educated then he may be placed under the supervision of the education authority who are required to advise, assist and befriend the child and to give directions to the child and parents that will secure the child's proper education. The wishes of the child and parents are to be taken into account but parents are required to comply with directions.

Failure to do so, without an appropriate defence (listed in Part III of Schedule 3 to the Act) is a criminal offence.

Part III of Schedule 3 to the Act specifies the details of education supervision orders.

2.8 INVESTIGATIONS ORDERED BY THE COURTS

Issues concerning the welfare of children may arise in any family proceedings eg divorce, domestic violence. Section 37(1) gives the court the power to direct local authorities to investigate the circumstances of a child where it appears that a care or supervision order may be necessary.

As part of this investigation the local authority must consider whether to apply for a care or supervision order; whether to provide services and assistance for the family, or whether to take any other action.

If the authority decides not to apply for a care or supervision order it is required to provide reasons to the court and also to inform the court of any other assistance provided for the family and/or child. The authority is also required to consider whether the case should be reviewed at a later date.

2.9 PROTECTING CHILDREN AT RISK

The child abuse inquiries of the late 80s highlighted problems with the statutory framework for protecting children at risk and Part V of the Act provides local authorities and the police with statutory powers designed to protect children from abuse whilst also recognising the rights of parents and giving them the ability to challenge the use of law in this area.

The Department of Health's Introduction to the Act describes the objectives of these powers in the following terms:

> . . . the Children Act tries to find a better balance between the need to protect children and the other interests of the individuals involved. The conditions which must be satisfied before an emergency protection or child assessment order may be made are closely linked to the purpose of these orders; where practicable parents and others

are given a right of challenge; the duration of the orders is shorter than the place of safety order; and the legal effect of both of these orders is more clearly spelt out.

2.9.1   A duty to investigate

The Act imposes on local authorities a duty to investigate where they have reasonable cause to suspect that a child in their area is suffering or is likely to suffer significant harm.

Section 47(1) provides:

Where a local authority —

b)   have reasonable cause to suspect that a child who lives, or is found, in their area is suffering, or is likely to suffer, significant harm,

the authority shall make, or cause to be made, such enquiries as they consider necessary to enable them to decide whether they should take any action to safeguard or promote the child's welfare.

2.9.2   Court orders

Three orders are provided by the Act; a child assessment order, an emergency protection order and a recovery order. The latter order is principally concerned with child abduction. Appropriate entry and search warrants are also available.

Child assessment order

The order must be sought in a full court hearing by a local authority or the NSPCC. The criteria for the grant of such an order are set out in section 43:

43 (1)   On the application of a local authority or authorised person for an order to be made. under this section with respect to a child, the court may make the order, if, but only if, it is satisfied that —

a)   the applicant has reasonable cause to suspect that the child is suffering, or is likely to suffer significant harm;

b)   an assessment of the state of the child's health or development, or of the way in which he has been treated, is required to enable the applicant to determine whether or not the child is suffering, or is likely to suffer, significant harm; and

c) it is unlikely that such an assessment will be made, or be satisfactory, in the absence of an order under this section.

Because the application is made at a full court hearing parents and other interested parties are able to be present and resist the application if they so wish. If the order is granted the child must be produced to the person named in the order and the order is likely to include directions regarding the necessary assessments including a medical examination. A child, with sufficient understanding to make an informed decision, may refuse to consent to such an examination or any other form of assessment.

Emergency protection order

Section 44 sets out the grounds on which such an order may be granted by the court:

44 (1)   Where any person (the applicant) applies to the court for an order to be made under this section with respect to a child, the court may make the order if, but only if, it is satisfied that —

a)   there is reasonable cause to believe that the child is likely to suffer significant harm if —

i)   he is not removed to accommodation provided by or on behalf of the applicant; or

ii)   he does not remain in the place in which he is then being accommodated;

In addition to this power local authorities may apply for an emergency protection order in the circumstances set out in part (b) of section 44(1):

b)   in the case of an application made by a local authority —

i)   enquiries are being made with respect to the child under section 47(1)(b); and

ii)   those enquiries are being frustrated by access to the child being unreasonably refused to a person authorised to seek access and that the applicant has reasonable cause to believe that access to the child is required as a matter of urgency; or

   c) in the case of an application by an authorised person:

      i) the applicant has reasonable cause to suspect that a child is suffering, or is likely to suffer, significant harm;

      ii) the applicant is making enquiries with respect to the child's welfare and;

      iii) those enquiries are being frustrated by access to the child being unreasonably refused to a person authorised to seek access and the applicant has reasonable cause to believe that access to the child is required as a matter of urgency.

Applications for an emergency protection order are normally made by a local authority social worker but the section is wide enough to allow any person with an interest in the child to do so. Applications are normally made to the court but may be made to a single JP who is a member of the family proceedings panel.

Where appropriate an order may authorise the applicant to enter specified premises and search for the child.

Under section 48(9) warrants may be issued by the court where attempts to exercise powers under an emergency protection order have been or are likely to be prevented. Such warrants authorise a police constable to assist the applicant for the order to exercise their powers under the order. The warrant may direct that the constable is accompanied by a doctor, nurse and/or health visitor.

Effect of the order.   The order requires production of the child and it also authorises the removal of the child from, or retention in, particular accommodation. The order gives the applicant parental responsibility for the child.

There is a presumption that during the currency of the order reasonable contact will continue between parents and child though this may be limited by the court. The court may also direct (or prohibit) medical examinations and assessment of the child during the period of the order.

During the order the applicant is under a duty to return the child or allow him or her to be removed to the parents or the person who had care prior to the order being granted where it appears safe to do so. The child can be taken back again by the applicant, if that is necessary, so long as the order remains in force.

Duration and discharge of the order. The order is limited to a maximum of eight days though there are limited circumstances in which this may be extended for a further seven days. The parents, the child and other strictly specified people, may apply to the court to have the order discharged though only after the order has been in existence for 72 hours. No application to discharge may be made by anyone who had notice of the original application or by anyone who was present at the hearing.

2.9.3 Police powers

The powers of the police in relation to children at risk are contained in section 46 of the Act and may be exercised without a court order on the basis that the officer has reasonable cause to believe that a child would be likely to suffer significant harm unless his or her powers were exercised.

In such circumstances police officers may take a child into police protection, for a maximum of 72 hours, by removing the child to suitable accommodation or by preventing the child's removal from a particular place. Responsibility for the child should be passed onto the local authority as soon as possible during the 72 hours.

Police protection under section 46 does not include a right of entry. If this is required it must be obtained by attaching a warrant to an emergency protection order. The police retain their power under section 17(1)(e) of the Police and Criminal Evidence Act 1984 which restates a common law power to enter and search premises for the purpose of saving life or limb.

3   THE CHILDREN ACT AND SOCIAL WORK
PRACTICE: some issues for discussion

3.1   WORKING IN PARTNERSHIP WITH FAMILIES

Local authorities have, under the Children Act 1989, a general duty to safeguard and promote the welfare of children within their area who are in need and so far as is consistent with that duty to promote the upbringing of such children by their families. As parental responsibility for children is retained notwithstanding any court order short of adoption, local authorities must work in partnership with parents, seeking court orders when compulsory action is indicated in the interests of the child but only when this is better for the child than working with the parents under voluntary arrangements.[4]

The principle of partnership is central to social work practice under the Act and should be manifested in a number of ways including the provision of information, consultation with children and families, parental participation in reviews concerning children who are being looked after by a local authority and the drawing up of written agreements relating to children who are being accommodated. Despite the importance of the principle and the requirements of regulations and guidance made under the Act, monitoring of the first year of the Act by the Family Rights Group suggests that partnership principles are not always reflected in practice.

Though the Group acknowledges that the information upon which they base their comments comes from their advice and advocacy service and therefore relates to people who are dissatisfied with the way in which they are being treated by local authorities, they point to recurrent problems, the wide geographical source of complaints and the unhelpful response from social workers to enquiries from the Group.

> Important decisions are made without consultation with children or their families and plans, if made, are not written down and copies are not made available to families. Written agreements are not made or if they are made are frequently the old style list of stipulations imposed on parents rather than the genuinely negotiated agreement, indicating what all the parties to the agreement should do, which is required by the regulations. People find out about important meetings and reviews by chance rather than being invited and in many cases still find that they are not allowed to bring an advocate or supporter with them to the meeting.[5]

---

[4] 'Working Together Under the Children Act. A guide to arrangements for inter-agency co-operation for the protection of children from abuse'. Home Office, Department of Health, Department of Education and Science, Welsh Office. 1991. HMSO.

[5] Mary Ryan, Family Rights Group 'Is Partnership Being Put Into Practice', The Magistrate, October 1992.

The Group is happy to acknowledge 'that there are many good practitioners who see the Act as providing essential tools for partnership work with families . . .'[6] but concludes that:

> Our casework experience indicates that there has not as yet been a major change in the way that families are treated by local authorities. We are clear that effort must continue to go into changing the attitudes of professionals so that they are not only familiar with the legislation and guidance but are genuinely enthusiastic about putting it into practice.[7]

Monitoring of the Act since implementation is being carried out by the Department of Health and it is to be hoped that evidence collected and received by the Department will show that the partnership principle is being increasingly evidenced in models of good social work practice.

3.1.1 Care orders and partnership

Care proceedings under the Act may be seen as evidence that partnership between local authorities and families with children in need has not been successful. The Act has established significant harm as the criterion for making a care order with the proviso that the harm is attributable to the care provided for the child by his or her parents. However, a number of the provisions of the Act make it clear that despite the criteria being established and a care order being granted to a local authority the options for work in partnership with parents remain.

Under a care order parental responsibility for the child is taken by the local authority but it also remains with the parent(s) so that it is shared between them. The purpose of this arrangement is that the parents of children in care continue to be involved in making decisions concerning their upbringing. Section 34 requires local authorities to facilitate reasonable contact between a child in care and his or her parents and section 23(6) requires that a local authority looking after a child (this includes a child in care) shall make arrangements for the child to live with their family so far as this is consistent with their welfare. Section 22(4) sets out a duty under which a local authority should consult

---

[6] Ibid, page 159.
[7] Ibid, page 160.

with the parents of children being looked after. Volume 3 of the Guidance on Family Placements and Volume 4 on Residential Care provide further details about the care of children being looked after by a local authority.

The expectation of the Act is that wherever possible partnership should continue even after a care order is made so that the order can be discharged where appropriate.

3.2   CHILD PROTECTION

Child abuse formed the focus for much public concern and comment prior to the passing and implementation of the Children Act. Concern about the need to protect children from abuse was tempered by concern not to intrude into family life unnecessarily. This concern has been taken up in the Guidance on Child Protection Work published by the government departments concerned. The preface to 'Working Together' declares:

> It is important for all professionals to combine an open-minded attitude to alleged concerns about a child with decisive action when this is clearly indicated. Intervention in a family, particularly if court action is necessary, will have major implications for them even if the assessment eventually leads to a decision that no further action is required. Public confidence in the child protection system can only be maintained if a proper balance is struck avoiding unnecessary intrusion in families while protecting children at risk of significant harm.[8]

Though the guidance is not law local authorities are required to work to it unless exceptional local circumstances justify variations. 'Working Together' identifies a number of principles which should inform child protection work stressing that such work should be undertaken against a background of partnership between local authorities and families. The necessity for inter-agency co-operation is clearly stated as is the need to develop close working relationships between social services departments, the police service, doctors, community health workers, schools, voluntary agencies and others. Area Child Protection Committees are identified as the forum for developing, monitoring and

[8]   Ibid, page iii.

reviewing child protection policies. Social work practitioners involved in child protection are required to work within a complex framework of statutory law, regulations, guidance and circulars from central government, and agency policy and practice. They continue to be accountable for their actions to families, parents and children; to the courts and ultimately to a society which imposes significant responsibility for preventing abuse to children on the social work profession.

The statutory framework of the Act and the detailed guidance contained in 'Working Together' represent a formidable attempt to provide for the protection of children from abuse whilst recognising the interests of parents and families. In many respects the messages from the child abuse inquiries of the late 80s have been taken on board in the Act so that the exercise of emergency procedures is now recognised as a last resort when work in partnership with families cannot by itself provide children with the necessary protection from abuse.

It is too early to assess whether the emphasis on partnership and the provision of services to families with children in need has reduced the necessity for local authorities to take emergency child protection procedures. The first Annual Report of the Children Act Advisory Committee, which was published late in 1992, reported on initial trends in the operation of the Act but warned against drawing firm conclusions from early experience. The Committee commented on the surprisingly few public law applications during the first 6 months of operation. The Children Act Report 1992, published by HMSO in February 1993, tends to confirm this trend. Changes in the law make pre and post Act comparisons difficult though statistics for the first year of operation show that there were 2300 emergency protection orders granted as against approximately 5000 place of safety orders a year under the previous legislation. The figures for care orders show that 1600 were made in the first year of the Children Act compared to 6200 orders in the previous year, though the number of new care orders being sought during the year had risen. The logic of the Act is that partnership between local authorities and families, in which local authority services are made available for children in need, operates to reduce the incidence of child abuse. The monitoring of the first year of the Act's operation has provided some early statistical indication that this might be happening though it will be some years before the existence of any link between these factors can be firmly established.

4   CASE STUDIES

1.   Robert and Maria are in the process of getting divorced but cannot agree arrangements concerning their two children. Martin (8 years) has said he wants to stay with his father whilst Kate (5 years) cannot express a coherent view. Robert is intending to remarry and would like to have the children at weekends. Maria, who wants both children to live with her, does not want the children to have any contact with Robert's new partner and is thinking of moving to the north of England where her parents live. Robert's parents, who have been very close to their grandchildren are horrified by this prospect fearing they will lose touch with them. The children are currently living with their mother but go to stay with their father and his new partner at weekends despite their mother's objections.

What proceedings and orders are available under the Children Act to resolve this dispute?

2.   Marcus who is three years' old has been looked after by the local authority for the last two months because his mother, Sue, has been mentally ill. She is due to leave hospital today and has told the authority that she will come and collect him early next week when she has had a chance to sort her flat out. You are seriously concerned about her ability to properly care for Marcus. Sue is not married.

What statutory powers and duties, under the Children Act, are relevant to such circumstances?

3.   Derek and Jenny are married and have one child, Angela, who is four. Their relationship is often violent and as a result of information you have received from the health visitor you suspect that Angela may sometimes be assaulted by Derek. The health visitor has also expressed concern about Angela's emotional and psychological development.

You are a local authority social worker.

Do you have a duty to investigate the situation?

If Derek and Jenny refuse to allow you to see Angela or co-operate in any other way do you have grounds for a child assessment order?

What would you seek to establish within such an order?

4. Natalie is 23, single and a heroin addict. She has just given birth to a baby girl who is displaying all the signs of addiction. She lives in a squat with her boyfriend who is the father of the baby. Natalie has not sought or received any ante-natal care and is completely indifferent to her baby. She is due to leave hospital tomorrow.

What rights does Natalie have under the Act if the local authority decides to seek an emergency protection order?

Are there grounds for the local authority to seek a care order?

What is the position of the father if he expresses a wish to be concerned with the baby's future?

How will the interests of the baby be represented in any court proceedings concerning her?

5. Sylvie is 13 and attends the local comprehensive school. One day the school welfare assistant rings your office to say that Sylvie has broken down at school and is claiming that she is being sexually abused by her stepfather and that her mother knows about it but does nothing.

What are you going to do in the short and medium term?

6. Jeanette is three years' old and has been accommodated by the local authority for the past four months since her mother left her with a neighbour and disappeared. It has now emerged that the mother is serving a prison sentence for drug and vice offences. She is due to be released in six months' time.

What are the powers and duties of the local authority in relation to Jeanette and what rights does the mother have?

7. Kylie is 18 months' old and is living with her mother Christine and the latest of a succession of boyfriends. You have been involved with the mother and daughter since Kylie's birth and you are concerned about the violent character of Christine's current boyfriend and in particular about the health and welfare of Kylie. At her last medical checkup the health visitor reported

that she was failing to thrive and that she was bruised on her back and legs. Christine was very defensive and could not provide an adequate explanation about the bruises. When you called at the flat last week the boyfriend told you that Christine and Kylie were asleep and refused you entry. They failed to keep an appointment to see you at the office yesterday and when you called at the flat in the afternoon the boyfriend refused you entry; he was abusive and threatened you with violence.

What are your powers under the Act in this situation?

8. Priscilla has three children aged four, seven and nine; they live in a tower block next to her friend Maggie. Earlier this month Maggie heard Priscilla shouting at the children and later saw her running down the stairs crying. Later that evening the eldest child knocked on Maggie's door and told her that her Mum had left. The local authority has accommodated the children and they are currently living with foster parents.

Priscilla has now contacted Maggie and told her that she has had a breakdown but is better now. She wants to know where the children are so that she can have them back. Maggie passes the message on to you as the duty social worker.

What is the legal situation?

What issues are you going to be concerned about?

9. Beverley is 17 years old and is currently living with her 3-month old baby son in a mother and baby unit run by the local authority. She is obviously having great difficulty in coping with the baby and there is particular concern about her rough handling of the baby and her inability to control her own temper. She has had fights with other residents and has been heard to threaten to kill her baby if he doesn't stop crying. On three occasions before she came into the unit she asked that the baby be 'taken into care' as she was frightened that she would harm her son but on each occasion she took him back after a couple of days.

The local authority have now decided to seek a care order over her child and have told her that they have started court proceedings and the first hearing will be next month.

Beverley is angry and confused; she knows that she doesn't want
her baby taken into care and that her father will do all he can
to support her in this. She wants to know all about the
proceedings: who will be involved, what could happen and what
she can do to stop her baby being taken into care.

How will you answer her questions?

10.   Sonia is a persistent school non-attender. Despite extensive
work by an education welfare officer and the social services
department Sonia is still not attending school. The local authority
is also concerned about the sleeping arrangements in the two
bedroomed flat which Sonia shares with her younger sister and
with her older sister and mother, both of whom have live in
boyfriends. Whenever a social worker visits the home Sonia is
in her bedclothes and her mother seems unable to get her to
school even when transport is provided by the authority.

Explain the legal options available to the authority.

5 ACTIVITIES

1.   In attempting to understand family proceedings there is no
substitute for seeing such proceedings in the family proceedings
court. The public are not admitted to such proceedings so
permission will be needed. This may be arranged through
placement agencies or by means of a letter of introduction and
request for permission to the Clerk to the Justices of the local
magistrates' court.

Because of the complexity of the issues involved in care
proceedings and the large number of people often involved such
proceedings frequently last for two or three days. Applications
for interim care orders are usually much shorter.

Provide an observation report of the proceedings you see. Identify
the role and functions of those present in court and on the
suitability of such proceedings for deciding the issues involved.

2.   Design a leaflet for parents and children which explains care
proceedings in the family proceedings court.

3.   Construct a flow chart or other diagram detailing the various legal steps in applying for an emergency protection order.

4.   Identify the different people who might be involved in care proceedings and their respective roles and functions.

5.   How is a child protection register compiled?

6.   Who may be present at a child protection conference and what is discussed?

7.   Write to the Children's Legal Centre and other organisations working in this area for their publication lists.

8.   Subscribe to or look at Childright (published by the Children's Legal Centre) each month — this will keep you up to date with legal issues concerning child care practice.

9.   Write to the Family Rights Group for a publications list. The Group works to improve services for families and their children in public care or in contact with other statutory agencies. Membership includes receiving copies of all its publications.

10.   Get hold of a copy of the annual report of your Area Child Protection Committee and a copy of their local procedural handbook.

6   ADDRESSES

British Agencies for Adoption and Fostering,
11 Southwark Street,
London SE1 1RQ.
Phone: 071 407 8800.

Children's Legal Centre,
20 Compton Terrace,
London N1 2UN.
Phone: 071 359 6251.
There is a free advice service available on this number between 2 and 5pm weekdays.

Family Rights Group,
The Print House,
18 Ashwin Street,
London E8 3DL.
Phone: office 071 923 2628;
help line 071 249 0008.

Gingerbread,
35 Wellington Street,
London WC2E 7BN.
Phone: 071 240 0953.

National Council for One-
Parent Families,
255 Kentish Town Road,
London NW5 2LX.
Phone: 071 267 1361.

National Society for the
Protection of Cruelty to
Children (NSPCC),
67 Saffron Hill,
London EC1N 8RS.
Phone: 071 242 1626.

7 MATERIALS

7.1 BASIC LEGAL MATERIALS FOR ORDINARY SOCIAL WORK PRACTICE

Department of Health *An Introduction to the Children Act 1989* HMSO.

'Child Protection Procedures — what they mean for your family' (1992) Family Rights Group and NSPCC.

Allen, N. *Making Sense of the Children Act 1989* (1991) Longman.

'Promoting Links — Keeping Children and Families in Touch' Family Rights Group.

'The Children Act 1989, Guidance and Regulations'. In particular see:

Volume 2 — Family Support, Day Care and Educational Provision for Young Children (1991).

Volume 3 — Family Placements (1991).

Volume 4 — Residential Care. HMSO (1991).

When parents separate. Children's Legal Centre.

'Working Together Under the Children Act. A guide to arrangements for inter-agency co-operation for the protection of children from abuse'. (1991) HMSO.

'Working with young people — legal responsibility and liability'. Children's Legal Centre.

7.2 FURTHER READING

White, R. Carr, P. Lowe, N. *A Guide to the Children Act 1989* (1990) Butterworths.

'Children Act Report 1992' (1993) HMSO.

Bainham, A. 'Children — The New Law, The Children Act 1989' (1990) Family Law.

Dewar, J. *Law and the Family* (1992) Butterworths.

The Childern Act Advisory Committee, Annual Report 1991/92 (1992) Department of Health.

Hoggett, B. and Pearl, D. *The Family, Law and Society* (1991) Butterworths.

CHILDREN ACT PROCEEDINGS -COURT STRUCTURE

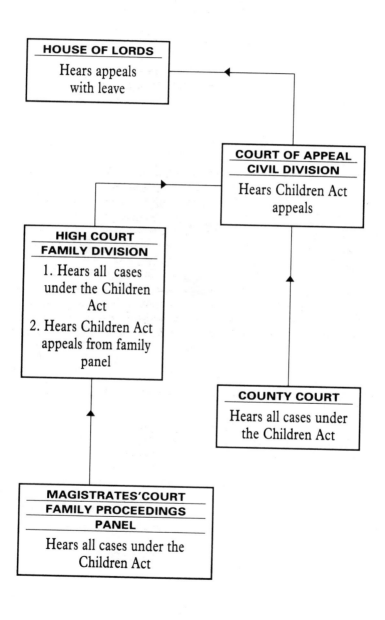

HOUSE OF LORDS

Hears appeals with leave

COURT OF APPEAL
CIVIL DIVISION

Hears Children Act appeals

HIGH COURT
FAMILY DIVISION

1. Hears all cases under the Children Act
2. Hears Children Act appeals from family panel

COUNTY COURT

Hears all cases under the Children Act

MAGISTRATES'COURT
FAMILY PROCEEDINGS
PANEL

Hears all cases under the Children Act

Application for a Care or Supervision Order

Section 31 The Children Act 1989   Date received by court

▶ Please use black ink.
The notes on page 8 tell you what to do when you have completed the form.

▶ If there is more than one child you must fill in a separate form for each child.

▶ A care / supervision order cannot be made if the child has reached the age of 17 or is 16 and married

▶ Please answer every part. If a part does not apply or you do not know what to say please say so. If there is not enough room continue on another sheet (put the child's name and the number of the part on the sheet).

▶ If you have any concerns about giving your address or that of the child or any other address requested in this form, you may give an alternative address where papers can be served. However, you must notify the court of the actual address on a separate form available from the court.

THE   CHILDREN   ACT

Application to   **The**   **[High] [County] [Magistrates'] Court**

for a   * care order   * supervision order

(delete which does not apply)*   **Case No.**

THE   CHILDREN   ACT

1   About the child

(a) The name of the child is
   Put the surname last

(b) The child is a   ☐ boy   ☐ girl

(c) The child was born on the   *day   month   year*   Age now

(d) Is the child married   ☐ yes   ☐ no

(e) The child usually lives at
   See note on addresses at top of this form

SPECIMEN

(f) The child lives with
   If the child does not live with a parent please give the name of the person who is responsible for the child   ☐ the child's mother   ☐ the child's father

(g) The child is also cared for by
   Put the surname last

(h) The child is at present   ☐ staying in a refuge (Please give the address to the Court separately)
                                    ☐ not staying in a refuge

(i) If the child is temporarily living away from usual address, please say where he / she is living at present
   See note on addresses at top of this form

(j) A Guardian ad litem   ☐ has not been appointed
                               ☐ has been appointed. The Guardian ad litem is
                               | Name | | |
                               | Address | | |
                               | Tel. | Fax | Ref |

(k) A solicitor   ☐ has not been appointed to act for the child
                      ☐ has been appointed to act for the child. The solicitor is
                      | Name | | |
                      | Address | | |
                      | Tel. | Fax | Ref |

THE   CHILDREN   ACT

1

2 About the applicant

(a) The applicant's full name is
   Put the surname last

(b) The applicant's title is   ☐ Mr ☐ Mrs ☐ Miss ☐ Ms ☐ Other *(say here))*

(c) The applicant is

   local authority

   ☐ an officer of the National Society for
   the Prevention of Cruelty to Children

   ☐ authorised by the Secretary of State to apply for this order.

(d) The applicant's official address is

(e) The applicant's telephone
   number and reference are   *Tel.*   *Ref*

(f) The applicant's solicitor is   *Name* *Address.*

   Tel.   *Fax.*   *Ref*

(g) The social worker is   *Name* *Address.*

   Tel.   *Fax.*   *Ref*

SPECIMEN

3 About the child's family

(a) The full name of the child's mother
   is   *Put the surname last*

(b) The mother usually lives at
   See note on addresses at top of page 1

(c) The full name of the child's father
   is   *Put the surname last*

(d) The father usually lives at
   See note on addresses at top of page 1

(e) The child's mother and father   ☐ are living together   ☐ are living apart

(f) The father is   ☐ married to the child's mother   ☐ married to someone else
   ☐ single   ☐ divorced

(g) The mother is   ☐ married to the child's father   ☐ married to someone else
   ☐ single   ☐ divorced

2

3 │ About the child's family (continued)

(h) The child has

☐ no brothers and sisters under 18

☐ brothers and sisters under 18. They are

See notes on addresses at top of page 1

Put the names , addresses and ages of all full brothers and sisters.

If the child has halfbrothers or halfsisters, stepbrothers or stepsisters say who they are in (i) below

If there are other children who are treated as children of the family say who they are in (i) below

The name(s) of the brother(s) and sister(s)	Age (years)	The address(es) of the brother(s) and sister(s)

Do not include adoption orders

☐ No order has been made for any brother or sister

☐ No order for a brother or sister has been applied for

☐ An order has been made for a brother or sister

☐ An order for a brother or sister has been applied for

The name(s) of the child(ren)	The type of order	The court which made the order and when or which will hear the application and the case number if known	✓ if the order has been applied for	is in force

(i) There are other children

☐ under 18 who do not live with the family

☐ under 18 who live with the family.

See notes on addresses at top of page 1

They are:

The name of the child	The age of the child	Please give reasons why the child lives / does not live with the family	Address of child not living with the family

4 **Section 37(1) directions**

(a) A section 37(1) direction for
the child's circumstances
to be investigated

☐ has not been made by a court
☐ has been made by a court

The court was

The direction was made on   Case no.

THE ■■■ CHILDREN ■■■ ACT

5 **Parental responsibility**

Some people have "parental responsibility" for a child.
The law says what "parental responsibility" is
and which people have it. These people include:

A the mother

B the father
if he **was** married to the child's mother
when the child was born

C the father
if he was **not** married to the child's mother
when the child was born
    but he now has a residence order
    or he now has a court order
      which gives him parental responsibility
    or he now has a formal "parental responsibility
      agreement" with the mother
    or he has since married the mother

D a guardian of the child

E someone who holds a custody or residence order

F a local authority which has a care order

G someone who holds an emergency protection order

H any man or woman who has adopted the child

SPECIMEN

The people who have parental
responsibility for this child
are believed to be

See note on addresses at the top of page 1

Name	Address

THE ■■■ CHILDREN ■■■ ACT

4

6 About other applications and orders which affect the child

(a) An Emergency Protection Order   ☐ is not in force

☐ is in force. The Court which made the order was

Case no.

The order ends on

(b) Other applications have   ☐ not been made

☐ been made or will be made

What the application was for or will be for	When an application was made or will be made	The court which heard the application or will hear the application and the case number if known	The result

SPECIMEN

(c) Other orders   ☐ have not been made

☐ have been made. The orders are

Please include orders that have been made but are no longer in force

Do not include adoption orders

The type of order	When was the order made	The court which made the order and the case number if known	✓ if the order has expired (say when)	is in force

THE   CHILDREN   ACT

9/91

7 About this application

(a) The grounds for applying for
a care / supervision order are

Delete one of * if appropriate

that the child concerned is suffering,
or is likely to suffer,
significant harm;
and that the harm, or likelihood of harm, is attributable to

*the care given to the child, or likely to be given to the child
if the order were not made, not being what it would be
reasonable to expect a parent to give to the child

*the child's being beyond parental control

(b) These grounds exist because

(c) If, as part of application for a
supervision order directions are
requested, please give details and full
supporting reasons

*Please say in part 8 what your plans are
for the child and the terms of the order you
are asking for*

6

9/91

7 **About this application** (continued)

(d) If you are also requesting an interim order tick the box and delete one of *

[ ] that there are reasonable grounds for believing that the circumstances with respect to the child are that the child concerned is suffering, *or* is likely to suffer, significant harm; *and* that the harm, or likelihood of harm, is attributable to

*the care given to the child, or likely to be given to the child if the order were not made, not being what it would be reasonable to expect a parent to give to the child

*the child's being beyond parental control

(e) These grounds exist because

SPECIMEN

(f) The following directions are requested for the interim order.

Please give full supporting reasons

(g) The respondents will be

- people with parental responsibility (see part 5)
- the child
- other people allowed by the Rules of court.

Please give details below

(i) Only give details of those respondents, whose names and addresses have not been given in part 5

(ii) Please put the address where the respondent usually lives or where papers can be served. See note on addresses at the top of this page.

(iii) You will have to serve a copy of this application on the respondents.

The name of the respondent	The respondent's address

8 **The plans for the child if a final order is made**

The plans for the child are

Please include the terms of the order you are asking for with supporting reasons.

Please make specific reference to arrangements for contact with the child.

THE ▬ CHILDREN ▬ ACT

9 **Declaration**

I declare that the information I have given is correct and complete to the best of my knowledge

Signed

Date

THE ▬ CHILDREN ▬ ACT

What you (the person applying) must do next

▶ There is a Notice of Hearing on page 9. Fill in the boxes on the Notice.

▶ Take or send this form and any supporting documentation to the court with enough copies for each respondent to be served. The top copy will be kept by the court and the other copies given or sent back to you for service.

▶ You **must** then serve the copies of the Application, the Notice of Hearing and any supporting documentation according to the rules. You may also be required under the Rules to give notice of the proceedings to other people.

In the [High] [County] [Magistrates'] Court

at

(When writing to the court please state the Case No.) **Case No.**

Tel. Fax

THE CHILDREN ACT

Notice of a [Hearing] [Directions Appointment]

You are named as a Respondent in these proceedings

about the child

☐ a boy ☐ a girl

born on the

You must read this Notice now

THE CHILDREN ACT

About the [Hearing] [Directions Appointment]

name of applicant

SPECIMEN

has made an application to the Court.

The Court has been asked to make ☐ a care order ☐ a supervision order

THE CHILDREN ACT

To be completed by the court

The Court will hear this at

on

at o'clock

the time allowed is

THE CHILDREN ACT

What you must do

▶ There is a copy of the application with this Notice. Read the application **now**. You do not have to fill in any part.

▶ You should obtain legal advice from a solicitor or, alternatively, from an advice agency. The Law Society administers a national panel of solicitors to represent children and other parties involved in proceedings related to the children. Addresses of solicitors (including panel members) and advice agencies can be obtained from the Yellow Pages and the Solicitors Regional Directory which can be found at Citizens Advice Bureaux, Law Centres and any local library.

▶ You may be entitled to legal aid. For certain Children Act proceedings, children, parents and those with parental responsibility will usually be eligible for legal aid automatically.

date

THE CHILDREN ACT

Application for Emergency Protection Order

Section 44 The Children Act 1989

Date received by court

▶ Please use black ink. The notes on page 7 tell you what to do when you have completed the form.

▶ If there is more than one child you must fill in a separate form for each child

▶ Please answer every part. If a part does not apply or you do not know what to say please say so. If there is not enough room continue on another sheet (put the child's name and the number of the part on the sheet).

▶ If you have any concerns about giving your address or that of the child or any other address requested in this form, you may give an alternative address where papers can be served. However, you must notify the court of the actual address on a separate form which you can get from the court office.

Please speak to the court official immediately if you wish this application to be heard without giving notice of the application to any other party.

THE CHILDREN ACT

Application to **The**   [High] [County] [Magistrates'] Court

for an Emergency Protection Order   **Case No.**

THE CHILDREN ACT

1   About the child

(a) The name of the child is
Put the surname last

(b) The child is a   ☐ boy ☐ girl

(c) The child was born on the   *day month year*   Age now

(d) The child usually lives at
See the note on addresses at the top of this form

SPECIMEN

(e) The child lives with   ☐ the child's mother ☐ the child's father
If the child does not live with a parent please give the name of the person who is responsible for the child

(f) The child is also cared for by
Put the surname last

(g) The child is at present   ☐ staying in a refuge. (Please give the address to the Court separately)

☐ not staying in a refuge

(h) If the child is temporarily living away from home, please say where he/she is living at present
See the note on addresses at the top of this form

(i) If a child's identity is unknown state any details that identify the child
You may attach a recent photo of the child for the use of the court

(j) A Guardian ad litem
☐ has not been appointed
☐ has been appointed. The Guardian ad litem

Name
Address
Tel.   *Ref*

(k) A solicitor
☐ has not been appointed to act for the child
☐ has been appointed to act for the child. The solicitor is

Name
Address
Tel.   *Fax*   *Ref*

THE CHILDREN ACT

CHA 34   1

Inchbrook Printers Limited 0453 843621

2   About the applicant

(a) The applicant's title is

☐ Mr ☐ Mrs ☐ Miss ☐ Ms ☐ Other *(say here)* [   ]

(b) The applicant's full name is
Put the surname first

(c) The applicant is

☐ an officer of the [   ] local authority

☐ an officer of the National Society for
the Prevention of Cruelty to Children

☐ a designated police officer
on behalf of [   ] local authority

☐ authorised by the Secretary of State

☐ other *(say here)* [   ]

(d) The applicant's address is

State home or office

(e) The applicant's telephone
number and reference are

Tel.   Ref

(f) The applicant's solicitor is

Name

Address.

Tel.   Fax   Ref

THE   CHILDREN   ACT

3   About the child's family

(a) The name of the child's
mother is
Put the surname last

(b) The mother usually lives at
*See the note on addresses at the top
of this form*

(c) The name of the child's
father is
Put the surname last

(d) The father usually lives at
*See the note on addresses at the top
of this form*

(e) The child's mother and father   ☐ are living together   ☐ are living apart

| 3 | About the child's family (continued) |

(f) The father is

- [ ] married to the child's mother
- [ ] single
- [ ] married to someone else
- [ ] divorced

(g) The mother is

- [ ] married to the child's father
- [ ] single
- [ ] married to someone else
- [ ] divorced

(h) The child has

- [ ] no brothers and sisters under 18
- [ ] brothers and sisters under 18. They are

Put the names, addresses and ages of all full brothers and sisters

If the child has halfbrothers or halfsisters stepbrothers or stepsisters say who they are in (i) below

If there are other children who are treated as children of the family say who they are in (i) below

See the note on addresses at the top of page 1

The name(s) of the brother(s) and sister(s)	Age (years)	The address(es) of the brother(s) and sister(s)

SPECIMEN

- [ ] No order has been made for any brother or sister
- [ ] No order for a brother or sister has been applied for
- [ ] An order has been made for a brother or sister
- [ ] An order for a brother or sister has been applied for

Do not include adoption orders

The name(s) of the child(ren)	The type of order	The court which made the order and when, or which will hear the application, and the case number(s) if known	✔ if the order has been applied for	✔ if the order is in force

CHA 34

3   About the child's family (continued)

(i)   There are other children   ☐ under 18 who do not live with the family
☐ under 18 who live with the family.

They are

See the note on addresses at the top of page 1.

The name of the child	The age of the child	Please give reasons why the child lives/does not live with the family	Address of child(ren) not living with the family

THE   CHILDREN   ACT

4   Parental responsibility

Some people have "parental responsibility" for a child.
The law says what "parental responsibility" is
and which people have it.   These people include:

A   the mother

B   the father
if he was married to the child's mother
when the child was born

C   the father
if he was **not** married to the child's mother
when the child was born
   but he now has a residence order

   or he now has a court order
      which gives him parental responsibility

   or he now has a formal "parental responsibility
      agreement" with the mother

   or he has since married the mother

D   a guardian of the child

E   someone who holds a custody or residence order

F   a local authority which has a care order

G   someone who holds an emergency protection order

H   any man or woman who has adopted the child

SPECIMEN

The people who have parental
responsibility for this child
are believed to be

See the note on addresses at the top of page 1

Name	Address

THE   CHILDREN   ACT

5 | About other applications and orders which affect the child

(a)   Other applications have   ☐ not been made

☐ been made or will be made

What the application was for or will be for	When an application was made or will be made	The court which heard the application, or which will hear the application, and the case number if known	The result

SPECIMEN

(b)   Other orders   ☐ have not been made

Please include orders that have been made but are no longer in force.   ☐ have been made.   The orders are

Do not include adoption orders.

The type of order	When the order was made	The court which made the order and the case number if known	✓ if the order has expired (say when)	is in force

THE   CHILDREN   ACT

6 | About this application

(a)   The grounds for making
this application are

Delete one if it does not
apply*

1

☐ that there is reasonable cause to believe that the child is likely to suffer significant harm if

  *the child is not removed to accommodation provided by or on behalf of the applicant

  *the child does not remain in the place in which the child is currently being accommodated

*Only an officer of a local
authority should tick box 2*

2

☐ that enquiries are being made with respect to the child's welfare under section 47(1)(b)
  and
  that those enquiries are being frustrated by access to the child being unreasonably refused to a person authorised to seek access and that there is reasonable cause to believe that access to the child is required as a matter of urgency

*Only an authorised person
under section 31 should
tick box 3*

3

☐ that there is reasonable cause to suspect that the child is suffering, or is likely to suffer, significant harm
  and
  enquiries are being made with respect to the child's welfare
  and
  those enquiries are being frustrated by access to the child being unreasonably refused to a person authorised to seek access and there is reasonable cause to believe that access to the child is required as a matter of urgency.

(b)   These grounds exist because

SPECIMEN

(c)   The applicant would like the court
to order that

If you would like the Court to give directions on

- *contact*
- *a medical or psychiatric examination or other assessment of the child*
- *information on the whereabouts of the child*
- *authorisation for entry of premises*
- *authorisation to search for another child on the premises*

put these here.

6 | About this application (continued)

(d)   This application will be heard

☐   without notice being given to the other side

☐   with notice being given to the other side

(e)   A report or relevant documentary evidence

☐   is attached

☐   is not attached

(f)   The respondents will be

● people with parental responsibility (see part 4)

● the child

● other people allowed by the Rules of the Court.

Please give details below

(i) Only give details of those respondents, whose names and addresses have not been given in part 4.

(ii) Please put the address where the respondent usually lives or where papers can be served. See the note on addresses at the top of page 1.

(iii) You will have to serve a copy of this application on each of the respondents.

The name of the respondent	The respondent's address

SPECIMEN

THE   CHILDREN   ACT

7 | Declaration

I declare that the information I have given is correct and complete to the best of my knowledge.

Signed

Date

THE   CHILDREN   ACT

What you (the person applying) must do next

▶   There is a Notice of Hearing on page 8. Fill in the boxes on the Notice.

▶   Take or send this form, and any supporting documentation to the court with enough copies for each respondent to be served. The top copy will be kept by the court and the other copies given or sent back to you for service.

▶   Unless you are asking for this application to be heard without giving Notice to any other party, you **must** then serve the copies of the Application, the Notice of Hearing and any supporting documentation according to the Rules. You may also be required under the Rules to give notice of the proceedings to other people.

In the

at

(When writing to the Court please state the Case No.)

Tel.

[High Court of Justice]
[County Court]
[Magistrates' Court]

| Case No. | |

Fax

THE CHILDREN ACT

Notice of a Hearing

You are named as a respondent in these proceedings

about the child

☐ a boy   ☐ a girl

born on the

description of child if details unknown

You must read this Notice now

THE CHILDREN ACT

About the Hearing

name of applicant

SPECIMEN

has made an application to the Court.

The Court has been asked to make an Emergency Protection Order.

THE CHILDREN ACT

| To be completed by the court |

The Court will hear this at

on

at   **o'clock**

The time allowed is

THE CHILDREN ACT

What you must do

▷ There is a copy of the application with this Notice. Read the application **now**. You do not have to fill in any part.

▷ You should obtain legal advice from a solicitor or, alternatively, from an advice agency. The **Law Society** administers a national panel of solicitors to represent children and other parties involved in proceedings relating to children. Addresses of solicitors (including panel members) and advice agencies can be obtained from the Yellow Pages and the Solicitors Regional Directory which can be found at Citizens Advice Bureaux, Law Centres and any local library.

▷ You may be entitled to legal aid. For certain Children Act proceedings, children, parents and those with parental responsibility will usually be eligible for legal aid automatically.

date

THE CHILDREN ACT

CHA 34   8

CHAPTER 4

The breakdown of domestic relationships

1 INTRODUCTION

The breakdown and ending of domestic relationships provides the focus for a considerable amount of social work though there are relatively few specific statutory powers and duties. It is clear though that the personal, financial and child care complexities and difficulties experienced by those involved in the breakdown of a relationship are such that social work intervention is often needed. Problems involving accommodation, the care of children and the organisation of satisfactory financial arrangements, are all areas in which social workers can provide information and expertise in any short term crisis and in the longer term. The only real 'professional law' for social work in this area is that which arises from the fact that many court proceedings dealing with the breakdown of marriage and other domestic relationships are 'family proceedings' for the purpose of the Children Act 1989. There is also the important civil work of the probation service in which probation officers act as court welfare officers providing welfare reports for the courts in family proceedings. Through this statutory duty the probation service has become involved in the important development of mediation and conciliation services which seek to reduce the conflict often involved in matrimonial litigation and family proceedings.

It is possible to suggest some examples of social work involvement in the legal aspects of relationship breakdown.

a) A substantial number of clients are involved or have been involved in matrimonial breakdown; this involves adult clients as well as children. The breakdown of domestic relationships may involve emergency social work intervention to protect a child or children under the Children Act 1989 or arranging the accommodation of children under the same Act. It may also encompass work with women and children who are living in a refuge having left the matrimonial home because of domestic violence.

b)   Where a court hearing family proceedings considers that a care or supervision order may be needed it can require a local authority to investigate the circumstances of the child to establish whether either order is appropriate.

c)   Social workers may be involved in the supervision of contact orders made under the Children Act 1989.

d)   Probation officers or social workers may be involved in the administration of a family assistance order made under the Children Act 1989. The order requires the practitioner to advise, assist and befriend any person named in the order.

e)   Work by probation officers as court welfare officers and the provision of welfare reports for the courts.

f)   The development of conciliation and mediation schemes by the probation service as part of the civil work of the probation service.

1.1   CONTENT

It is clear then that social work in the field of relationship breakdown is varied and can be complex. This chapter will give some explanation of the law which seeks to organise and provide for the consequences of such breakdown and will identify and explain the incidences of social work involvement required by both the law and by definitions of good practice.

It is necessary therefore to look at divorce in the county court and its consequences for both spouses and for children and at the matrimonial jurisdiction of the magistrates' courts. The Children Act 1989 has had a substantial impact on this area of law and practice by defining court proceedings dealing with these issues as family proceedings. The result is significant; where children are involved section 8 orders, such as residence and contact orders, are available; and section 1 principles apply so that the welfare of the child is paramount and there is a presumption of no order unless making an order is considered to be better for the child(ren).

The Child Support Act 1991 was implemented in April 1993 and an outline of the system of child support established by the legislation will be provided.

Domestic violence will be considered as a separate matter as will the statutory duties of probation officers and social workers as report writers and the involvement of the probation service in the development of conciliation and mediation services.

2 THE LAW

2.1 DIVORCE

The facility of a divorce is only available to couples who are married. In this sense the law favours marriage as a form of domestic relationship by providing the services of the law to arrange and regulate the consequences of its breakdown. Such arrangements include the protection and enforcement of important rights for the divorcing spouses as well as for their children, such as accommodation, financial provision and appropriate care for children. In contrast to the favouring of marriage the law tends to disadvantage cohabitation. Couples who are not married cannot get divorced and are not able to avail themselves of all the facilities of the law outlined above.

2.1.1 Grounds

The Matrimonial Causes Act 1973 specifies that the sole ground for divorce is the irretrievable breakdown of marriage. This is to be established by one of five 'facts':

— that the respondent has committed adultery and the petitioner finds it intolerable to live with them;

— that the respondent has behaved in such a way that the petitioner cannot be expected to live with them;

— that the respondent has deserted the petitioner for a continuous period of two years;

— that the parties have lived apart for a continuous period of two years and that the respondent consents to the decree being granted;

— that the parties have lived apart for at least five years.

2.1.2 Petition stage

One of these facts, or a combination of two or more of them, will form the basis of the divorce petition which will be presented to a local divorce county court. A divorce petition may not be presented during the first year of marriage. Procedural rules specify the steps to be taken and time limits for the conduct of what is known as the petition stage of a divorce. This stage does not involve a court appearance by the parties and legal aid is not available for this part of a divorce unless proceedings are contested, though advice and assistance under the green form scheme may be. As a result social work customers may need advice, assistance and support during this phase of divorce.

In the simplest divorce the petition is unopposed, there are no children and the parties have made mutually satisfactory arrangements for property and financial matters. In such circumstances the divorce court will be able to pronounce a decree nisi which can be made absolute after a short period of time. The spouses may remarry only after the divorce decree has been made absolute.

2.1.3 Ancillary proceedings

The unfortunate fact is that most divorces do not follow this simple path; the petition itself may be opposed, though this is rare these days; much more common is agreement between the parties about divorcing, but disagreement about the arrangements proposed for the matrimonial home, financial matters and the children. Such disputes are the basis of what are known as ancillary proceedings and legal aid is available for such proceedings.

If there are children of the marriage the court, under section 41 of the Matrimonial Causes Act 1973, must consider whether, in the light of any arrangements that have been made for the children, to exercise any of its powers under the Children Act. These might include making a section 8 order, a family assistance order, or requiring the local authority to investigate the circumstances of the child.

The parties to divorce proceedings are encouraged to reach their own agreements on the issues of property, finance and children. In relation to any order it makes for a child the divorce court is subject to the principles set out in section 1 of the Children Act: primarily that the child's welfare is the paramount consideration and no order is to be made unless the court considers that doing so would be better for the child than making no order.

Where there is agreement concerning the arrangements for the children between the parties they must file a statement with the court setting out the terms of the agreement.

Where the parties to a divorce are unable to reach agreement on the children then either or both parents may apply for a section 8 order. The court may make a section 8 order on its own motion or it may direct the local authority to investigate the circumstances of the children.

In relation to property and finance the parties are free to make their own arrangements. The terms of such agreements are subject to the provisions of the Child Support Act which means that maintenance arrangements must not be agreed which have the impact of reducing the liability of one party to maintain the children to the extent that the other party is required to claim social security benefits. Failing agreement the court has wide powers to make appropriate orders under the 1973 Act.

The litigation of such disputes is complex and often bitterly contested and it is only possible here to give the broadest outline of the relevant legal principles. It should also be noted that such disputes often arise before or at the time that a divorce petition is served so that disputes concerning the right to occupy the matrimonial home, the right to maintenance, or issues concerning the children need to be regulated by the divorce court during the divorce proceedings and pending any final resolution of the issues. Such regulation is available through the ability of the court to make appropriate interlocutory orders as soon as the divorce proceedings begin.

2.1.4   Property and financial orders

Property

Upon divorce, or a judicial separation, the court can make orders concerning the matrimonial home and the necessary financial arrangements. In relation to the matrimonial home the court has extensive powers to order the transfer of ownership of a home or the tenancy of a rented property between the parties, or it may order the sale of the property and allocate the proceeds of the sale between the parties, or order that the home be settled on trust so that its sale can be postponed until, for instance, the children reach adulthood or finish full time education. The court's powers in relation to the matrimonial home are wide and varied but under section 25 of the Matrimonial Causes Act it is under a duty, when making orders in relation to property and finance, to give its first consideration to the welfare of any child of the family.

Finance

Court orders in relation to the financial arrangements consequent upon divorce are again varied and if anything the law is more complex than in relation to property orders. The court is subject to the principle of section 25 described above and to a more general 'clean break' objective set out in the Matrimonial and Family Proceedings Act 1984 which aims to terminate financial responsibility of one party for the other as soon as possible after the divorce. There are additionally a series of specific statutory criteria in section 25 which the court is required to consider when deciding on an order for periodic (maintenance) and/or lump sum payments. These criteria include the financial resources and circumstances of the parties; their financial needs in the future which may depend on their age and health; any non-financial contribution made to the marriage eg child care and other domestic duties; the conduct of each of the parties if it would be unfair to ignore it and the value of any future financial benefits such as a pension which will be lost upon divorce.

The law is designed to provide principles which will allow the court to make arrangements and orders which are appropriate to the individual circumstances of any divorce. However, for many social work clients the reality of divorce is determined by the availability of local authority accommodation and the level of social security benefits for the parent who will care for the children after the divorce.

2.1.5 Children Act orders for children: residence and contact

The notion of parental responsibility emphasised by the Act is based on a responsibility for children that is continuing notwithstanding the divorce of a child's parents, so that both parents are expected to be involved in the major decisions about their child(ren). The expectation underlying the provisions of the Act is that divorcing parents will make their own arrangements for the care of their children post divorce and that the courts will only intervene where the welfare of the child requires such intervention.

Where disputes between divorcing parents arise and agreement cannot be reached the court may have to consider making a section 8 residence or contact order. A residence order will regulate the arrangements for where a child is to live and may specify a situation where a child resides with both parents at different times. A contact order requires a person with whom a child is living to allow contact between the child and another person, the other parent for example.

Before the court makes such orders it may require a welfare report to be prepared by the court welfare service. There are a number of factors which are acknowledged to influence both the recommendations made in such reports and the orders ultimately made by the court. These factors are dominated by the welfare principle but may also include the views of the child, a reluctance to disturb existing child care arrangements if they are working well, some evidence of a 'maternal preference', a concern with the behaviour of the parents only if it is relevant to the child's welfare, the standard of care available and a desire to keep siblings together.[1]

---

[1] For a more detailed discussion of these issues and of the law concerning children and divorce see Dewar, J. *Law and the Family* (2nd edn, 1992).

2.1.6 Care and supervision orders

Because divorce proceedings are family proceedings for the purposes of the Children Act it is possible for the court to make a care or supervision order. Such orders can only be made upon application by a local authority and then only on proof of the criteria set out in section 31(2) of the Children Act:

> A court may only make a care order or a supervision order if it is satisfied —
>
> a) that the child concerned is suffering, or is likely to suffer, significant harm; and
>
> b) that the harm, or likelihood of harm, is attributable to —
>
> > i) the care given to the child, or likely to be given to him if the order were not made, not being what it would be reasonable to expect a parent to give to him; or
> >
> > ii) the child's being beyond parental control.

Where the divorce court considers that either of these orders might be appropriate it will require the local authority to investigate the circumstances of the child(ren). If the local authority, as a result of its investigations, decides not to apply for a care or supervision order then it must inform the court of its reasons for not making such an application, and of the services it is providing for, and the work it is undertaking or intending to undertake with, the child(ren) and the family.

2.1.7 Divorce law reform

The Law Commission has recently been considering the operation of divorce law and its possible reform.[2] Criticism of the current law centres on its emphasis on the issue of fault and the fact that the law requires little consideration by the parties of the consequences of the divorce and planning for its impact on issues of property, finance and children until late in the process.

The Law Commission proposes what has been termed 'divorce

---

[2] 'Facing the Future: A Discussion Paper on the Grounds for Divorce'. 1988. 'The ground for divorce'. 1990.

over time'. Under its proposals a divorce would be granted no sooner than a year after one or both parties had served notice with the court that they consider that the marriage has broken down. The minimum one year period would be used to sort out and agree issues concerning children, property and money. The Law Commission favours agreement between the parties, with the help of mediation if necessary, rather than the imposition of court orders, though the necessary orders will be available to deal with issues such as the occupation of the matrimonial home and the consequences of domestic violence. Orders concerning children are, of course, available under the Children Act.

The Law Commission has included a draft Bill in its reform proposals and a parliamentary initiative is awaited at the time of writing.

2.2 THE MATRIMONIAL JURISDICTION OF THE MAGISTRATES' COURTS

Divorce is a matter only for the county courts, but magistrates' courts have an important jurisdiction to deal with a number of matrimonial disputes short of divorce. This work is undertaken by the family proceedings panel of magistrates under the Domestic Proceedings and Magistrates' Courts Act 1978. The Act provides the court with a number of orders where a married applicant can establish that:

— the respondent has failed to provide reasonable maintenance for the applicant or the children of the family; or

— the respondent has behaved in such a way that the applicant cannot reasonably be expected to live with the respondent; or

— the respondent has deserted the applicant.

Subject to the provisions of the Child Support Act, which takes the majority of child maintenance matters out of the jurisdiction of the family proceedings court, orders can be made to provide maintenance for the applicant (and children). Orders can also be made for lump sum payments. When it is deciding on these orders the court is required to consider a number of criteria which are similar to those considered by the divorce courts when making property and financial orders. The magistrates also have a power to formalise agreements made by the parties themselves for maintenance and lump sum payments by means of a consent order.

Within this, now limited, jurisdiction the family proceedings court is required by section 8 of the Domestic Proceedings and Magistrates' Courts Act 1978 to consider whether to exercise any of its powers under the Children Act 1989. These powers include section 8 orders and the power to require a local authority to investigate the circumstances of the child(ren).

2.2.1 Child support

The Child Support Act 1991 was implemented in April 1993 and its provisions are likely, in time, to have a significant impact on the issue of child maintenance. The objectives of the legislation are said to be twofold; enforcing the obligation of parents to maintain their children, and thereby reducing the expenditure the state currently makes to fulfill that role where parents are defaulting on their responsibility.

The normal situation will be where a child's parents have separated, the child is living with its mother and the father is not paying maintenance for the child. In such circumstances the mother of the child can apply to the Child Support Agency for a maintenance assessment against the father which the agency will collect and enforce if necessary. The assessment of maintenance is made on the basis of a means test and a formula detailed in regulations.

A parent, or person with parental responsibility, who is claiming Income Support, Family Credit or Disability Working Allowance is required to apply to the Agency for child maintenance and is therefore obliged to use its assessment, collection and enforcement services unless there are reasonable grounds for believing that compliance would involve a risk of harm or undue distress to the applicant or child. A person against whom an order is made has a right to have the decision reviewed and may appeal to a Child Support Appeal Tribunal.

The introduction of child support means that the courts have only a residual jurisdiction concerning child maintenance in a number of special circumstances where child support does not operate. Divorcing couples are still able to agree on the issue of maintenance for their children post divorce though such agreements may not have the effect of increasing reliance on welfare benefits above the level which would be established if a child support assessment were in force.

2.3   THE WORK OF PROBATION OFFICERS IN THE COURT WELFARE SERVICE

2.3.1   Reports

The probation service has an important role providing, as the court welfare service, reports for the courts in a number of proceedings including divorce in the county courts, in domestic/family proceedings in the magistrates' courts under the Domestic Proceedings and Magistrates' Courts Act 1978, family proceedings under the Children Act 1989 and in wardship proceedings in the High Court. The function of the court welfare officer in this respect is to help the court resolve disputes so that the welfare of the child(ren) is promoted or safeguarded. This is achieved firstly by investigation and then by the submission of a welfare report to the court. Their work is determined by the principles set out in section 1 of the Children Act 1989 that the welfare of the child is the paramount consideration, that no order should be made unless the making of such an order is for the benefit of the child, and the principle that delay is likely to prejudice the interests of the child.

2.3.2   Mediation

In divorce and other family proceedings the investigation and inquiry process and the preparation of a welfare report is a difficult matter which requires sensitivity and skill. Where there are disputes between the parents over the children the adversarial nature of divorce proceedings can mean that such disputes become entrenched and bitter. This feature of divorce litigation has been recognised for some time and a number of initiatives have been made with the broad objective of reducing conflict in disputes about children and of increasing areas of agreement between divorcing couples. It is thought that ultimately divorced parents are more likely to adhere to an agreement about the care of their children which has been mutually agreed than to an arrangement which has been imposed by court order. Underpinning the development of mediation schemes, designed to achieve these objectives where possible, is the belief that a child's welfare is better served by the continuation of a relationship with both parents after their divorce. Agreement between them about the care of their child is more likely to encourage such continuing relationships. The principle of continuing parental responsibility enshrined in the Children Act reflects these beliefs.

A number of mediation schemes have been developed 'out of court' in the sense that they are not formally connected to the divorce courts. The development of 'in court' conciliation schemes has largely resulted from an interpretation by some divorce court welfare officers of their professional role to encompass the promotion of agreement between divorcing couples on the future care of their children. It is argued that such agreement will in turn promote the welfare of the child. This development, and involvement in mediation services, is seen as the best method of achieving agreement and promoting the interests and welfare of children.

The availability of mediation services, both 'out of court' and 'in court' has grown significantly in recent years though the character of such schemes is varied. There are a number of well established criticisms of mediation and the courts have made it clear that court welfare officers should not combine the roles of mediator and report writer. Nonetheless the benefit of mediation is now widely accepted and it seems that some form of mediation process may be formally incorporated into divorce court proceedings.

The extension of mediation from disputes concerning children to encompass financial and property matters now seems firmly established. It is also clear that many family proceedings panels hearing matrimonial disputes and family proceedings under the Children Act in the magistrates' courts are using the services of the court welfare service to attempt a mediation of disputes before a formal hearing in court.[3]

---

[3] For more information on mediation see Dewar, J. *Law and the Family* (2nd edn, 1992) pp 280-290.

2.4 THE IMPLICATIONS OF THE CHILDREN ACT 1989

The Children Act 1989 has a considerable impact on the way in which the law seeks to regulate the breakdown of domestic relationships. The breakdown of such relationships has a number of consequences and the Act provides a statutory code for all issues concerning children however they arise, eg as a result of divorce or as a result of domestic violence. So in divorce proceedings the Matrimonial Causes Act 1973 will provide for the issues concerning the parties, their property and their money and the Children Act provides principles and provisions for the divorce court to settle issues concerning the care of the children where this cannot be agreed by the divorcing parents.

A central concept of the Children Act is the notion of parental responsibility which is described as 'the collection of duties, rights and authority which a parent has in respect of his child'.[4] In relation to marital breakdown the Act makes it clear, both in principle and in detail, that the parental responsibility of both parents for their children will continue despite their separation or divorce; it can only be restricted by specific orders of the court. The Act provides four orders under section 8, known as 'section 8 orders', which can be made to control and restrict parental responsibility where this is necessary for the welfare of the children. The important principles are that both parents will continue to exercise full parental responsibility for their children, except where that has been limited by a section 8 order, and that no order will be made unless it is necessary for the welfare of the child.

Section 8 orders are available in a wide range of family proceedings dealing with issues arising from the breakdown of domestic relationships. These family proceedings include divorce and separation proceedings under the Matrimonial Causes Act 1973, proceedings arising from domestic violence under the Domestic Violence and Matrimonial Proceedings Act 1976, matrimonial and domestic violence proceedings under the Domestic Proceedings and Magistrates' Courts Act 1978 and issues concerning the occupation of the matrimonial home under the Matrimonial Homes Act 1983. Section 8 orders can be made in

[4] See Department of Health 'An Introduction to the Children Act 1989'. HMSO.

family proceedings heard in the High Court, the county court and the magistrates' court.

The court may make a section 8 order itself without anyone having made an application though normally an application will be made in family proceedings by a parent, a guardian or anyone in whose favour a residence order has been made. These applicants do not need the leave of the court to make an application. The Act recognises that other people may have an interest in the upbringing of a child and provision is therefore made for a person with a genuine interest in the child's welfare to make an application with the leave of the court.

2.4.1 Family assistance orders

A family assistance order may be made under the terms of section 16. Such an order is designed to 'provide short-term help to parents following separation or divorce, to smooth the transition period for them and to encourage cooperation between them'.[5] The order is made in family proceedings and normally requires a probation officer or local authority social worker, or some other person, to advise, assist and befriend a person named in the order ie parent, child, person with whom the child is living, or a person in whose favour a contact order has been made. The consent of anyone named in the order, except the child, is required and the order lasts for a maximum of six months. The order is directed to increasing co-operation between parents to the advantage of the children.

2.5 DOMESTIC VIOLENCE

Domestic violence has been an important social issue during much of recorded history; as a legal issue it seems to have been rediscovered in the early 1970s. Domestic violence may well constitute a criminal assault and in theory such an assault can be prosecuted as a criminal offence. There is some evidence that the Crown Prosecution Service is reluctant to charge the perpetrators of such assaults where they believe that the victim may be unwilling to give evidence against their partners. Indeed

[5] Bainham, A. 'Children — The New Law, The Children Act 1989' (1990) Family Law.

it may be that the criminal law does not offer women sufficient protection from domestic violence for it is geared to the punishment of the assailant rather than the protection of the victim, with the result that a conviction and sentence may exacerbate the violence and increase the threat to women.

The disadvantages of the criminal law response to domestic violence led pressure groups working in this area in the early 1970s to look to the civil law for appropriate remedies and protections. A number of civil actions such as divorce provided the possibility of an injunction against a violent husband but because it was necessary to seek such orders as part of other proceedings they did not provide the speed, convenience and particular remedies sought by women who had been assaulted. The other important defect of using established matrimonial law actions was that they were unavailable to women who were not married to their partners. The inappropriateness of the criminal law and the disadvantages of the existing civil law procedure became the basis for a well orchestrated pressure group campaign to provide a specially designed civil law action for the victims of domestic violence. The campaign resulted in a private members' Bill becoming law as the Domestic Violence and Matrimonial Proceedings Act 1976.

Social workers have no specific powers or duties in relation to domestic violence though there are important duties under section 37 of the Children Act which require social work investigation where information is received that a child is suffering or likely to suffer significant harm. Social workers also have the right to apply for a child assessment order under section 43 of the Act and for an emergency protection order under the terms of section 44 of the Act. Notwithstanding the emergency child protection provisions of the Children Act the victims of domestic violence may often need the support and help of a social worker who understands the legal implications of their position.

2.5.1 Domestic Violence and Matrimonial Proceedings Act 1976

The 1976 Act, commonly known as the Domestic Violence Act, provides the county court with the power to give appropriate injunctions (court orders) to victims without the necessity of their having to take other proceedings. Both married and cohabiting women (and men) may apply to the court under the Act for the necessary orders. The court has a number of orders at its disposal including:

—   non-molestation orders to protect the applicant and /or the children from further violence, threats and harassment;

—   exclusion or ouster orders which can exclude a man from the home, regulate the use of the home, prevent the man from coming within a specified area, or allowing the woman and children to re-enter the home.

The law in this area has unfortunately been confused by case law so that applications for ouster orders by spouses may only be made under the Matrimonial Homes Act 1983. In considering whether to make any such orders the court is required to consider criteria contained in the Act ie the conduct of the parties, their respective needs and financial resources, the welfare and needs of the children and to all the circumstances of the case. Applications for ouster orders by non-spouses are made under the 1976 Act but are also subject to the same criteria.[6]

Powers of arrest may be attached to the orders granted under the 1976 Act if there has been actual bodily harm to the victim and there is a likelihood of future violence.

An application for the orders available under the Act may be made ex parte so that the man is not given notice of the first hearing in the proceedings. This facility may be important where notice of the proceedings might trigger another assault.

2.5.2   Domestic Proceedings and Magistrates' Courts Act

The jurisdiction of the county court, in relation to domestic violence, has been supplemented by the Domestic Proceedings and Magistrates' Courts Act 1978 which gives powers to the family proceedings panel in magistrates' courts which are similar to those of the county court:

[6]   The Matrimonial Homes Act 1983 provides for the High Court and the county court to regulate the rights of spouses to occupy the matrimonial home. Under this jurisdiction the court can make a variety of orders concerning occupation similar in effect to those available under the Domestic Violence Act 1976.

— A personal protection order where the applicant can establish that the respondent (the husband) has been violent or threatened violence towards the applicant or the children and that the order is necessary to protect them.

— An exclusion order which requires the respondent to leave the matrimonial home or prevents him from entering the home.

The grounds for an exclusion order are the respondent's violence to the applicant or children, or a threat of violence to them and actual violence to a third party, or the breach of the terms of a personal protection order. Again a power of arrest may be attached to the orders where the respondent has physically injured the applicant and is likely to do so again.

The ability of the victim to establish the allegations which form the basis of the application for an order is obviously important for the powers of the court are substantial eg to exclude a person from their own home. It may be that a social worker involved with the family will be in a good position to provide independent evidence of the allegations made.

Though both the 1976 and 1978 Acts provide some remedies for women and children who have been assaulted or threatened with violence within a domestic relationship, they are directed towards short term relief rather than to permanent solutions. Indeed exclusion orders merely suspend rights of occupation while the order is in force and do not interfere with the ownership of property or tenancy rights. In practice such orders will not normally be made for more than three months. When an exclusion order expires the person against whom it was made is free to return to the home.

Long term legal solutions may be achieved in other ways which involve the permanent break up of the violent relationship such as divorce, or by the provision of safe and permanent alternative accommodation. It may be that such accommodation has to be sought under Part III of the Housing Act 1985, which is designed to provide housing for the homeless. A woman, with children, who has been assaulted by her partner and as a result is homeless, should not have serious difficulty in establishing a priority need under the Act and therefore an entitlement to permanent accommodation from the appropriate housing authority.

3   THE LAW AND SOCIAL WORK PRACTICE: some issues for discussion

3.1   THE CIVIL WORK OF THE PROBATION SERVICE

The involvement of the probation service in running the court welfare service has a much lower profile than the involvement of the service in the criminal justice system. Statistics suggest that about 12% of all reports prepared are for the civil courts. In 1990 the Middlesex Area Probation Service prepared 733 welfare reports for the civil courts in what can broadly be termed family law proceedings.[7] Such work clearly requires particular expertise and the involvement of the probation service in mediation work has meant that civil probation work has become increasingly specialised.

Research published in 1989 described different approaches to civil work by probation services and by individual officers. James and Dingwall identified a traditional approach which they describe as 'investigating the circumstances of parents and children on behalf of the court, reporting and making recommendations to courts, and trying to reduce the conflict and reach agreements in the process, if appropriate'.[8] The authors of the research also identified a different more therapeutic service or approach which gives supremacy to the wishes and agreements of the parents who are seen as the legitimate definers of the welfare of the child. The traditional approach would allocate major decisions about the welfare of the child to the court whilst the other approach would seek to establish parental agreement about arrangements for the children and would have an expectation that the court will confirm such agreement in the terms of its orders. It is to be expected that, over a period of time, the philosophy of the Children Act, which seeks to encourage parents to agree on arrangements for their children post divorce and to prevent the court from making any order unless it can be shown that a positive benefit will accrue to the child(ren), will have an impact on the work of the court welfare service and the models of practice adopted by individual probation officers.

[7] See 'Middlesex Area Probation Service: A Service to the Courts and the Community' 1990.
[8] See James, A. Dingwall, R. 'Social Work Ideologies in the Probation Service; The Case of Civil Work' (November 1989) Journal of Social Welfare Law.

3.1.1 The future of civil work

One of the elements of the argument for a family court is the chance it would provide for the creation of an independent social work service attached to it. The creation of family proceedings by the Children Act 1989, whilst not creating such a family court, nevertheless provides a much clearer focus for such specialist social work in the preparation of welfare reports and the further development of mediation services. The court welfare service is involved in a significant number of family proceedings in the magistrates' courts and provides the opportunity for couples who have sought a court hearing to try to reach some agreement at the very earliest stage of legal proceedings. It is often the case that a disputed hearing need not take place because couples have reached some solution to their dispute at a pre-trial appointment with the court welfare service.

3.2 DOMESTIC VIOLENCE, THE LAW AND SOCIAL WORK PRACTICE

Domestic violence provides an example of how the quality of social work practice in a particular area can be enhanced by an appropriate understanding of the law. In work with the victims of domestic violence the boundaries of such knowledge are not restricted to legal provisions designed to deal with domestic violence itself but also include an understanding of legal services, the law on child protection, the law relating to relationship breakdown, social security and housing law.

A very brief pathway can be indicated which will illustrate the need for a social worker to develop legal knowledge and practice skills which together provide good quality social work practice.

A social worker with a female client who has been assaulted may well need to initiate an immediate response which could include, in no particular order of priority:

— contact with the police;

— finding a place in a refuge for the woman and her children;

— contacting a sympathetic lawyer with appropriate knowledge and skills;

— arranging for medical attention;

— triggering the emergency child protection measures in the Children Act;

— arranging for children to be accommodated by the local authority;

— providing help, information and support at any court hearing where an injunction is sought;

— providing evidence to the court of injuries sustained;

— supporting and possibly assisting the client in claiming social security benefits where necessary.

Longer term involvement with such clients may involve dealing with the housing department in securing accommodation under the homelessness provisions of the Housing Act 1985 and supporting the client during divorce proceedings.

The complexity and variety of legal knowledge and practice skills is clear and most if not all of the work described above involves the law in one way or another. An understanding of the legal implications of a client's situation will enable the social worker to make appropriate practice decisions and with the help of a sympathetic lawyer, to provide the necessary support and protection.

4 CASE STUDIES

Here are a series of case studies which may be used to consolidate work done in the areas covered in this chapter.

1. Desmond and Barbara have been married for ten years and have two children, Rufus (8) and Rebecca (6). They have been separated for three years and Barbara wishes to get divorced. The children have been sharing their time between both parents and wish to continue such a pattern. The matrimonial home is owned by Desmond who has been living with his new girlfriend in her flat for the last two years. You have become involved with

Barbara and her children as both Rufus and Rebecca have been having problems at school.

Barbara is anxious about how to proceed with the divorce and about what might happen to the house and the children. Barbara does not work and has been living on money given to her by Desmond.

What advice would you give to Barbara?

Would your advice be any different if a) Barbara petitions on the basis of Desmond's adultery and b) Desmond makes it clear that he wishes to have the children exclusively?

2.   Rosanna has three children and lives with Mick. She rings the office from a local refuge where she is staying with her children after leaving her local authority flat because Mick has been violent towards her children and has threatened her and the children should they return.

Rosanna 'wants him out' and asks you what can be done.

3.   Neil and Ruby have been married for 16 years and have one child, Charlie (11). Ruby has petitioned for divorce but she and Neil are in dispute over what should happen to Charlie who is currently living with Ruby. The court welfare officer has rung both Ruby and Neil to arrange a meeting to talk about Charlie.

Provide some information on the role of the court welfare officer. If Neil and Ruby cannot agree, what orders are available under the Children Act to provide for the children and what principles will the court take into account when it makes any decision about Charlie?

4.   Ricky and Lorraine have been married for five years and have one child, Steven, aged three. As the duty social worker you receive a phone call from a call box; Lorraine is very upset on the phone and tells you that Ricky has assaulted both her and Steven. You tell her to come to the office where in conversation it transpires that there has been a long history of violence. Lorraine is scared to go back to the home (a local authority flat with a joint tenancy) and she fears for her and Steven's safety in the light of threats made to them by Ricky.

What advice and assistance would you be able to provide in the short term crisis situation and in the longer term?

Would your answer be any different if Ricky and Lorraine were not married?

5.   Terry and June have one child, Hannah, aged six. Terry left the matrimonial home (which they jointly own and subject to a substantial mortgage) two years ago and June has just instructed a solicitor to begin divorce proceedings. Terry is delighted as he has moved in with a new girlfriend. Terry has been seeing Hannah on a weekly basis but June does not want Hannah to meet his new girlfriend and so she has refused to let Hannah see Terry.

How might the court seek to solve the dispute between Terry and June over Hannah?

6.   Marcus and Lorretta, who are married, have lived in a council flat for five years and they have three children aged five, three and two. One month ago they had yet another row and Marcus left. Lorretta has heard nothing from him since, though she knows that he is staying with a friend of his. She has no money and has been living on her child benefit and money borrowed from her mother. She is getting desperate for money but has decided that she does not want Marcus to return or see the children because his aggressive behaviour upsets the children and since he has been away they have been much better. Lorretta is a devout Roman Catholic and would not contemplate beginning divorce proceedings.

What can she do?

5   ACTIVITIES

1.   Ring your local divorce county court and ask whether they produce a booklet to help people undertake their own divorce petitions.

2.   Look in your local telephone book and see if there is a local divorce mediation scheme. Look under 'mediation', 'conciliation'

or 'divorce'. If so contact them for any information they might be able to provide. The addresses and phone numbers for national organisations working in this area are set out below.

3.   Contact your local probation service and ask for any information they can provide on their civil work. It may be possible to spend a day with a court welfare officer.

4.   With the help of the local social services department, women's refuge (if there is one), CABx and any other sources try and compile a list of local lawyers who you would feel able to refer a client to.

5.   Is there a law centre in your area ? Does it deal with domestic violence work?

6 ADDRESSES

British Agencies for Adoption
and Fostering (BAAF),
11 Southwark Street,
London SE1 1RQ.
Phone: 071 407 8800.

Children's Legal Centre,
20 Compton Terrace,
London N1 2UN.
Phone: 071 359 6251. Advice
service 2-5pm weekdays.

Family Mediators Association,
North and Central London —
Phone: 081 954 6383;
South and Central London —
Phone: 081 789 9111;
All other areas —
Phone: 0272 500140.

Law Centres Federation,
Duchess House,
18-19 Warren Street,
London W1P 5DB.
Phone: 071 387 8570.

Legal Aid Board,
5th and 6th Floors,
29-37 Red Lion Street,
London WC1R 4PP.
Phone 071 831 4209.

National Council for One
Parent Families,
255 Kentish Town Road,
London NW5 2LX.
Phone: 071 267 1361.

National Family Conciliation
Council,
Shaftesbury Centre, Percy
Street,
Swindon,
Wiltshire SN2 2AZ.
Phone: 0793 514055.

Solicitors Family Law
Association,
P.O.B. 302,
Keston,
Kent BR2 6EZ.
Phone: 0689 850227.

Rights of Women.
52/54 Featherstone Street,
London EC1.

7 MATERIALS

7.1 MATERIALS FOR EVERYDAY SOCIAL WORK PRACTICE

Legal Aid Board *Legal Aid Guide.*

Allen, N. *Making sense of the Children Act 1989* (1990) Longman.

National Welfare Benefits Handbook Child Poverty Action Group.

Undefended divorce. A guide for the petitioner acting without a solicitor Lord Chancellor's Department. Available free from county courts.

7.2 FURTHER READING

Department of Health *An Introduction to The Children Act 1989* (1989) HMSO.

Bainham, A. 'Children — The New Law. The Children Act 1989' (1990) Family Law.

Dewar, J. *Law and the Family* (1992) Butterworths.

Parkinson, L. *Separation, Divorce and Families* (1987) BASW/ Macmillan.

CHAPTER 5

The law of community care

1 INTRODUCTION

Historically this area of social work and the law which regulates much of it has received relatively little attention. This situation changed in the early 1980s due in many respects to the work of pressure groups such as Age Concern, the Disability Alliance, MENCAP and the Royal Association for Disability and Rehabilitation (RADAR) who succeeded in increasing public recognition of the interests of people who are chronically ill, have a physical disability or learning difficulty.

Social work in this area and with this group of clients constitutes an important element of professional practice. It is regulated by a complex variety of statutory provisions, some imposing duties, some according rights and others giving discretionary powers to local authorities. The National Health Service and Community Care Act 1990 (hereafter known as the Community Care Act), which was implemented in April 1993, establishes local authorities as the lead agency in the provision of community care services but does nothing to reduce the complexity of the law which regulates this area of practice. In some respects the Act increases the complexity by grafting new powers and duties on to those that are already in place under existing legislation such as the Chronically Sick and Disabled Persons Act 1970.

1.1 COMMUNITY CARE: ORGANISATION AND REFORM

Community care is not new. So, for example, it is possible to understand the provisions of the Chronically Sick and Disabled Persons Act 1970 as being directed to allowing people with a disability to live relatively independent lives in their own homes with the help of services provided by the local authority social services department. The trend in social policy toward care in the community rather than in residential institutions was confirmed by the Disabled Persons (Services, Consultation and Representation) Act 1986 (hereafter known as the Disabled Persons Act 1986) and by the programme to close many long stay psychiatric hospitals which has been implemented during the 1980s and early 90s. The introduction of the Social Fund can also be understood as part of a rolling community care programme that is itself seen by some commentators as an element of the privatisation and domestication of the welfare state. This 'rolling programme' of community care has been implemented in an incremental fashion, often without proper resourcing. The failure to implement the key sections of the Disabled Persons Act can be seen as an example of this. It is no surprise therefore to find that the organisation of community care for people with a chronic illness, physical disability, learning disability or for people who are elderly and vulnerable has been the subject of sustained criticism for some time.

In 1986 an Audit Commission report on community care provided an alarming picture of escalating demand for services, increasing costs, particularly for residential provision, and gross underprovision of community care services and facilities. In many ways the Audit Commission's work provided the initiative for the 1988 report on community care by Sir Roy Griffiths which identified confusion in responsibility for community care which was shared between local and national government, the national health service, the voluntary and private sector and informal carers. The Griffiths report recommended that local authorities, through their social services departments, should become the lead agency for community care. Griffiths argued that local authorities should not be the monopoly providors of community care services but act as the arrangers and purchasers of them.

> Elected local authorities are best placed, in my judgement, to assess local needs, set local priorities and monitor local performance. ... What is needed is strengthening and buttressing of their capacity to do this by clarifying and where necessary, adjusting responsibilities and to hold them accountable.[1]

The Griffiths report was published in March 1988 but it is thought that the recommendation of a lead role for local authorities was not well received by government and it was not until November 1989 that a White Paper was published setting out government

[1] 'Community Care: An Agenda for Action'. (1988). HMSO.

legislative proposals for the organisation of community care services. 'Caring for People — Community Care in the Next Decade and Beyond' proposed that a substantial element of care services be supplied by the voluntary and private sectors with local authority social services departments organising and purchasing individual provision in response to their assessment of individual need. However, in other sections the White paper asserted that service provision would have to take account of what is available and affordable.

Provision by the voluntary and private sector was to be extended beyond residential care to include those domicillary care services provided by social services departments. The White Paper fell short of requiring competitive tendering for care provision and recognised that local authorities should retain the power to provide care services themselves particularly for people with high level specific needs. To encourage the use of the voluntary and private sectors the government required local authorities to produce an annually updated three year community care plan. The Secretary of State has the power to intervene by issuing directions and giving guidance.

Part III of the Community Care Act 1990, which was fully implemented in April 1993, provides the legislative framework for community care in England and Wales. The nine sections contained in this part of the Act do not constitute a code of community care law, rather they are a variety of provisions which are grafted onto the legislative framework of community care law that existed prior to the Act.

1.2 LEGAL STRUCTURE

The complex legal structure of community care is built upon a number of powers and duties imposed principally on local authorities and health authorities. The extent of community care law is varied and considerable and, as an example of its scope, can be understood to extend to the duty of housing authorities to provide accommodation for vulnerable people who are homeless and have a priority need under the homelessness provisions of the Housing Act 1985.

The law contains a number of enabling powers which impose duties on local authorities but contain discretion over how and to what extent that duty is performed, eg section 2 of the Chronically Sick and Disabled Persons Act 1970 requires a local authority to make arrangements for the provision of appropriate aids, assistance and facilities to a large category of people who are ill, have a physical disability or learning difficulty. Indeed there has been considerable criticism of this provision arising from the difficulties encountered by people seeking to enforce the duties of local authorities under this section. There are also some discretionary legal powers where local authorities can decide whether they wish to do something, eg section 31 of the National Assistance Act 1948 gives a local authority the power to decide whether it wishes to give funds to voluntary organisations for the provision of recreational facilities or meals for old people.

1.3   CONTENT

One of the difficulties in understanding this area of law arises from the fact that the statutory provisions cover a number of different groups of people. In some respects the different groups constitute distinct client groups for social work. The nature of practice with elderly people who are vulnerable may have some similarities with social work with young people who have a physical disability but there are important differences in the skills and knowledge needed for effective work with both groups. Despite these differences much of the law is the same and though, for example, it would make sense to have a chapter specifically dealing with vulnerable elderly people the information contained in it would in many respects duplicate that presented in a chapter on people with a chronic illness, physical disability or learning difficulty.

The availability of social security benefits specifically designed for people with a disability is considered briefly in this chapter.

2   THE LAW

2.1   THE STATUTORY FRAMEWORK FOR SOCIAL WORK PRACTICE

There are a number of statutory provisions which together constitute the boundaries and framework for social work practice with people who have a chronic illness, a physical disability or learning difficulty.[2]

2.1.1   National Assistance Act 1948: section 29: a general duty to promote welfare

Section 29(1) requires local authorities to make arrangements to promote the welfare of 'persons who are blind, deaf or dumb (or who suffer from mental disorder of any description) and other persons who are substantially and permanently handicapped by illness, injury or congenital deformity or such other disabilities as may be prescribed by the minister'.

2.1.2   Health Services and Public Health Act 1968: section 45: the promotion of the welfare of old people

Section 45 gives local authorities the power to promote the welfare of old people. This may be achieved by the provision of meals on wheels, home helps, transport services, adaptations to the home and social work support. However, a government circular (DHSS 19/71) makes it clear that, in the light of limited financial resources and knowledge and staff shortages, it is 'both impracticable and undesirable for all authorities to seek to provide from the outset all possible services for all the elderly'.

2.1.3   Chronically Sick and Disabled Persons Act 1970: section 1: duty to identify need

Section 1 requires a local authority to identify the needs of those persons identified in section 29 of the National Assistance Act 1948. Section 1 also requires the local authority to publish information about the services it provides for these client groups.

2.1.4   National Health Service and Community Care Act 1990: section 46

This section requires local authorities to publish community care plans which are subject to review and modification. Local

---

[2] On people with learning difficulty see also the chapter on Mental Health.

authorities are required to consult a wide constituency before initial publication and in keeping the plan under review, including health authorities and the voluntary and private sectors.

2.1.5   National Health Service and Community Care Act 1990: section 47

This section establishes a system of assessment of needs for community care services and a requirement that local authorities inform the person assessed of the result of the assessment and their proposals for the provision of community care services.

2.2   SPECIFIC LEGAL PROVISIONS

Within these general powers and duties Parliament has legislated for the provision of more specific services and facilities.

a)   Part III accommodation under section 21 of the National Assistance Act 1948:

> a local authority may with the approval of the Secretary of State, and to such an extent as he may direct shall, make arrangements for providing —
>
> a) residential accommodation for persons who by reason of age, illness, disability or any other circumstances are in need of care and attention which is not otherwise available to them; . . .

The duty has been extended by the Community Care Act to cover expectant and nursing mothers.

b)   Providing home helps and laundry facilities under Schedule 8 of the National Health Service Act 1977.

c)   Arrangements for the provision of welfare services under section 2 of the Chronically Sick and Disabled Persons Act 1970: these include adaptations to accommodation, the installation of a telephone, transport services and help in the home.

d)   Car stickers for the disabled under section 4(1) of the Chronically Sick and Disabled Persons Act 1970.

e)   The provision of invalid cars under section 5(2) and Schedule 2 of the National Health Service Act 1977.

f)   The provision of training and occupation facilities, including day centres, meals, social work support and accommodation for the prevention of physical illness and/or mental disorder under Schedule 8 of the National Health Service Act 1977.

2.3   CARE AND AFTER CARE

Legislation also requires local authorities and health authorities to provide care and after care services. The importance of such services is increasing substantially with the continuing switch to community care as an alternative to residential or institutional care particularly in the mental health field.

a)   The National Health Service Act 1977, Schedule 8 requires local authority social services departments to provide prevention, care and after care services in relation to physical and mental illness.

b)   The Mental Health Act 1983, section 117 places a duty on health authorities and social services departments to provide after care services for patients discharged from psychiatric hospital having been detained for treatment.

2.4   OTHER GENERAL RIGHTS

More general rights include the right to social security benefits eg income support, and of the vulnerable homeless to housing under Part III of the Housing Act 1985. This chapter provides an outline of those social security benefits which have particular relevance to people with a chronic illness, physical disability or learning difficulty.

2.5   COMPULSORY POWERS

There are circumstances in which the law can be exercised against members of these client groups so that social workers become involved in exercising compulsory powers against eg people who have learning difficulty and are unable to care for themselves.

The right of an approved social worker to apply for the compulsory admission to psychiatric hospital of a person who is mentally disordered is discussed in the chapter on mental health.

In relation to other clients section 47 of the National Assistance Act 1948 provides for the compulsory removal from home of those who:

(a) are suffering from grave chronic disease or being aged, infirm or physically incapacitated, are living in insanitary conditions, and

(b) are unable to devote to themselves, and are not receiving from other persons, proper care and attention.

The removal must be for the purpose of securing the necessary care and attention for the person.

The power is substantial and the procedure for using it is complicated. The community physician must certify to the local authority that institutional care is required by a person satisfying the conditions detailed above in their own interests or for preventing injury to the health of or serious nuisance to others. The local authority may then apply to a magistrates' court, or to a single JP, for an order under which the person is removed to a hospital or other suitable place (subject to the agreement of the institution to take the patient) and the order allows their detention there for up to three months. Seven days' notice to the person of the application for the order is normally required but there is an accelerated procedure which excludes the need for seven days' notice. If this procedure is used the order expires after three weeks but can later be replaced by a three month order on application to the court.

Evidence suggests that these compulsory powers are rarely used.

2.6   COMMUNITY CARE SERVICES

The Community Care Act (section 46(3)) defines the term 'community care services' to cover services provided under:

— Part III of the National Assistance Act;

— section 45 of the Health Services and Public Health Act 1968;

— section 21 of and Schedule 8 to the National Health Service Act 1977;

— section 117 of the Mental Health Act 1983.

Services available under these statutory provisions are identified elsewhere in this chapter.

A wider definion of the phrase is adopted in this chapter so that the phrase is taken to include, among other provisions, section 2 of the Chronically Sick and Disabled Persons Act 1970.

2.6.1 The provision of services under the Chronically Sick and Disabled Persons Act 1970

This Act is acknowledged as one of the primary legislative provisions for the provision of community care services which enable and encourage those identified under section 29 of the National Assistance Act 1948 to live reasonably independent lives in their own homes. These services include:

— practical help in the home;

— the provision of or help in obtaining a radio, television or other recreational facilities;

— the provision of lectures, games, outings or assistance in using educational facilities;

— assistance in travelling to such activities;

— assistance in arranging adaptations or the provision of equipment in the home;

— holidays;

— meals in the home or elsewhere;

— the provision of or assistance in obtaining a telephone and special equipment to facilitate its use.

Despite the fact that rights to an assessment and to the provision of services under the 1970 Act have been confirmed by section 4 of the Disabled Persons Act 1986 the promise of the 1970 legislation has never been realised. Indeed there has been sustained criticism of the failure of local authorities to meet their duties under the Act.[3] Rights to an assessment and to the provision of community care services are now further confirmed by duties imposed on local authorities by section 47 of the Community Care Act 1990 though section 2 of the 1970 Act remains in force. It is to be hoped that the default powers of section 7 of the Local Authority Social Services Act 1970 as amended by section 50 of the Community Care Act 1990 will finally provide a means by which people can enforce their rights under section 2.[4]

2.7   THE DISABLED PERSONS ACT 1986: assessment, advocacy and after care

In an attempt to strengthen the notion of entitlement of people with a disability to the services specified under the 1970 Act the Disabled Persons Act 1986 was introduced to provide such people with a stronger voice so that their interests could be properly protected and their needs met.

The 1986 Act provides for the appointment of a representative or advocate for a disabled person who will be able to act on their behalf in connection with the provision by the local authority of any social services. These provisions are contained in sections 1 and 2 of the Act which to date have not been implemented.

Section 3 provides that before making an assessment of needs a local authority should listen to representations made to them by the person with a disability or his or her representative. By this section local authorities are also under a duty to provide a written statement of the needs they accept as requiring provision and their proposals for meeting those needs. Alternatively the local authority must provide written reasons for their decision that the person with a disability does not have needs which require the provision of services by them. Section 3 has never been implemented.

[3] See Keep, J. *Stand and Deliver* (27.8.92) Community Care.
[4] These default powers are discussed later in this chapter.

Section 4 of the Disabled Persons Act confirms the provisions of section 2 of the 1970 Act which itself imposes a duty on local authorities to assess the requirements of people with a disability as defined by section 29 of the National Assistance Act 1948.

Section 7 provides for an assessment by health authorities and social services departments of the needs of patients who have been discharged from hospital having been detained for treatment for a mental disorder for 6 months or more. The use of the term 'mental disorder' in the section is designed to include assessment of people with a learning disability. Upon publication of the White Paper, 'Caring for People — Community Care in the Next Decade and Beyond', in November 1989, the government announced that section 7 will not be implemented arguing that the needs of all people will be assessed under the new system based on the White Paper and existing legislation. That decision continues save for an undertaking to review the situation in the light of experience of the new community care system.

2.8 RESIDENTIAL CARE

Section 21 of the National Assistance Act 1948 provides the legal basis for the provision of local authority residential accommodation (known as Part III accommodation) for those who are in need of care and attention which they would not get if such accommodation was not provided.

Under section 26 a local authority may, as an alternative to its duties under section 21, make arrangements with the voluntary or commercial sector to provide the necessary residential or nursing care accommodation for a person falling within the terms of section 21.

Section 22 provides that where accommodation is provided by the private or voluntary sector residents pay for the accommodation from their income support which includes a residential allowance. The local authority pays the balance. Residents are able to keep a personal allowance for their day to day expenses.

Residents in local authority accommodation are required to pay the authority for their accommodation from their income support subject to a protected personal allowance.

The regulation of private residential and nursing homes takes place under the provisions of the Registered Homes Act 1984. The 1984 Act provides for the registration of private residential and nursing home accommodation where 'board and personal care are provided in residential accommodation for those in need of such personal care by reason of old age, disablement, past or present dependence on alcohol or drugs, or past or present mental disorder'. For residential accommodation the registration authority is the local authority whose duties are exercised by the social services department. The registration and inspection of residential care homes is concerned with the quality and safety of facilities and services and is influenced by the Code of Practice, Home Life, issued by the Department.[5] The Code establishes principles of care that can be seen as a set of 'rights' for residents ie fulfilment, dignity, autonomy, individuality and esteem.

Small residential care homes (where board and personal care for less than 4 persons is provided) have been brought within a modified system of registration by the Registered Homes (Amendment) Act 1991.

In relation to private nursing homes the supervision and registration are carried out by health authorities under the terms of the Act and the influence of the Code of Guidance: *Registration and Inspection of Nursing Homes; A Handbook for Health Authorities.*[6]

2.9   INSPECTION UNDER THE NATIONAL HEALTH SERVICE AND COMMUNITY CARE ACT 1990

Section 48 of the Community Care Act provides for a system of inspection for premises in which community care services are provided. Inspectors are authorised by the Secretary of State to enter and inspect premises except those registered under the Registered Homes Act 1984; the system therefore extends to premises in the voluntary and private sector and to all premises which are not covered by other legislation.

[5] For further detail see Brooke Ross, R. 'Regulation of Residential Homes for the Elderly in England and Wales' (March 1985) Journal of Social Welfare Law.

[6] For critical comment on the Registered Homes Act 1984 see Carson, D. 'Registering Homes: Another Fine Mess?' (March 1985) Journal of Social Welfare Law.

The main function of inspecting the provision of community care services is undertaken by local authorities under powers granted in existing community care law and by arrangements for monitoring and inspection negotiated in contracts for the provision of community care services.

2.10   GUARDIANSHIP UNDER THE MENTAL HEALTH ACT 1983

The guardianship provisions of the Mental Health Act are contained in sections 7-10 and provide a mechanism by which the interests of someone who is over 16 and has a mental disorder can be protected. This protection is afforded by placing the person in the guardianship of the local authority social services department or some other person approved by them. The guardian will have considerable control over that person's life.

Reception into guardianship can only take place where it is for the welfare of the patient or the protection of other people and requires a diagnosis of mental disorder as defined by the Mental Health Act. Under the Act there are four categories of mental disorder: mental illness, severe mental impairment, mental impairment and psychopathic disorder. The utility of guardianship orders in the provision of care for people with learning disability is restricted by the definition of mental impairment in the Act. This is defined as a state of arrested or incomplete development of mind (not amounting to severe mental impairment) which includes significant impairment of intelligence and social functioning and is associated with abnormally aggressive or seriously irresponsible conduct of the person concerned. As a result a client with learning disability who does not display abnormally aggressive or seriously irresponsible conduct is not mentally impaired for the purposes of the Act and therefore cannot be received into guardianship under it.

These limitations have had the effect of severely restricting the use of guardianship by local authorities (possibly as few as 200 orders are made each year) though it also seems that many authorities are reluctant to use guardianship because of the compulsion attached to it. The stigma attached to the use of compulsory powers under the Mental Health Act is significant and challenges proposals to extend guardianship powers to those people with learning difficulty who currently fall outside the definition of mental impairment and also perhaps to seriously confused elderly people who exhibit bizarre behaviour.[7]

2.11 EDUCATION

The legal framework for the education of children and young people who have special educational needs as a result of their physical disability or learning difficulty is contained in the Education Act 1981. This area of law and practice is discussed in Chapter 11.

The Disabled Persons Act 1986 requires the local education authority to notify the social services department of the date that the young person with a statement of special educational needs will be leaving full time education. The provisions of section 5 of the Act also require the social services department to carry out an assessment of the needs of the young person.

2.12 THE MANAGEMENT OF PROPERTY AND AFFAIRS FOR THOSE UNABLE TO DO SO THEMSELVES

One difficult aspect of illness, physical disability or learning difficulty concerns the ability of people to manage their own affairs either temporarily or permanently. The law provides a number of procedures and facilities to overcome this problem.[8]

2.12.1 Day to day

The weekly collection of social security benefits or pensions may be undertaken by someone nominated as an agent. This may be the local authority where a long term agent is needed for someone living in Part III accommodation.

Where a person is unable to undertake more complex dealings with the Department of Social Security eg claiming benefit,

---

[7] For an extended discussion of guardianship in relation to the elderly see Age Concern *The Law and Vulnerable Elderly People* Section 3, Chapter 2. (1986).

[8] For further detail see Age Concern *Legal Arrangements for Managing Financial Affairs* Fact Sheet Number 22.

because of their incapacity then the Department may appoint someone else to exercise that person's rights in respect of social security benefits. Dealings with banks or building societies may require what is known as a third party mandate; essentially a permission to act on behalf of the person.

2.12.2 Power of Attorney

Broader powers to act on behalf of someone else may be given under a Power of Attorney; the power may be limited to specific matters or unlimited. The power may only be given and exercised while the donor of the power has mental capacity in the sense that they are able to understand what they are doing and what the effects will be. A Power of Attorney will come to an end when the donor no longer has the necessary mental capacity as described.

2.12.3 Enduring Power of Attorney

This disadvantage, which is considerable, has been addressed by the Enduring Power of Attorney Act 1985. Under the Act a person with mental capacity (the donor) may appoint someone else (the attorney) to manage their affairs when they lose the mental capacity to do so themselves. The form of this appointment is governed by regulations. When the donor becomes mentally incapable the enduring Power of Attorney must be registered with the Court of Protection. Notice of the intention to register must be given by the attorney to the donor and to at least three of the donor's nearest relatives. Both the donor and his or her relatives are entitled to object to the registration or to the attorney. The attorney must act on behalf of the donor and in their interests and the Court of Protection will consider complaints against an attorney.

2.12.4 The Court of Protection[9]

The task of the Court of Protection is to protect and manage the financial affairs and property of people who are unable to do so themselves because of their mental incapacity. The Court

[9] The Court of Protection is briefly discussed in the chapter on Mental Health. The work of the Court is equally important in relation to the customer groups considered in this chapter so that a further discussion is presented here.

is regulated by the Mental Health Act 1983 and the Court of Protection Rules.

An application to have someone placed under the jurisdiction of the Court may be made by anyone, including a local authority, though normally it will be by the nearest relative. There must be a medical diagnosis that the person is 'incapable, by reason of mental disorder, of managing and administering his property and affairs'. A person under the jurisdiction of the Court is known as a patient. The Court is likely to appoint a receiver to manage the patient's property; this may be a relative, solicitor, bank or the Director of a local authority social services department. Before appointing a receiver the Court will notify the patient of what is proposed so that objections can be made. The task of the receiver is to administer the patient's money and affairs in their best interests and according to the Court's instructions. The patient may make a valid will if the Court considers that they have 'testamentary capacity'; if this is not the case then the Court will make a statutory will on their behalf. Receivers must normally submit annual accounts to the Court and administration fees are payable to the Court. A receivership will end on the death of the patient or on recovery of mental capacity.

Where the estate is small or the administration is simple the Court may use what is known as a short procedure order under which authorisation for particular transactions is given by the Court without the need for the appointment of a receiver.

There has been some concern over the work of the Court centering on the inadequacy of staff to properly deal with the approximately 22,000 cases under its jurisdiction, the level of fees charged and the lack of public awareness of its work.[10]

2.13   SOCIAL SECURITY BENEFITS

Entitlement to benefit is an issue of considerable importance to a substantial number of people with a chronic illness, physical disability or learning difficulty. Despite concerted pressure by a number of pressure groups representing such claimants (and

[10] For a more detailed criticism and discussion of the work of the Court see Age Concern *The Law and Vulnerable Elderly People* Section 3, Chapter 1. (1986).

clients) and notwithstanding the introduction of disability living allowance there is no unified disability benefit available, instead claimants have to establish entitlement to individual benefits designed to meet specific need. Some of these benefits are contributory in the sense that entitlement depends in part on adequate national insurance contributions, others are non-contributory; whilst the basic benefit of income support is means tested. In this chapter consideration will concentrate on those benefits which are specifically designed for claimants with a long term illness, physical disability or learning difficulty.

2.13.1 Income support[11]

This means tested benefit provides a subsistence level of income to all those whose resources (both capital and income) do not meet a level set by the state. Benefit is paid at a rate which is fixed by reference to designated categories of need.

The level of benefit paid may be increased by a premium payment which reflects special categories of need. Two premium categories are of particular relevance here, they are age and ill-health. Premiums are paid in respect of a disabled child, to pensioners and in respect of disablement.

The disabled child premium is paid if a child is receiving disability living allowance or is registered blind.

Disability premium is paid on the basis of disability or long term sickness and can be established by entitlement to disability benefits such as attendance allowance, disability living allowance and severe disablement allowance or the long term sickness benefit or invalidity pension. There is also a severe disability premium for those who are treated by the income support regulations as severely disabled which in essence requires receipt of disability living allowance and that no one is being paid by the state, through invalid care allowance, to look after them.

[11] Only the briefest outline is provided here. The law in relation to income support is complex; the best claimants' guide, which includes details on the Social Fund and Housing Benefit, is the *National Welfare Benefits Handbook* published annually by the Child Poverty Action Group. Social security benefits for people with a disability are detailed in the *Disability Rights Handbook* published annually by the Disability Alliance.

The pensioner premium is paid on the basis of an age entitlement and the higher pensioner premium is paid on the basis of age and disability.

2.13.2   Benefits for short term sickness

Statutory sick pay or sickness benefit are benefits paid to those who are incapable of work for a short period of time (usually up to 28 weeks). Statutory sick pay is paid by employers to their employees who are incapable of work due to sickness or disability whilst entitlement to sickness benefit depends on an adequate contribution record and is paid to claimants who are not in employment and cannot seek or take employment because of their incapacity.

2.13.3   Benefits for long term or permanent sickness or disability

For claimants who develop a long term or permanent incapacity for work their entitlement to statutory sick pay or sickness benefit is likely to be superseded by an entitlement to invalidity benefit. This benefit is made up of a basic pension together with an allowance the value of which relates to age at the time of incapacity. Dependency allowances in respect of adults and children may be added to the pension and age related allowance.

2.13.4   Severe disablement allowance

This is a benefit which does not depend on a contribution record, nor is it means tested. The claimant must have been incapable of work for at least 28 weeks and, except for those whose incapacity began before their twentieth birthday, be classed as 80% disabled. This level of disablement is automatically satisfied by receipt of attendance allowance, disability living allowance, or by being registered blind.

2.13.5   Disability living allowance

Disability living allowance has replaced mobility allowance and will eventually replace attendance allowance. It is designed for people who need help with looking after themselves and for those who find it difficult to walk or get around. Disability living allowance therefore has two components — a care component and a mobility component; both have different disability tests and both have different levels of payment. The benefit is non means tested, non contributory and is paid on top of income support and other social security benefits.

There are strict age tests: there is no lower age limit for the care component; the claimant must be 5 or over for the mobility component. Disability living allowance is payable for life but the claimant must have started to qualify for the benefit before his or her sixty-fifth birthday; the claimant must have been under 66 on 6 April 1992 and the claim must be made no later than the day before the claimant's sixty-sixth birthday.

The care component disability tests are:

— the claimant must be so severely disabled physically or mentally that he or she requires from another person:

DURING THE DAY

No 1 — frequent attention throughout the day in connection with bodily functions; or

No 2 — continual supervision throughout the day in order to avoid substantial danger to themselves or to others; or

AT NIGHT

No 3 — prolonged or repeated attention in connection with bodily functions; or

No 4 — in order to avoid substantial danger to themselves or to others the claimant requires another person to be awake for a prolonged period or at frequent intervals for the purpose of watching over themselves; or

PART TIME DAY CARE

No 5 — the claimant requires in connection with bodily functions attention from another person for a significant portion of the day (whether during a single period or a number of periods); or

No 6 — the claimant cannot prepare a cooked main meal for themselves if they have the ingredients.

The higher rate of care component is paid to claimants who satisfy either or both 1 and 2 and either or both 3 and 4.

The middle rate is paid to claimants who satisfy either or both 1 and 2 or either or both 3 and 4.

The lower rate is paid to claimants who satisfy either or both 5 and 6.

The mobility component tests are:

The higher rate tests are:

1. inability to walk ; or

2. virtual inability to walk; or

3. the exertion required to walk would constitute a danger to life or would be likely to lead to a serious deterioration in health; or

4. the claimant has no legs or feet (from birth or through amputation); or

5. the claimant is both deaf and blind; or

6. the claimant gets higher rate care component and is severely mentally impaired with extremely disruptive and dangerous behavioural problems; or

7. the claimant is switching from the pre-1976 invalid vehicle scheme and still meets those rules.

The lower rate mobility test is:

— the claimant may be able to walk but be so severely disabled physically or mentally that, disregarding any ability the claimant may have to use routes which are familiar to the claimant on their own, the claimant cannot take advantage of the faculty out of doors without guidance or supervision from another person most of the time.

2.13.6 Attendance allowance (for claimants who were aged 65+ on 6 April 1992)

This benefit, which is non-contributory and is not means tested, is paid where the claimant is severely disabled physically or mentally and as a result needs to be looked after either during the day or the night or during both the day and the night. Being 'looked after' involves what the Social Security Act 1975 calls 'frequent or prolonged or repeated attention with bodily functions' or 'continual supervision to avoid substantial danger to self or to others'. The benefit is paid at a lower or higher rate depending on whether the help is needed for the day or night or for the whole 24 hours.

2.13.7 Disability working allowance

This benefit which is tax free and non-contributory is paid on top of low wages or self employed earnings to people whose disabilities put them at a disadvantage in getting a job. The person with a disability must be working for more than 16 hours a week.

2.13.8 Invalid care allowance

This benefit is paid to the carer of someone who is receiving attendance allowance or disability living allowance. The care must be 'regular and substantial' and in effect is the equivalent of a full time job for the law deems caring for 35 hours a week to satisfy this requirement and disqualifies from entitlement anyone who is gainfully employed or in full time education. This is a non-contributory non-means tested benefit.

2.13.9 Those who are sick or disabled because of an industrial injury or disease

The Social Security Act 1975 provides a series of benefits for those who have been injured at work or who have contracted one of a number of specified industrial diseases. In many respects the benefits are the equivalent of those already mentioned eg constant attendance allowance is the industrial equivalent of disability living allowance and attendance allowance; in addition claimants of these benefits may also be entitled to non-industrial benefits such as the mobility component of disability living allowance whilst carers may be entitled to invalid care allowance.

2.13.10   The social fund

The social fund is a Department of Social Security benefit to help people on a low income meet exceptional expenses. The fund is largely discretionary and comprises of community care grants, budgeting loans and crisis loans.

Community care grants can be made to 'promote community care' which is defined by the department to include helping someone establish themselves in the community after discharge from residential or institutional care, or helping someone remain in the community rather than be admitted to residential or institutional care. Such grants are said to be designed to complement, not replace, provision by health authorities and social services departments.

Budgeting loans are designed to assist claimants meet occasional expenses for which it might be difficult to budget. They are repayable to the department.

Crisis loans can be made by the department to help with expenses following an emergency or disaster.

The statutory social fund provides entitlement to grants paid in respect of maternity expenses, funeral costs and cold weather.

3   COMMUNITY CARE, THE LAW AND SOCIAL WORK PRACTICE: some issues for discussion

3.1   ENFORCING RIGHTS TO COMMUNITY CARE SERVICES

The difficulty of enforcing rights to community care services has been a cause for concern for many years. Section 50 of the Community Care Act amends section 7 of the Local Authority Social Services Act 1970 to provide for: i) the Secretary of State to issue directions to local authorities concerning the exercise of their social services functions; ii) for local authorities to establish a complaints procedure; iii) the Secretary of State to establish an inquiry to consider the exercise of social services functions by any local authority; and iv) for default powers under which the Secretary of State can order a local authority to comply with their statutory duties.

The Secretary of State may issue directions to local authorities concerning the exercise of their community care functions and authorities must exercise their functions in accordance with such directions. It seems that the government intends that this power should only be used infrequently to safeguard the interests of users of services and their carers.

Local authorities must have a complaints procedure concerning the assessment of community care services and their provision. The procedure must have an independent element to it.

Section 7D specifies the default powers of the Secretary of State. Their operation has been explained by the Parliamentary Under-Secretary of State for the Department of Health in the House of Lords debate on the Community Care Bill.

> We expect the default procedures in this section to work in the following way. The first stage will be when it comes to the Secretary of State's attention that an authority is failing to discharge its functions. This may come from a number of directions — the work of the social services inspectorate, information received from organisations representing disabled people or by direct representations to the Secretary of State by users of services. The first thing the Secretary of State needs to do is to satisfy himself that the authority has failed without reasonable cause to exercise its functions. This will entail some form of further investigation or enquiry and may, if the Secretary of State feels it would be useful, include using the general powers of direction to direct the authority to exercise its functions in a particular way.

> It will only be after these processes have been exhausted and work with the authorities through the social services inspectorate has failed to secure any improvement in the situation that the use of the default powers will be considered. ..... When these powers are used the Secretary of State first has to issue an order then, if it is not complied with, he can seek an order from the court to enforce it.

Service users may conclude that these default powers, which are seen by government as a last resort when the other procedures of section 50 have been gone through, are too slow and cumbersome to provide an effective remedy for a person with a chronic illness, physical disability or learning difficulty who needs community care services which they are not receiving or for which they have not been assessed.

Complaints to the Commissioner for Local Administration (the local government ombudsman) concerning delays in carrying out assessments have generated reports which are critical of local authority delay in the assessment process. Perhaps more significantly the Divisional Court has ordered a judicial review of a case involving Hereford and Worcester County Council where the authority failed to provide the full time carer the authority's assessment had established was necessary for a client. The case was settled out of court on the basis that the authority provided the full time carer and compensated the client.[12]

The situation now seems to be that the 'mixed economy' of community care is matched by a 'mixed economy' of enforcement procedures. To the possibility of using default powers, complaints procedures, local ombudsman complaints and judicial review applications, recourse might be had to particular procedures established under legislation that relates to specific groups of clients such as children with special educational needs under the Education Act 1981 and children with a disability under the Children Act 1989. The possibilities are varied, though complexity and confusion might ensnare the client with a legitimate grievance and an unmet need for community care services.

3.2   PEOPLE WITH LEARNING DIFFICULTY

The ambiguous legal position of people with learning difficulty is discussed at some length in the chapter on mental health particularly in relation to the case involving the death of Beverley Lewis. However it is worth restating some of the points of that discussion in the context of this chapter.

The legal position of people with learning difficulty currently means that unless they display abnormally aggressive or seriously irresponsible conduct they do not come within the compulsory powers of the Mental Health Act 1983. It is argued that, in relation to people who because of their age, physical disability or learning

---

[12] See John Keep 'Stand and Deliver' (27.8.92) Community Care.

difficulty are unable to care for themselves, compulsory powers should be available and used where appropriate to protect their interests and promote their care. This paternalistic basis for compulsory intervention is evidenced in the removal from home powers in section 47 of the National Assistance Act as well as in the compulsory admission and guardianship powers of the Mental Health Act 1983. The Beverley Lewis case provides disturbing evidence that despite these compulsory powers and general community care services a number of people with learning difficulty are not receiving the care services they need. The closure of long stay beds in psychiatric hospitals has meant that a substantial number of patients/residents have been discharged into the community where the under funding of community care services has meant that many do not receive appropriate care. This feature is compounded where health authorities and social services departments have been unable to properly assess their needs. Assessment of needs is important and it is to be regretted that upon publication of its White Paper on community care the government announced that section 7 of the Disabled Persons Act 1986, which requires assessment of the needs of a patient, including someone who has learning difficulty who is to be discharged from psychiatric hospital, was not to be implemented.

The Beverley Lewis case has led to calls for the reform of the guardianship provisions of the Mental Health Act. The guardianship order is designed to provide mentally disordered patients with a less restrictive alternative to hospital detention. However, the definition of mental impairment adopted in the Act, in an attempt to distance people with learning difficulty from the compulsory powers of the Act, has meant that very few guardianship orders are made by local authorities. Reform of the Act to bring people with learning difficulty within its compulsory provisions would frustrate the intentions of the legislators and those who argued on their behalf.[13]

MENCAP have argued that the issue of guardianship, beyond the limited context of the Mental Health Act, be urgently considered so that people with learning difficulty will be

[13] For an argument that particular interpretations of the guardianship order or of section 47 of the National Assistance Act 1948 might have allowed compulsory intervention to protect the interests of Beverley Lewis see Phil Fennell 'The Beverley Lewis Case: was the law to blame?' (17.11.89) New Law Journal, pp 1557–1558.

adequately protected. They cite concern about the ability of people with learning difficulty to consent to operations and the legal basis on which the courts have permitted sterilisations to be carried out, as particular issues and suggest that the concept of guardianship might be used as a means by which the interests of people with learning difficulty may be protected.[14] The consideration by the Law Commission of the law concerning vulnerable mentally disordered people is to be welcomed if it provides some adequate protections for people with learning difficulty and for others who because of their mental disorder are not able to properly provide for themselves.

3.3   DISCHARGING PATIENTS WHO HAVE OR HAVE HAD A MENTAL ILLNESS: AFTER CARE AND COMMUNITY CARE

In the House of Lords debate on the Community Care Act, Baroness Hooper, the Parliamentary Under-Secretary of State for the Department of Health, outlined the expected position under the Act.

> . . . because we recognise the need for a seamless service for patients being discharged from hospital and in particular the special needs of those who have had treatment for a mental disorder, we have taken steps to address the situation. First, we have issued guidance on discharge planning for all patients (The Discharge of Patients from Hospital). It covered the care of patients released after a short spell in hospital as well as those who have received long term care. Secondly, our draft guidance on community care planning . . . specifically mentions discharge procedures as an area on which health and local authorities should make planning agreements. As part of such agreements, health and local authorities will need to reach agreement on assessing the needs for care services provided by local authorities. Thirdly, in relation to mentally ill people, we have made it clear that mentally ill people discharged into the community should have a precise plan drawn up for their after care. This should help both to prevent inappropriate discharge and also lessen the risk of people losing touch with the caring services at a later stage. We have recently issued for consultation with local authorities, district health authorities and other interested bodies draft guidance on care programmes for mentally ill people. ... Fourthly, section 117 of the Mental Health Act 1983 already imposes a duty on district health authorities and local authorities to provide, in collaboration with

---

[14] See Whelton, M. Mann, G. *Mental Handicap and the Law* MENCAP, pp 19–20.

voluntary agencies, after care services for certain categories of mentally disordered patients who have ceased to be detained and who leave hospital. The duty on the authority is to provide such after care services until they are satisfied that the person concerned is no longer in need of them.[15]

This extended quotation has been included because it identifies the expectations of government concerning the provision for one category of client needing community care services and also because it provides a good example of how the assessment and provision of community care services should work in practice. Assessment, consultation, joint planning, statutory after care and community care service provision here characterise the structure and practice of community care.

3.4 PROTECTING THE RIGHTS OF PEOPLE WHO ARE ELDERLY

Age Concern, in its 1986 report, 'The Law and Vulnerable Elderly People', called for legislation similar to child care law to protect vulnerable elderly people from neglect and abuse. The report acknowledged the improvements that might be generated by the Disabled Persons Act 1986 but nonetheless called for specific legal powers and duties to be imposed on local authorities. The general power to promote the interests of people who are elderly under the Health Services and Public Health Act 1968 could be amended to include a power to give advice, guidance and assistance in the same way that such powers are provided in relation to children in need by the Children Act 1989. There may also be a need for a provision similar to that in section 47 of the Children Act which requires a local authority to investigate where they have reasonable cause to suspect that a child is suffering or is likely to suffer significant harm. The Age Concern report acknowledged the difficulty of enforcing duties to assess needs and provide services by calling for an intervention order by which a court could require the local authority to provide the services detailed in an order.

It is entirely legitimate to argue that the provisions of the Community Care Act, particularly the duty to assess and the enforcement procedures, render the call from Age Concern

---

[15] Hansard, H.L. Vol 520, cols 489-90; quoted in Current Law Annotated Statutes 1990 c 19 19/46.

redundant. Experience of the Act over its first years will determine its utility and effectiveness but the placing of legal duties on local authorities to provide or arrange for the provision of community care services without proper funding will mean that concerns on behalf of vulnerable elderly people will remain. There are some who fear that an under-funded community care service might increase the pressure on those who look after vulnerable elderly people to an extreme in which the incidence of elder abuse could increase.[16]

3.5   ASSESSMENT FOR COMMUNITY CARE SERVICES

Section 47 of the Community Care Act sets out the assessment duty of local authorities in seemingly circular terms.

> . . . where it appears to a local authority that any person for whom they may provide or arrange for the provision of community care services may be in need of any such services, the authority —
>
> (a)   shall carry out an assessment of his needs for those services; and
>
> (b)   having regard to the results of that assessment, shall then decide whether his needs call for the provision by them of any such services.

The trigger to assessment is whether a person is someone for whom an authority may provide community care services. This is a matter of law so that where there is a refusal to assess that decision can be challenged in the courts by way of an appliction for judicial review. The form of assessment to be used is a matter of choice for the local authority though arrangements for assessment will have to be published in an authority's community care plan and the consultation requirement for the compilation of such plans should enable the views of all parties including carers to be taken into account in the design of the assessment arrangements.

Assessment is a multi-disciplinary undertaking. The government spokesperson in the House of Lords debate on the Act identified government expectations of the process of assessment by referring to the White Paper:

---

[16] For comment on the existence and reality of elder abuse see, for example Polly Neate *Home Truths* (13.6.91) Community Care.

... all agencies and professions involved with the individual and his or her problems should be brought into the assessment procedure when necessary . . .

The White Paper lists: social workers, GPs, community nurses, hospital staff such as consultants in geriatric medicine, psychiatry, rehabilitation and other hospital specialities, nurses, physiotherapists, occupational therapists, continence advisors, community psychiatric nurses, staff involved with vision and hearing impairment, housing officers, the Employment Department's resettlement officers and its employment rehabilitation service, home helps, home care assistants and voluntary workers.[17]

The process of assessment is concerned to identify whether there is a need for community care services in relation to a particular client and if so to identify those services that are needed. Following an assessment local authorities are obliged to take into account their duties under section 2 of the Chronically Sick and Disabled Persons Act 1970 and other legislation such as the National Assistance Act 1948, section 21 and Schedule 8 to the National Health Service Act 1977 and section 117 of the Mental Health Act 1983. However local authorities under the Community Care Act are not obliged to meet all needs and are told by government that they should take into account priorities and resources though obligations under the Chronically Sick and Disabled Persons Act are mandatory and must be complied with notwithstanding an authority's financial circumstances.

Funding for the first year of community care (1993/94) is set at £539 million, based on government estimates of 110,000 elderly and disabled people who during the year would have gone into residential care. Based on figures produced by the Institute of Health Services Management, which argues that £750 million is needed to properly implement community care reforms, the Royal Association for Disability and Rehabilitation has expressed concern about the plight of service users.

Community care should mean choice and a system that provides options for choice to be genuine — but will it? If local authorities are to be assessors and providers of resources for community care how will conflicts of interest be avoided? What safeguards will there be to ensure user led assessment rather than resource led assessment?[18]

[17] 'Caring for People — Community Care in the Next Decade and Beyond' (1989) quoted in Current Law, Annotated Statutes 1990 c 19 19/47.
[18] RADAR Bulletin No 221 November 1992.

3.6   IMPLEMENTATION OF THE DISABLED PERSONS ACT 1986

The failure of government to implement some of the major provisions of the Act is cause for serious concern. The Act is designed to improve the position of 'disabled persons', a wide group of people defined by reference to section 29 of the National Assistance Act as the 'blind, deaf or dumb, and other persons who are substantially and permanently handicapped by illness, injury or congenital deformity or who are suffering from a mental disorder within the meaning of the Mental Health Act'. One of the strategies for achieving this improvement is the appointment of a representative or advocate who could articulate the desires and wishes of the disabled person for the provision of care services. The appointment of representatives is provided for in section 1 of the Act and the rights of that person are specified in section 2. These sections have not been implemented.

Section 3 of the Act provides for the assessment of needs of disabled persons and similarly has not been implemented. The government has announced that section 7, which would have required the assessment of persons, including people with learning difficulty, leaving psychiatric hospital after treatment as an inpatient for 6 months or more, will not be implemented.

3.7   ADVOCATING RIGHTS TO COMMUNITY CARE SERVICES

The Disabled Persons Act 1986 recognises the need for some community care clients to have a person appointed to represent their interests in the process of establishing service provision for their community care needs. It is much to be regretted that these particular sections of the Act, sections 1, 2 and 3, have never been implemented. Nonetheless the interests of a representative or advocate are implicitly recognised in the Community Care Act which requires wide consultation in the drafting of community care plans and in the process of assessment.

Citizen advocacy is a relatively new development in Britain though its impact in the era of community care established by the implementation of the Community Care Act 1990 promises to be considerable. Terry Philpot, writing in the Guardian quotes

Wendy Booth of the Huddersfield Citizen Advocacy Group on the philosophy of the movement:

> . . . a process through which the interests of devalued people are represented and protected . . . Advocates do not assess their partner's best interests but work with them to discover how they see things, either assisting them to express their needs directly or making representations on their partner's behalf.[19]

Advocacy should complement the role of local authorities and social workers in assessing the need of individual clients for community care services and ensuring that proper service provision is made. In this way advocates and practitioners can be instrumental in making sure that vulnerable people and those with a chronic illness, physical disability or learning difficulty can have the optimum level of control over their own lives.

4 CASE STUDIES

1. Anny is an elderly woman living on her own in a privately rented flat. She is chronically ill and you are concerned that she is not looking after herself and is forgetting to turn off the gas fire at night. She also refuses to go to the hospital appointments that her GP makes for her. The GP has asked you, as a social worker, to try to help. He expresses the view that Anny cannot carry on in this way much longer. She appears to have no living relatives.

What can you do to help Anny?

2. Joan is an elderly woman living in a small house with her daughter Mary. The house is owned by Joan. In the past year Joan has developed a condition that has made it very difficult for her to get up the stairs to the bedroom and bathroom. Joan has written to the council for help, but they have told her that the waiting list for a visit is nine months due to lack of staff. Joan can no longer get out to the shops because she cannot walk that far and can no longer do any housework. Mary, who is out at work all day, is becoming very worried about Joan's mobility and her general condition. Joan lives on her pension.

[19] Terry Philpot 'A partner, friend and voice'. (17.9.92) Guardian.

You work for a charity that provides advice to elderly people and Mary has approached you with a number of specific enquiries:

a) will the council install a stairlift?

b) will the council provide a home help for her mother?

c) will the council provide and install a personal alarm for her mother?

d) as a last resort will the council provide a place in a residential home for Joan?

e) what social security benefits are available for their situation?

3. Alice is 84 years' old and lives on her own in a local authority flat. She has been referred to the social services department for the first time by her GP and the case has been allocated to you. She has very bad arthritis and her flat is damp and draughty and has not been modified in any way to help her. She has trouble using the bath and the toilet and she cannot get out to collect her pension.

Identify the statutory provisions which you would consider in determining the ways in which you could help Alice continue to live in her own flat.

In what circumstances would she be entitled to residential accommodation?

4. Peter is 73 years' old and is living in a private residential care home. He is becoming increasingly confused and is withdrawing large sums of cash from his substantial bank account. He sends the money to his son asking him to look after it for him because the woman who is running the home is trying to steal it from him. His house has been empty since he went into the home and his stockbroker is asking for instructions with regard to his investments.

The son asks you for a detailed explanation of the possible legal arrangements that can be made for someone in his father's position.

Consider also the situation if Peter were 85, currently in good physical and mental health but concerned that in the near future he may begin to lose his mental faculties and not be able to manage his personal and financial affairs.

5. Robert is 24 years' old, blind, deaf and has learning difficulty. Since he left his special school at the age of 19 he has lived at home and been cared for by his mother. Over the last two years it has become increasingly difficult to visit Robert; his mother is very aggressive and refuses to allow anyone to enter the house. Last year you were so concerned that you managed to get Robert admitted to psychiatric hospital for assessment but he was discharged three days later after his mother pleaded with the psychiatrist to let him return home. You understand from Robert's elder sister that he spends all his time lying on a sofa in the front room in squalid conditions and she is concerned about the standard of care being provided for him by their mother who she thinks is mentally ill. The house is in a bad state of disrepair and is owned by the local authority.

As a local authority field social worker (and an approved social worker) what can you do?

5   ACTIVITIES

1. Get a copy of your local authority's community care plan and check through the arrangements it has made for the provision of community care services.

This will give you a picture of provision by the statutory, voluntary and private sector.

2. Which voluntary groups are working in your area? What community care services do they provide?

For example, is there a local Age Concern or MENCAP group?

3. Write to the pressure groups and voluntary organisations working with the client groups discussed in this chapter and get hold of their publication lists.

Age Concern have a comprehensive list of publications and they produce a number of free fact sheets which provide important information concerning people who are elderly.

RADAR has a comprehensive publications list.

The Disability Alliance produces an annual edition of its *ESSENTIAL Disability Rights Handbook*.

4. How does the complaints procedure work in your local authority?

5. How does the inspection system work in your local authority?

6. Look at Community Care on a regular basis. The implementation of the Act will be monitored and the first year(s) of experience evaluated.

7. Subscribe to RADAR's monthly Bulletin.

6   ADDRESSES

Age Concern,
Astral House,
1268 London Road,
London SW16 4EJ.
Phone: 081 640 5431.

Centre for Policy on Ageing,
25-31 Ironmonger Row,
London EC1V 3QP.

Court of Protection,
The Public Trust Office,
Protection Division, Stewart House,
24 Kingsway,
London WC2B 6JX.

National Association for
Mental Health (MIND),
22 Harley Street,
London W1N 2ED.
Phone: 071 637 0741.

The Disability Alliance
Educational and Research
Association,
Universal House,
88-94 Wentworth Street,
London E1 7SA.
Phone: 071 247 8776.

The Royal Association for
Disability and Rehabilitation
(RADAR),
25 Mortimer Street,
London W1.
Phone: 071 637 5400.

MENCAP,
123 Golden Lane,
London EC1Y 0RT.
Phone: 071 253 9433.

7 MATERIALS

7.1 BASIC LEGAL MATERIALS FOR ORDINARY SOCIAL WORK PRACTICE

Age Concern *Age Concern Fact Sheets.*

'Dealing With The Estates of People Suffering From Mental Disorder' Public Trust Office.

Disability Rights Handbook 'Disability Alliance' (New edition published annually in April/May.) ESSENTIAL.

Luke Clements 'Duties of social services departments' Legal Action. September 1992.

'Enduring Powers of Attorney' Public Trust Office.

'Handbook for Receivers' Public Trust Office.

'If Only I'd Known That A Year Ago. A guide for newly disabled people, their families and friends' RADAR.

RADAR Fact Sheets.

'Sick or Disabled? A guide to benefits if you are sick or disabled for a few days or more' Department of Social Security Leaflet FB28.

Your local authority Community Care Plan.

7.2 FURTHER READING

'Home Life: A Code of Practice for Residential Care' Department of Health Circular LAC (89) 8. Published by Centre for Policy on Ageing.

Brooke Ross, R. 'Safeguarding and Promoting the Welfare of Residents? The Contribution of the Registered Homes Act in England and Wales' (1989) No 5 Journal of Social Welfare Law.

Fennell, P. 'The Beverley Lewis case: was the law to blame?' (17.11.89) New Law Journal.

Griffiths, A., Grimes, R., and Roberts, G. *The Law and Elderly People* (1990) Routledge.

Greengross, S. *The Law and Vulnerable Elderly People* (1986) Age Concern.

CHAPTER 6

The criminal justice system

1 INTRODUCTION

1.1 SOCIAL WORK INVOLVEMENT IN THE CRIMINAL JUSTICE SYSTEM

Social work involvement in the criminal justice system centres on the work of the probation service. Other social workers may also have clients who are facing a criminal prosecution, are victims of a crime or are seeking to discharge a sentence of the court such as a fine. This chapter, which is concerned with the adult criminal justice system,[1] will provide information specifically concerned with probation work but will also give an outline of the jurisdiction of the criminal courts and of criminal procedure. The sentencing options of the courts will be discussed and the principles of sentencing outlined. The chapter does not provide a comprehensive discussion of probation work.

Whilst the probation service provides specialist social work practice skills in the criminal justice system the involvement of other social workers most often takes place vicariously through clients. To give clients the information and support they may need as they face the criminal justice system it is necessary for social workers to have a reasonable knowledge of the system so that they can answer enquiries about it. For example: does the client know at what stage they are in the system; do they know what might happen next; do they appreciate the significance of what has happened; should they be legally represented; can they appeal?

---

[1] Defendants between the ages of 10 and 17 inclusive are dealt with in the youth court.

1.2 REFORM OF THE SYSTEM

The criminal justice system has always been the site of political controversy with public concern centering on crime rates and sentencing practice, and government policy concerning itself with the costs of the system and the image of the 'law and order' industry. Other issues, such as the public accountability of the police and the nature and impact of policing policies, continue to interest commentators on the criminal justice system.

Change is a characteristic of the criminal justice system. A White Paper, 'Crime, Justice and Protecting the Public', was published in February 1990 just a few days before a Green Paper, 'Supervision and Punishment in the Community: A Framework for Action', on the future of the probation service. Both documents contained proposals for reform with the general objective of reducing the number of offenders sentenced to prison and the introduction of community based sentences as alternatives to custody. The objective of government policy in relation to the probation service was indicated by the comments of John Patten, the Home Office Minister, who said on publication of the Green Paper:

> Probation officers will continue to need the personal skills which help them work effectively with offenders, but more than ever they will have to function as part of a criminal justice agency, delivering a service to the public and the criminal justice system as a whole as well as to individual offenders.

Many of the changes proposed in these papers formed the basis of the Criminal Justice Act 1991 which was implemented on 1 October 1992. It is clear that the Act is changing sentencing policy and practice and significantly affecting the nature of probation work in the criminal justice system.

In addition the Royal Commission on Criminal Justice, which was established in the wake of the release of the Birmingham Six, is currently sitting and is expected to report in 1993. The balance between adversarial and inquisitorial processes may be radically changed as a result of the recommendations of the Royal Commission.

1.3 PRINCIPLES OF CRIMINAL JUSTICE AND CRIMINAL LAW

Most criminal offences have two elements which have to be established for a defendant to be found guilty. The prosecution must establish both the actus reus, the commission of the criminal act, and the mens rea, the necessary criminal intent. There are, however, a number of offences, which are described as strict liability offences, where a criminal intent is not required as an element of the crime eg going through a red traffic light.

There is a presumption of innocence in the criminal law. A defendant is innocent of a charge until s/he has been proved guilty. The burden of proof is therefore on the prosecution who must prove their allegations beyond a reasonable doubt.

Criminal procedure in the English legal system is adversarial in character. This means that any trial is by way of a contest between the prosecution and the defence in which the prosecution is seeking to establish its allegations by evidence and the defence is seeking to undermine the worth of the allegations and the evidence. There is no objective finding of truth by the court which has to rely on the prosecution and the defence for the evidence on which it must make a decision. If, therefore, the prosecution is unable to bring evidence of its allegations the case must be dismissed.

2 THE LAW

2.1 THE CATEGORIES OF CRIMINAL OFFENCES

Criminal prosecutions are decided in either the magistrates' courts or the Crown Courts. The venue will depend on the type of offence and in certain circumstances on the choice of the defendant.

2.1.1 Summary offences

These are the least serious criminal offences and they can only be dealt with in the magistrates' courts.

2.1.2   Either way offences

Such offences may be tried in the magistrates' court or in the Crown Court. The venue for trial will be decided at what is called a 'mode of trial' hearing in which brief facts of the allegation will be given to the magistrates and they will decide whether the case is suitable to be heard by them or whether the nature of the allegation or their limited powers of sentencing require that it be heard by the Crown Court. If the magistrates decide to 'accept jurisdiction' then the defendants must decide whether they wish the case to be heard at the magistrates' court or at the Crown Court. In such circumstances defendants are therefore able to choose to be tried by a judge and jury, or by the magistrates.

2.1.3   Indictable offences

These are the most serious criminal offences and they can only be tried in the Crown Court. In relation to such offences magistrates have a preliminary jurisdiction to commit the case to the Crown Court. In essence a committal hearing is designed to establish that the prosecution have a case of sufficient worth for the defence to have to answer the allegation. In practice most committals these days are completed by the prosecution serving the case papers on the court and the defence, and the magistrates announcing to the defendants that they are committed for trial at the Crown Court.

2.2   BAIL

The issue of bail is of fundamental importance for the refusal of bail means that a person is deprived of liberty despite a presumption of innocence. Initially bail is granted or refused by a senior police officer but as soon as a defendant appears in court for the first time the issue is one for the court.

The Bail Act 1976 provides that a person charged with an imprisonable offence shall be granted bail unless one of the exceptions specified in the Act is established. These are:

there are substantial grounds for believing that the accused would, if released on bail:

i)   fail to surrender to custody; or

ii)   commit an offence while on bail; or

iii) interfere with witnesses or otherwise obstruct the course of justice, whether in relation to himself or any other person.

Bail may be granted unconditionally or subject to conditions such as residence or a surety, or the defendant may be remanded in custody. Because bail is such an important issue defendants should be legally represented where there is a chance that they could be remanded in custody following an unsuccessful bail application. Such representation may be provided by the duty solicitor where a defendant does not have his or her own solicitor. The issue of bail is first decided in the magistrates' courts but a defendant refused bail by the magistrates may apply to a Crown Court judge for bail.

A number of probation committees provide bail hostels though the availability of hostel places varies throughout the country and the conditions of acceptance are often very specific. Nonetheless the availability of a place in a probation hostel is often influential in persuading magistrates to grant bail with a condition of residence at the hostel.

2.3 PRE-TRIAL PROCEDURE

The prosecution of minor summary offences may be dealt with in a single court hearing without the need for the defendant to be represented. However, in many cases an adjournment of the proceedings may be needed so that the defendant's solicitor can take instructions from his or her client. Such adjournments may be for a short period of time enabling the case to progress on the same day or for a week or more where such time is necessary for the defence solicitor to consider the strength of the prosecution's case as disclosed by 'advance disclosure' and to take appropriate instructions from the defendant. The defence is entitled to advanced disclosure from the prosecution in all either way and indictable offences. On the basis of such instructions, and the legal advice given, the defendant will plead guilty or not guilty to the allegation as put by the prosecution.

A plea of not guilty means that a date for trial must be fixed and the proceedings adjourned so that witnesses may attend court to give evidence. Upon any adjournment of a case where the offence is imprisonable, the issue of bail will need to be decided.

If the defence in an either way matter decides to opt for a jury trial the case must be committed for trial at the Crown Court and the arrangements for such a hearing will normally require another adjournment.

In indictable offences the pre-trial procedure will be the same as for an either way offence where the defence opts for a jury trial except there will be no mode of trial hearing. It should be borne in mind that the more serious the offence the more likely it is that bail will be a contested issue.

This very brief outline of the pre-trial procedures will serve to show that it is only in the simplest matters that a defendant will appear in court, have the allegation put to them, plead guilty and be sentenced at one hearing. Criminal prosecutions can often be protracted matters particularly where there is a trial, a finding of guilt and a request for pre-sentence reports.

2.4   THE CRIMINAL TRIAL

2.4.1   The magistrates' court

The majority of prosecutions in the magistrates' courts are conducted by the Crown Prosecution Service and will be opened by the crown prosecutor outlining the allegations to a bench of lay magistrates or to a single stipendiary magistrate. The evidence to sustain the allegations will be presented by prosecution witnesses who will be taken through their evidence by the crown prosecutor. Once they have given their evidence each prosecution witness will be available to be cross-examined by the advocate for the defence. After cross-examination the prosecution may re-examine their witnesses and the magistrate(s) may question witnesses to clarify issues of doubt in the evidence they have given. The case for the prosecution will close when all their witnesses have given their evidence and any cross-examination and re-examination has taken place.

At the end of the case for the prosecution the defence may address the magistrate(s) on the basis that the prosecution have failed to make out a case for the defence to answer. This will be the situation for example, where the defence is of the opinion that the evidence brought by the prosecution fails to establish either of the elements, the actus reus or mens rea, of the crime. If the magistrate(s) agrees then the case will be dismissed at this stage. If they reject this application by the defence the case continues with the evidence of the defence witnesses. Again each witness is available to be cross-examined by the crown prosecutor and may be re-examined by the defence advocate.

When all the evidence has been presented the defence will address the magistrate(s) on the evidence, the burden of proof and points of law if necessary. The prosecution may also address the magistrate(s) on points of law.

The magistrate(s) will normally retire to make their decision on the facts as they find them and on the law which will be explained to them by their clerk. If they find the defendant not guilty that is the end of the matter, unless the issue of costs needs to be decided, and the defendant is free to leave the court. If the finding is one of guilt the offender (as s/he now is) must be sentenced for the offence. The options available to the magistrate(s) are considered below but prior to sentence the defence advocate may wish to address the magistrate(s) in mitigation of the offender and the crown prosecution will provide information about the offender's criminal record, if any.

The magistrate(s) may decide, and in some circumstances must decide, to adjourn for the preparation of reports before deciding upon the sentence. Pre-sentence reports, which are prepared by the probation service, may be supplemented by psychiatric or other reports.

2.4.2 The Crown Court

In essence the procedure of a trial in the Crown Court is the same as that in the magistrates' court though for those involved it is a very different experience.

A defendant who pleads not guilty to a charge in the Crown Court will be tried by a jury. The first task is therefore to choose a jury; their task is to decide the question of guilt on the basis of the evidence presented and the law as explained to them by the judge. In the Crown Court the judge decides questions of law while the jury decides questions of fact.

The presentation of evidence by witnesses and their cross-examination and re-examination is essentially the same as in the magistrates' court though the questioning is done by barristers instructed by defence solicitors and by the Crown Prosecution Service, and it proceeds much more slowly. At the end of the presentation of evidence both the prosecution and defence will address the jury. The judge will then direct the jury by explaining the law and by reviewing the evidence. The jury will retire to reach a verdict. Juries are expected to reach a unanimous verdict though if that proves impossible the judge may be willing to accept a majority (10-2) verdict.

If the jury find the defendant not guilty that is the end of the matter except for the issue of costs. A finding of guilt means that the judge must consider the question of sentence. Again it may be necessary to adjourn the case for the preparation of reports as in the magistrates' court. Maximum sentences are set by Parliament but judges have considerable discretion in the choice and severity of sentence.

2.5   SENTENCING IN THE ADULT CRIMINAL COURTS

The Criminal Justice Act 1991 is the latest in a long line of legislation designed to tackle the problematic issues of sentencing policy and practice. The government has declared that the new Act provides a 'coherent statutory framework for sentencing which is based on a coherent set of principles.'[2] and the Home Office's General Guide to the Act describes the Act in the following terms:

> The Criminal Justice Act 1991 makes important changes to sentencing procedures and practice; to the way in which custodial sentences are administered; to the way in which young people are dealt with in the criminal justice system; and in the administration of criminal justice services — in particular the magistrates' courts, the probation service and the guarding of remand prisoners.

The Guide identifies six principles that form the basis of the

[2] John Patten MP, Minister of State, Home Office 'The Criminal Justice Act 1991' (23.11.1991) Justice of the Peace.

Act and therefore should determine the sentencing practice of the criminal courts and influence the practice of those working within the criminal justice system.[3]

(i) the severity of the sentence in an individual case should reflect primarily the seriousness of the offence which has been committed. Whilst factors such as preventing crime or the rehabilitation of the offender remain important functions of the criminal justice process as a whole, they should not lead to a heavier penalty in an individual case than that which is justified by the seriousness of the offence or the need to protect the public from the offender;

(ii) a sharper distinction than hitherto should be drawn between property offences and offences against the person — that is crimes of a sexual or violent nature. The Act recognises that additional restrictions may need to be placed on the liberty of a sexual or violent offender in order to protect the public from serious harm from the offender;

(iii) the procedures for administering sentences once they have been imposed should be both rigorous and fair so as to ensure that the sentencer's intentions are properly reflected in the way in which the sentence is served;

(iv) community penalties should play a full part in their own right in the structure of penalties. They should not be viewed as 'alternatives to custody';

(v) the way in which young people are dealt with in the criminal justice system should more closely reflect their age and development, as should the extent to which their parents should be expected to take responsibility for their actions;

(vi) criminal justice services should be administered as efficiently as possible, and without discrimination on improper grounds, particularly those of race and sex.

Within these principles it is worth acknowledging those that represent significant change for they will have the greatest impact on practice. The link between the seriousness of the offence and the severity of the punishment, sometimes known as the principle of proportionality or 'just deserts' has the impact of shifting the emphasis of sentencing policy away from the overt objectives of crime prevention and rehabilitation and firmly toward the principle of sentencing to punish. The explicit distinction that

---

[3] A full quotation from the Guide, paragraph 1.2 is provided here.

is made between offences against property and violent or sexual offences is important for in repect of the offences against the person the Act recognises that the principle of sentencing to fit the seriousness of the crime may not be sufficient to provide proper protection to the public and provides for more severe sentencing when such protection is necessary. Community sentences are recognised by the Act as a category of sentences in their own right and not as alternatives to custody.

The Act establishes that sentences under the Act are to be understood in terms of their restriction on liberty. Custody clearly falls within this notion and fines may be seen as restricting the offender's liberty to choose how his or her resources are spent. Community sentences are required by section 6(2) to be 'such as in the opinion of the court are commensurate with the seriousness of the offence' and should be understood as restricting liberty.

The Act provides for four categories of sentence, discharges (absolute and conditional), fines, community sentences and custody. The principle of sentencing commensurate with the seriousness of the offence operates across the range of sentences so that a community sentence can be imposed only if the offence concerned is serious enough to justify the level of restriction of liberty involved in complying with the sentence. Equally custody can be ordered only where the offence is so serious that only a custodial sentence can be justified for it or where the offence is a violent or sexual offence so that only a custodial sentence would provide adequate protection for the public from serious harm from the offender.

When a court imposes a community sentence it must be satisfied, in addition to the requirement that the sentence is commensurate with the seriousness of the offence, that the particular sentence chosen is also the most suitable for the offender.

In deciding the seriousness of an offence the court must take account of all aggravating and mitigating circumstances. Section 28(1) provides that in mitigating a sentence the court may take into account any matters which it considers to be relevant. The same section allows the sentencing court when it is sentencing an offender for more than one offence to consider the total impact of the orders.

The 'just deserts' principle, which requires sentences to reflect the seriousness of the offence, is reinforced by section 29(1) which provides that an offence shall not be regarded as more serious by reason of previous convictions or a failure to respond to previous sentences. This provision has caused much concern particularly as it reverses sentencing practice under previous legislation and because subsection (2) allows the court to take aggravating factors disclosed by the circumstances of other previous offences into account in fixing the seriousness of the current offence. The ambiguity of these two subsections of section 29, when taken together, has prompted much criticism.

The importance of the new sentencing principles, and the significant departure from old principle and practice that they represent, should not be underestimated by probation officers and other practitioners in the criminal justice system. The principles will shape the sentencing practice of the criminal courts and therefore must be taken into account in the preparation of pre-sentence reports by the probation service. The work of the service will also be significantly influenced by the new community sentences available under the Act, by the introduction of National Standards for the Supervision of Offenders in the Community and by the expectation of government that the Act means that the probation service will be 'centre stage' in the criminal justice system. Discussion of these, and other issues, will be undertaken after an examination of the sentences available to the courts.

2.6   SENTENCES AVAILABLE IN THE ADULT COURT

2.6.1   Discharges and financial penalties

Absolute and conditional discharges

An absolute discharge is a decision by the court, following a plea of guilty or a finding of guilt, that no punishment is necessary.

A conditional discharge is a decision by the court that it will not impose a sentence for the offence committed on condition that the offender commits no further offence during the period of discharge (a maximum of three years). Should a further offence be committed during that period the offender is liable to be sentenced for the original as well as the subsequent offence.

Fines

The Criminal Justice Act 1991 introduces a new system of unit fines for magistrates' courts which allows the fine imposed on an individual offender to reflect both the seriousness of the offence and the offender's means. As a general proposition unit fines will not be used in the Crown Court.

There are five levels of offence with a maximum number of available units of seriousness within each level as set out below:

Up to 2 units for a level 1 offence (max. fine of £200).
Up to 5 units for a level 2 offence (max. fine of £500).
Up to 10 units for a level 3 offence (max. fine of £1000).
Up to 25 units for a level 4 offence (max. fine of £2500).
Up to 50 units for a level 5 offence (max. fine of £5000).

Each level of offence has a maximum ceiling for fines as indicated in the above table.

The level of seriousness determined by the court for a particular level of offence is multiplied by a figure derived from the offender's weekly disposable income to reach a fine amount which represents both seriousness and ability to pay. The Act lays down a minimum value of £4 and a maximum value of £100 for each unit of seriousness.

The offender's ability to pay is determined by the calculation of their weekly disposable income. This figure is calculated on the basis of information supplied by the offender and it is an offence not to provide such information without reasonable excuse or to make a false declaration of means or fail to disclose any material fact.

The Act provides that fines may be recovered by the attachment of income support subject to a maximum deduction.

In the Crown Court the 'old' fine system continues to apply. In deciding the level of any fine to be imposed the court must first consider the gravity of the offence. However, the court is also required to consider the financial circumstances of the offender. Consideration of these factors will allow the court to fix an appropriate fine and terms of payment.

Compensation orders

Financial orders to compensate the victims of crime have an increasing prominence in sentencing policy and practice as a greater consideration of the victim has become a feature of the criminal justice system. Section 104 of the Criminal Justice Act 1988 amends section 35 of the Powers of the Criminal Courts Act 1973 to encourage the criminal courts to make compensation orders to the victims of crime. Courts are now under a duty to give reasons for not making a compensation order when they have an opportunity to do so.

The Home Office issued a circular in 1988 (85/1988) which shows the levels of compensation for personal injury awarded by the civil courts. The majority of these figures have been adopted by the Magistrates' Association as guidelines for compensation orders in the magistrates' courts.

The maximum compensation order in the magistrates' court is £5000 and where an offender has limited means a compensation order will take precedence over a fine as a sentence choice and in payment. The value of a compensation order should reflect the loss of the victim but must also take the offender's means to pay into account. There is no limit to the amount of a compensation order made in the Crown Court.

2.6.2 Community sentences

Probation

A probation order may be made on adult offenders for a minimum of 6 months and a maximum of 3 years. The offender must consent to the order. Section 8(1) of the Criminal Justice Act 1991 substitutes a new section 2 into the Powers of the Criminal Courts Act 1973 specifying the conditions for making a probation order:

> . . . supervision of the offender by a probation officer is desirable in the interests of —
>
> a) securing the rehabilitation of the offender; or
>
> b) protecting the public from harm from him or preventing the commission by him of further offences.

There are now five types of additional requirements which may be included in an order: residence; to refrain from or take part in specified activities; attend a probation centre; a requirement that sexual offenders take part in specified activities or attend a probation centre; to submit to treatment for a mental condition; to submit to treatment for drug or alcohol dependency.

Community service

Such an order is available as a sentence for an imprisonable offence and requires the offender to consent to undertake unpaid work for the community. Orders can vary between 40 hours and 240 hours work to be completed in one year and are carried out under the supervision of a community service organiser. National Standards identify the objective of such orders to be the re-integration of the offender into the community through positive and demanding unpaid work and reparation to the community.

Combination order

This new order, introduced by section 11 of the Criminal Justice Act 1991, combines probation supervision and community service. The Home Office's General Guide to the Act sets out the thinking behind this order:

> The combination order is intended for offenders who the courts believe should make some reparation to the community, through a community service order, and who also need probation supervision to tackle problems that underlie their offending and thus to reduce the risk of further offending in the future. Given the considerable restriction on liberty inherent in a combination order, such an order will be appropriate for amongst the most serious offenders likely to be given a community sentence.

The order is available for offenders who have committed an imprisonable offence. The probation element is for a minimum of 12 months and a maximum of three years and the community service element for between 40 and 100 hours.

Attendance centre order

Attendance centre orders may be made on offenders up to the age of 20. The minimum sentence is for 12 hours and the maximum for 36 hours. The order is served by attendance at the centre, normally on a Saturday afternoon, to undertake directed activities in a disciplined environment usually run by the police. Such orders cannot be made where there is no centre geographically available for the offender to attend.

Curfew orders

This new order is introduced by section 12 of the Criminal Justice Act 1991 which also provides, by section 13, for such orders to be electronically monitored by 'tagging'. The order is for a minimum of 2 hours and a maximum of 12 hours a day; it may be made for any period up to six months. The order, which requires the offender to be in a specified place at and for a specified time, cannot be made unless the offender is willing to comply with it.

Pre-sentence reports

The sentencing court must obtain a pre-sentence report from a probation officer before it can make a probation order with additional requirements, a community service order or a combination order. The preparation of such reports is covered by the National Standards which specify that a report should address the current offence, relevant information about the offender, a conclusion and where relevant a proposal for the most suitable community sentence.

Enforcing and revoking community sentences

Offenders who breach the requirements of a community sentence may be fined up to a maximum of £1000, or receive up to 60 hours community service, or be given an attendance centre order if they are under 21. If the court is of the opinion that the breach is serious it may revoke the original order and sentence anew for the original offence. Where the court finds that the offender has wilfully and persistently failed to comply with the order then the court may assume that the offender has not consented to a community order thus leaving the offender liable to a custodial sentence.

The commission of a further offence whilst an offender is serving a community sentence does not, in itself, constitute a breach of the order but may be the basis for revoking the order and re-sentencing for the original offence.

Community orders may be revoked in the interests of justice and Schedule 2 of the 1991 Act specifies that a probation order may be revoked under this provision on the grounds of the good progress of the offender.

2.6.3   Custodial sentences

Custody

Custodial sentences for summary and either way offences can only be imposed after the court has obtained a pre-sentence report. In the case of indictable only offences the court must obtain a pre-sentence report unless, in the circumstances of the case, the court considers it is unnecessary. The court must consider and take into account the contents of the report, other information about the offence and the offender that is available including aggravating and mitigating factors before deciding on sentence.

Section 1 of the Criminal Justice Act 1991 sets out the criteria which must be met for a custodial sentence to be imposed:

(2) Subject to subsection (3) below, the court shall not pass a custodial sentence on the offender unless it is of the opinion —

a)   that the offence, or the combination of the offence and one other offence associated with it, was so serious that only such a sentence can be justified for the offence; or

b)   where the offence is a violent or sexual offence, that only such a sentence would be adequate to protect the public from serious harm from him.

(3)   Nothing in subsection (2) above shall prevent the court from passing a custodial sentence on the offender if he refuses to give his consent to a community sentence which is proposed by the court and requires that consent.

In reaching its conclusion that the offence is so serious that only a custodial sentence can be justified, the sentencing court may take into account one other associated offence. Such offences are defined by section 31(2) to cover:

a)   the offender is convicted of it in the proceedings in which he is convicted of the other offence, or (although convicted of it in earlier proceedings) is sentenced for it at the same time as he is sentenced for that offence; or

b)   the offender admits the commission of it in proceedings in which he is sentenced for the other offence and requests the court to take it into consideration in sentencing him for that offence.

Section 3 sets out a number of procedures that must be gone through before it can impose a custodial sentence. In reaching the conclusion that an offence is so serious that only a custodial sentence is justified the court is required to take aggravating and mitigating factors into account. When deciding that a custodial sentence is necessary to protect the public from serious harm from a violent or sexual offender, the court may take into account any information it has about the offender. The court is required to obtain a pre-sentence report and consider its contents before making either of these two decisions, though there is no obligation to do so in indictable only cases where the court considers that it is unnecessary to have a report.

Section 4 sets out additional requirements to safeguard the interests of offenders who have a mental disorder.

In cases where custody is a possible sentence the pre-sentence report is particularly important. Such a report will contain information concerning aggravating and mitigating factors surrounding the commission of the offence. The Guide to the Criminal Justice Act 1991, published by the Home Office, in the section on Custodial Sentences and the Sentencing Framework suggests factors which should be considered by the court and which must therefore be canvassed in a pre-sentence report: '. . . the presence or absence of pre-meditation, or whether the offender was the ringleader or a junior partner in the crime.' Such reports must cover the issue of the risk of harm to the public posed by a violent or sexual offender.

It should also be noted that under section 1(3) a court may impose a custodial sentence on an offender who refuses to consent to the passing of a community sentence where his or her consent is required.

Courts may impose suspended custodial sentences under the amended provisions of section 22 of the Powers of the Criminal Courts Act 1973. The power to suspend is limited to cases where custody is firstly an appropriate sentence and suspension can be justified by the exceptional circumstances of the case. The second criterion can only come into play if the first criterion is satisfied. Where a court suspends custody it must consider whether to additionally impose a fine or compensation order.

Custodial sentences on offenders under 21 cannot be suspended.

2.7   THE CRIMINAL JUSTICE WORK OF THE PROBATION SERVICE

The probation service was first put on a statutory footing by the Probation of Offenders Act 1907. It now employs approximately 6500 probation officers, most of whom have a social work qualification. It is funded largely by the Home Office and is administered locally by committees comprising magistrates, local authority representatives, a Crown Court judge and other co-opted members.

The probation service provides a number of services, the majority of which are concerned in some way with the criminal justice system, and it is these services which are subject to the significant impact of the Criminal Justice Act 1991. The government has made it clear that it sees the probation service as a lead agency in the administration of the criminal justice system and much of its work is now subject to the 'National Standards for the Supervision of Offenders in the Community' published by the Home Office in 1992.

The major work of the probation service under the Act is in the preparation of pre-sentence reports for the courts, the supervision of offenders subject to community sentences, the supervision of offenders before and after their release from prison and the management of approved probation and bail hostels. All this work is subject to the National Standards.

The foreword to the National Standards sets out Ministerial intent:

> The publication of these national standards is an important step . . . We now have a clear statement of expected practice setting out the objectives of supervision. This forms a broad and consistent framework, within which probation and social services staff can exercise the initiative and professional judgment essential for the effective supervision of offenders in the community.

In addition, the standards are an important statement to which sentencers, offenders and the public can look as the basis on which such work should operate.

Objectives for the standards are set out in Chapter 1:

The objective of these national standards is to strengthen the supervision of offenders in the community, building on the skill and experience of practitioners and service managers:

* by setting a clear framework of expectations and requirements for supervision, understood by those carrying out the task and by others;

* by enabling professional judgment to be exercised within a framework of accountability;

* by encouraging imagination, initiative and innovation, and the development of good practice; and

* by ensuring that supervision is delivered fairly, consistently and without discrimination, and that positive steps are taken to ensure that this is the case.

2.7.1 Probation orders

Probation orders are made under sections 2 and 3 of the Powers of the Criminal Courts Act 1973 as amended by the Criminal Justice Act 1991. The criteria for making such an order are:

supervision of the offender by a probation officer is desirable in the interests of (a) securing the rehabilitation of the offender; or (b) protecting the public from harm from him or preventing the commission by him of further offences.

National Standards indicate the desired objectives of such an order:

Effective probation order supervision requires high standards both from probation services and from individual probation staff and should generally entail establishing a professional relationship, in which to advise, assist and befriend the offender with the aim of:

* securing the offender's co-operation and compliance with the probation order and enforcing its terms;

* challenging the offender to accept responsibility for his or her crime and its consequences;

* helping the offender to resolve personal difficulties linked with offending and to acquire new skills; and

* motivating and assisting the offender to become a responsible and law-abiding member of the community.

The courts have the power to impose additional requirements in a probation order as indicated above. Under this provision probation services have established a number of special programmes such as the Break With The Past offence based programme established by the Middlesex Area Probation Service for the London Borough of Hounslow which offers a 'period of structured and focused group work aimed at modifying the behaviour of serious offenders'.

2.7.2   Community service orders

The probation service is responsible for establishing, managing and operating community service orders. These responsibilities are subject to the National Standards which specify prompt commencement of work, a minimum work rate of five hours per week, standards of acceptable performance and behaviour, accurate and timely record keeping and enforcement including breach action where appropriate.

2.7.3   Combination orders

Combination orders are supervised by the probation service with the objective of securing the rehabilitation of the offender; protecting the public from harm from the offender; and/or preventing the offender from committing further offences. National Standards specify that there should be a supervising officer for the order who is responsible for reviewing the order every three months in consultation with other officers involved.

2.7.4   Supervision orders

Under the provisions of the Criminal Justice Act 1991 the probation service is involved in the supervision of offenders sentenced to a supervision order in the Youth Court. This work is discussed in the chapter on youth justice.

2.7.5   Management of approved probation and bail hostels

The probation service is responsible for the day to day running of probation and bail hostels under the direction of area probation committees or voluntary management committees. Probation hostels provide residential facilities for offenders who require enhanced supervision to live in the community. Such hostels are provided for, among others, high risk offenders who have been released from custody, or offenders on a probation order with an additional residence requirement order. Bail hostels provide accommodation for defendants on bail with a condition of residence at the hostel as an alternative to a remand in custody.

The management of such hostels is subject to the National Standards which specify appropriate objectives:

Hostel staff should develop a regime in consultation with their committee and the local probation service. This should provide a structured and supportive environment which will seek to:

*   promote a responsible and law-abiding lifestyle, and respect for others;

*   create and maintain a constructive relationship between the hostel's staff and residents;

*   facilitate the work of the probation service and other agencies aimed at reducing the risk that residents will offend or re-offend in the future;

*   assist the residents to keep or find employment and to develop their employment skills;

*   encourage and enable residents to use the facilities available in the local community and to develop their ability to become self reliant in doing so;

*   enable the residents to move on successfully to other appropriate accommodation at the end of the period of residence;

*   establish and maintain good relations with neighbours and the community in general.

National Standards also set clear specifications relating to supervision and enforcement which require staff to respond firmly and quickly to deal with non-compliance.

2.7.6   Supervision before and after release from custody

The probation service is involved with offenders while they are serving a custodial sentence and upon release from a prison establishment. The release provisions of the Criminal Justice Act 1991 establish a system under which custodial sentences are served partly in prison and partly in the community but subject to recall. Supervision by a probation officer is a central part of that part of a custodial sentence served in the community. National Standards set objectives for post-release supervision as:

   (i)   protection of the public;

  (ii)   prevention of re-offending;

 (iii)   successful re-integration in the community.

And:

Ensuring effective supervision requires high professional standards both from the probation services and from individual probation staff and should generally entail establishing a professional relationship, in which to advise, assist and befriend the offender with the aim of:

   (i)   enforcing the conditions of the licence and securing the offender's co-operation and compliance with those conditions;

  (ii)   challenging the offender to accept responsibility for his or her crime and gaining their co-operation in avoiding offending in the future;

 (iii)   helping the offender to resolve personal difficulties linked with offending and acquiring new skills;

 (iv)   motivating and assisting the offender to change for the better and to become a responsible and law-abiding member of the community; and

  (v)   assessing the risk of the offender re-offending and/or presenting a danger to the public, and responding appropriately.

Standards also specify liaison between the supervising probation officer, the prison probation officer and prison staff from the beginning of a sentence to facilitate preparation for and supervision after release. Further standards are set for the enforcement of licence conditions and for breach and recall to prison.

2.8 THE PREPARATION OF PRE-SENTENCE REPORTS BY THE PROBATION SERVICE

Pre-sentence reports are produced for the sentencing court to assist that court in determining the most suitable method of dealing with an offender. Under the Criminal Justice Act 1991 a pre-sentence report must be considered before a court imposes a custodial sentence, except in indictable only offences where the court considers a report to be unnecessary; and in the case of a community service order, a combination order, or a probation or supervision order with additional requirements. Pre-sentence reports should address the offence, relevant information about the offender, provide a conclusion and, where appropriate, a proposal for the most suitable community sentence.

3 CRIMINAL JUSTICE AND SOCIAL WORK PRACTICE: some issues for discussion

3.1 Reform of the criminal justice system

It can be argued that the criminal justice system is midway through a period of substantial reform. The Criminal Justice Act 1991 can be seen as the first phase of this reform; there is little doubt that its provisions have established a new era of sentencing policy and practice. Other phases in the reform of the criminal justice system are represented by the re-organisation of the administration of magistrates' courts and by the imposition of cash limited budgeting on those courts; the work of the Royal Commission on Criminal Justice and the proposals of the Lord Chancellor to reform the criminal legal aid scheme by the introduction of fixed fees for work in the magistrates' courts.

Though a number of these reforms will not have a direct effect on the probation service or other social work professionals working within the criminal justice service, there is little doubt that the service will be much changed if and when all the proposed reforms have been implemented. In 'A New Framework for Local Justice', a White Paper published in February 1992 the government outlined plans to reform the management of magistrates' courts in England and Wales. Reform is to be directed toward greater management efficiency and increased consistency in the provision of services. A new funding scheme for magistrates' courts is to be gradually introduced in which resources will reflect the amount of work undertaken by a court and its level of efficiency measured by reference to, among other factors, the number of cases completed and a court's success in collecting fines.

The Lord Chancellor's proposals to introduce fixed fees for some magistrates' court work to replace lawyers' fees based on hourly rates for work done is a response to the rising cost of legal aid. Other proposals include the franchising of criminal legal aid work to a small number of solicitors' firms who would tender for the business. Though the Lord Chancellor's proposals are argued from the need for efficiency and control of the legal aid budget, lawyers fear that their implementation will further restrict the availability of legal services for defendants in the magistrates' courts and the quality of the service funded through legal aid. If such fears were realised a greater emphasis might be placed on the probation service to provide quasi-legal advice and assistance to defendants in the magistrates' courts.

The Royal Commission on Criminal Justice, which is currently hearing evidence, is concerned with the principles and details of the criminal process. In its report, which is expected in 1993, the Commission will consider the balance to be adopted in England and Wales between an adversarial and inquisitorial criminal justice system, but it might also report on other suggestions which would have a significant impact on probation officers and social services staff working within the system. For example, Barbara Mills QC, the Director of Public Prosecutions, has argued for a significant extention to the cautioning system. In an interview reported in the Independent (22.9.92) she provides the example of a shoplifter who admits the offence being cautioned and paying a sum of money to the store. If such a proposal were to extend to social work involvement through, for example, voluntary intermediate treatment, or involvement with the probation service, then the impact would be considerable.

Her stated objective is to remove a significant number of minor cases from the courts. Many social work professionals would commend such an objective and there is much favourable comment on the impact of cautioning. It should be remembered though that cautioning systems are also criticised for their relative inability to provide 'due process' in the same way that such processes and rights are provided by the criminal courts.

3.2 THE IMPACT OF NATIONAL STANDARDS

Considerable reference in this chapter has been made to the National Standards for the Supervision of Offenders in the Community and there is no doubt that their publication and introduction constitute a significant statement of expected practice in this area of work. Despite its considerable misgivings concerning the principles behind the Criminal Justice Act expressed before its implementation, the probation service is publicly seeking to be positive about the impact of the Act on its work. An ambivalent welcome is given to the National Standards by the service:

> The Criminal Justice Act represents a continuum — a progression in terms of political and penal thinking. It is a big challenge which has promoted a considerable amount of upheaval in the service, but in the end I believe the Act and the National Standards will bring out the best in us. David Mathieson, Chief Probation Service for Merseyside.[4]

> Like it or not, a culture change is afoot and all agencies in the criminal justice system will have to go along with it. The move to deal with more offenders in the community is seen by probation service staff as a constructive one, and the concept of restriction on liberty as a sentencing baseline is welcomed. Reserving prison for the most serious offenders only is a concept which is also welcomed in probation circles . . . [5]

> The new legislation is an important contribution towards dealing with crime more effectively, but its impact will depend on goodwill and partnership between all the organisations and individuals involved in the criminal justice process. There is already much excellent probation practice around the country and the new National Standards will help to make this practice better still.[6]

[4] Anthony Ostler 'The Criminal Justice Act 1991 — A Probation Viewpoint' The Magistrate. October 1992.
[5] Ibid.
[6] Malcolm Bryant, Chief Probation Officer, Berkshire. Quoted in Anthony Ostler. ibid.

The introduction of the new Act and National Standards has had a significant impact on social workers and probation officers working in the criminal justice system. It is difficult though to assess how far National Standards build on established good practice and how far they signify new specifications for practice in the system. Though the standards are not legally enforceable law agencies are expected to work to them and where that becomes impossible to inform sentencers of the situation. The Standards declare that they seek to encourage good practice but avoid unnecessary prescription; it is to be hoped that their introduction will facilitate the further development of good professional practice within the criminal justice system.

3.3   ANTI-DISCRIMINATORY PRACTICE UNDER THE CRIMINAL JUSTICE ACT 1991

Section 95 of the Act requires the Home Secretary to publish information annually to help persons involved in the administration of justice to satisfy their duty to avoid discriminating against any person on the ground of race or sex or any other improper ground. The Home Office has now published the first two booklets in response to section 95 including: *Race and the Criminal Justice System and Gender and the Criminal Justice System*. The booklets contain information about the position of the ethnic communities and the differential position of men and women in our society. Both contain important statistical information about the criminal justice system and comment on the experience of the ethnic communities and women in their contacts with the criminal justice system. The terms of section 95 and the publication of these booklets mark an important recognition of the existence of discrimination in the administration of criminal justice and they will provide a useful annual benchmark for measuring whether discrimination on the grounds of race, ethnicity and gender is being tackled by the agencies of the system and by those employed within the system.

The anti-discriminatory declaration within section 95 is taken up in the National Standards with a clear equal opportunities statement in the introduction to the Standards.

The work of probation services and social services departments must be free of discrimination on the ground of race, gender, age, disability, language ability, literacy, religion, sexual orientation or any other improper ground . . . effective anti-discriminatory practice is essential to avoid further disadvantaging those already most disillusioned and disadvantaged in society.

This statement is backed up by particular specifications:

All services must have a stated equal opportunities policy and ensure that this is effectively monitored and reviewed. Effective action to prevent discrimination (anti-discriminatory practice) requires significantly more than a willingness to accept all offenders equally or to invest an equal amount of time and effort in different cases. The origin, nature and extent of differences in circumstances and need must be properly understood and actively addressed by all concerned — for example, by staff training, by monitoring and review and by making an extra effort to understand and work most effectively with an offender from a different cultural background.

The importance of official recognition of these issues should not be underestimated. The challenge for criminal justice agencies and for those who work within the system is to work toward an anti-discriminatory practice so that the statements and aims of the National Standards are not merely rhetoric.

4 CASE STUDIES

1.   Doug Richards is twenty-three and has been found guilty of burglary for the third time in two years. The magistrates have decided to adjourn the case for four weeks for a pre-sentence report having indicated that they think the offence serious enough for a community sentence.

Identify the issues which your report will have to address.

If you were to recommend a probation order identify the role of the probation officer and the offender in the administration of such an order.

2.   Mary Lewis has pleaded guilty to her first offence, theft by shoplifting. Mary is 34 and a single parent and has indicated to the magistrates that she took some food from Marks and Spencer because she had nothing to give her daughter for tea and no money to buy anything. She lives in a local authority flat; income

support and child benefit are her sole source of income. She has told the magistrates that she wants some help and they have asked for a pre-sentence report.

Indicate the issues you would address in your report particularly in view of your conclusion that this offence does not warrant a community sentence.

In the event that a one year probation order is made what powers are open to you if Mary fails to keep any of the appointments you make with her?

What could the consequences be for Mary?

3. Martin, who is 25, has been given 240 hours' community service having been found guilty of a 'domestic' burglary. On two occasions he has failed to turn up for work as directed and when he does turn up his work is unsatisfactory.

As a community service officer what powers do you have?

What might be the consequences for Martin?

4. You are a probation officer on court duty in your local magistrates' court. An 18 year old is brought up to the court from the cells. He was arrested by the police last night and has been charged with the theft of £5000. He is clearly confused but tells the magistrates that he is guilty and wants the matter dealt with today. When he is asked if he wants a lawyer he refuses. The bench is clearly concerned and decides to put the case back for an hour so that 'you can have a chance to speak to the probation officer'. They indicate that they do not think he realises the seriousness of his position and ask you whether you can help.

When you see him he has no idea of what is going on and asks you to explain what could happen to him.

What are you going to tell him?

What are you going to tell the magistrates when he appears in court again in an hour?

5 ACTIVITIES

1. Any Diploma student who has a probation placement will obviously have the very best experience of probation work. Other students might be able to arrange to visit a local probation office or sit in court with the duty probation officer and thereby gain some understanding of the nature of probation work and the criminal process.

The addresses and phone numbers of probation services in England, Wales and Northern Ireland appear in the back of 'Supervision in the Community: Probation Working' published by the National Association of Probation Officers.

2. Most probation services provide information and publications which explain their work. Get hold of as much information as possible from the probation service for your area. What particular schemes do they run for offenders ?

3. Some understanding of the criminal justice system at work can be achieved by undertaking observation reports of the magistrates' courts and the Crown Court. Particular attention might be paid to the role of the duty solicitor, other defence lawyers, the probation officer and the impact of recommendations in pre-sentence reports.

Those who are able to visit both the magistrates' courts and the Crown Court will notice substantial differences in the character and nature of proceedings in both courts. What is the quality of the summary justice provided in the magistrates' courts?

4. Keep up to date with changes in the criminal justice system. During 1993 and 1994 such changes are likely to focus on the report of the Royal Commission on Criminal Justice and on the criminal legal aid scheme. Any changes in the criminal legal aid scheme are likely to have an impact on social work clients who are involved in the criminal justice system.

5. Get publication lists from:

Association of Chief Officers of Probation;

Howard League for Penal Reform;

National Association for the Care and Resettlement of Offenders;

National Association of Probation Officers;

Liberty;

Prison Reform Trust.

These organisations produce high quality pressure group material on issues concerned with the criminal justice system. With a selection of the available materials it is possible to put together a substantial package of information about the criminal justice system which will be useful in social work practice.

6.   If you are thinking of working in the criminal justice system as a probation officer or social work professional you should get hold of a copy of the National Standards from the Home Office.

6   ADDRESSES

Association of Chief Officers of Probation,
20–30 Lawfield Lane,
Wakefield,
West Yorkshire.
WF2 8SP.
Phone: 0924 361156.

Her Majesty's Stationery Office,
PO Box 276,
London SW8 5DT.

Home Office, Probation Service Division.
50 Queen Anne's Gate,
London SW1H 9AT.
Phone: 071 273 3262.

Howard League for Penal Reform,
708 Holloway Road,
London N19 3NL.
Phone: 071 281 7722.

National Association for the Care and Resettlement of Offenders,
169 Clapham Road,
London SW9 0PU.
Phone: 071 582 6500.

National Association of Probation Officers,
3/4 Chivalry Road,
Battersea,
London SW11 1HT.
Phone: 071 223 3503.

Liberty (National Council for Civil Liberties),
21 Tabard Street,
London SE1 4LA.
Phone: 071 403 3888.

Prison Reform Trust,
59 Caledonian Road,
London N1 9BU.
Phone: 071 278 9815.

7 MATERIALS

7.1 BASIC MATERIALS FOR ORDINARY SOCIAL WORK PRACTICE (NB not for specialist criminal justice practice)

'A Quick Reference Guide to the Criminal Justice Act 1991' £3. Available from the Home Office or NACRO.

'Courts and Sentencing'; 'Police'; 'The Probation Service'; 'Prisons'. All are NACRO Factsheets.

'Know Your Rights! Liberty' (1990) £7.95.

'National Standards For The Supervision of Offenders In The Community' Home Office. 1992. £3.

'Race and Criminal Justice' (1991) NACRO.

'Women and Criminal Justice: Some Facts and Figures' (1992) NACRO.

7.2 FURTHER READING

Andrew Ashworth et al. 'Criminal Justice Act 1991. Legal Points. Commentary and Annotated Guide for Practitioners' (1992) Waterside Press.

'Custody, Care and Justice' (1991) The Howard League. £3.

'Gender and the Criminal Justice System' (1992) Home Office.

Ashworth, A. et al. 'Materials on the Criminal Justice Act 1991' (1992) Waterside Press.

'Pre-Sentence Reports' (1992) NACRO. £2.50.

'Race and the Criminal Justice System' (1992) Home Office.

CHAPTER 7

Youth justice

1 INTRODUCTION

1.1 SOCIAL WORK INVOLVEMENT IN YOUTH JUSTICE

The involvement of social workers in the youth justice system is both varied and extensive and it may be useful to start this chapter by identifying some of the areas of practice which bring social workers into contact with the criminal justice system as it affects children (10-13) and young persons (14-17) both inclusive.

a)   Social work clients under the age of 18 who are prosecuted for a criminal offence will have their case heard at the youth court. (The date which determines whether a case is to be dealt with in the youth court or in the adult criminal court is· the date on which a plea is taken. A plea taken before a young person's eighteenth birthday will mean that the case is dealt with in the youth court.) Such an experience can be very confusing and alienating and many youth defendants and their parents may benefit from the explanations and support of a social worker who is familiar with the system.

b)   Local authority social workers and probation officers may be required to prepare a pre-sentence report to help the court decide on an appropriate sentence and such a report will have to take into account both the offence and the circumstances of the youth offender.

c)   The court will often also require a school report. These are usually written by teachers but processed by the Education Welfare Service. In other circumstances pre-sentence reports may incorporate the comments of teachers.

d)   If the court makes a supervision order a local authority social worker or a probation officer will be appointed to act as the supervisor of the order. Probation officers supervise 16 and 17 year old offenders sentenced to a probation order.

e) The probation service, through the community service section, runs community service projects and community service is available as a sentence in the youth court for offenders aged 16 or 17.

f) Other social workers may be involved in running intermediate treatment projects some of which are used in the administration of supervision orders. A number of intermediate treatment projects are now specifically designed and used as alternatives to custody for youth offenders.

g) Social workers and probation officers working with youth offenders are increasingly developing links with legal practitioners so that cases can be jointly 'planned' to the advantage of the youth defendant/offender concerned.

h) Social workers and probation officers may be involved in the creation of action plans between social services departments, probation areas and voluntary organisations to supervise young offenders in the community.

i) Members of youth justice teams may be required to attend at a police station to act as an appropriate adult during the questioning of a child or young person who is suspected of having committed an offence.

The variety of practice outlined above is 'reactive' in the sense of responding to a child or young person already involved with the youth justice system either as a suspect, defendant or as an offender. In another, equally important respect, social work practice is also 'proactive' in its concern and work designed to keep children and young people out of the criminal courts and in a more general sense 'out of trouble'.

The establishment, in a number of areas, of inter-agency or cautioning panels which bring together the police, the social services, probation, the education welfare service and others with the common objective of keeping child and young offenders out of court, has been an important element in what are known as 'diversionary schemes'. The increased use of the official police caution as an alternative to prosecution can be seen as part of this diversionary objective though it can only be used where a child or young person admits an offence. Social work involvement in such work is far from universal and in many respects reflects the variety of models of diversionary schemes in operation (see below).

The Children Act 1989, in Schedule 2, places a duty on local authorities to take reasonable steps to reduce the need to bring criminal proceedings against children and young persons and to encourage children in their area not to commit criminal offences. Guidance published under the Act indicates that this duty involves local authority participation in diversionary schemes.

There is evidence that social services departments and probation officers are increasingly seeing their role in youth justice as including not only a responsibility to individual youth offenders but also to the management of the youth justice system. As part of this process of management social services departments and probation services are involved in constructing policy statements, in setting goals such as diverting youth offenders from court and reducing the number of custodial sentences.

In many areas social services and probation work with young people involved with the criminal justice system is now organised through a youth justice team which is responsible for court duty services, assessment for and the preparation of pre-sentence reports, supervision of community sentences, the development of bail support facilities, involvement in crime prevention initiatives and the cautioning panel and the supervision of young offenders before and after release from young offender institutions.

1.2   THE POLITICS OF YOUTH JUSTICE

Youth justice is a site of political controversy and as a result has experienced, or suffered, the effects of significant shifts in penal and social policy. The variety of constituencies with an interest in the youth justice debate is considerable and includes the 'caring professions', the 'law and order lobby', the legal profession, the prison service, the magistracy, the courts service and others. The periodic domination of particular constituents in the debate has been reflected in' these shifts in policy so that the essential character or philosophy of the youth system is difficult to define.

1.3 A MODEL FOR YOUTH JUSTICE?

A continuing debate centres on the search for an appropriate 'model' for youth justice. By simplifying the debate (which some commentators consider to be dated if not obsolete) it has been possible to identify the alternative models as the welfare model and the justice model. The welfare model saw intervention based on welfare or treatment as the appropriate response to a child or young person who commits a criminal offence. Offending was seen as symptomatic of some underlying problem which needed to be identified and responded to. Treatment was provided by the caring professions so that power in this model lay with the social work profession. The alternative model argued that the welfare response to youth crime contained far too much discretionary power in the sense that the offender could become a 'victim' of the caring professions as one of the unintended consequences of welfarism. Critics of the welfare model saw the adult criminal justice system which operates on the basis of rights for the defendant and determinate sentences for the offender as the appropriate model for the youth justice system.

This debate, which has been deliberately simplified, was itself overlaid by the necessity of government to be seen to be doing something about the incidence of criminal behaviour and the possibly conflicting desire of government to reduce prison overcrowding. The much vaunted 'short, sharp, shock' response of the 1980s to serious or habitual youth offending was no more successful in cutting the rates of re-offending than any other response and in the years before the introduction of the young offender institutions magistrates had been increasingly unwilling to sentence youth offenders to detention centres.

Currently there is difficulty in determining a coherence in policy underpinning the youth justice system despite the separation of the criminal youth court from the 'care proceedings court', consequent upon the implementation of the Children Act 1989 and the Criminal Justice Act 1991. The Children Act emphasises the welfare of children both in the community and in court proceedings and the Criminal Justice Act emphasises the 'just deserts' principle of sentencing within which the seriousness of an offence is reflected in the severity of the sentence. The possible tension between the philosophies of these two Acts must also be seen in the light of section 44 of the Children and Young Persons Act 1933 which is still in force, not having been repealed by the Criminal Justice Act 1991. Section 44 provides:

> Every court in dealing with a child or young person who is brought before it, either as an offender or otherwise, shall have regard to the welfare of the child or young person . . .

All those involved in youth justice will have to steer a pathway through the possibly conflicting philosophies of the three statutory provisions identified above.

1.4   THE PRINCIPLES OF THE CRIMINAL JUSTICE ACT 1991

The 1991 Act provides a sentencing framework for all criminal offenders and established a youth court to administer that framework for offenders aged 10 to 17. There are a number of features of the Act which, put together, may be said to constitute an important statutory element in a philosophy for youth justice:

— the principle of proportionality between the seriousness of the offence and the severity of the sentence applies to the sentencing of children (10–13) and young persons (14–17);

— this principle is to be balanced with the welfare principle of section 44 of the Children and Young Persons Act 1933 which continues to apply in the youth court;

— an emphasis on the responsibility of parents for the behaviour of their children under the age of 16;

— the establishment of a new category of offender; the 16–17 year old 'near adult' offender is subject to the full range of sentences;

— the introduction of National Standards to establish a base of good practice for the supervision of offenders in the community and for the preparation of pre-sentence reports;

— a statutory duty on all those working in the criminal justice system to avoid discriminating on improper grounds including race or gender;

— an encouragement to inter-agency co-operation in the development of diversionary initiatives and in the supervision of offenders in the community.

2 THE LAW

2.1 THE JURISDICTION OF THE YOUTH COURT

The youth court is part of the magistrates' court system but is constituted separately from the adult court and there are strict rules which seek to prevent children and young people coming into contact with adult defendants at court. Criminal proceedings against youth defendants are brought under the law contained in the Children and Young Persons Acts of 1933 and 1969 which specify that prosecutions are brought in the youth court. Exceptions are a charge of murder, where proceedings will be brought in the Crown Court, or where the charge is a serious one (where an adult would face a minimum of 14 years in prison) and the court feels that a substantial sentence, beyond its powers, is necessary then the child or young person may be committed for trial to the Crown Court. A child or young person may be tried in the adult criminal courts when s/he is jointly charged with an adult.

The age of criminal responsibility is set by Parliament at 10 and in prosecutions of those between 10 and 13 the court must be satisfied that the child committed the offence and also that s/he knew that what they were doing was wrong before they can make a finding of guilt. Young people aged 14 to 17 are fully responsible for their criminal acts. The Children and Young Persons Act 1969 contained a provision by which the age of criminal responsibility would have been raised to 14; the section was never implemented and has now been repealed. Nonetheless due to the increased use of cautioning the numbers of children under 14 who are prosecuted has dropped dramatically.

Proceedings in the youth court are governed by the Magistrates' Courts (Children and Young Persons) Rules 1988 and are subject to the principle set out in section 44(1) of the Children and Young Persons Act 1933 which requires the court to 'have regard to the welfare of the child or young person and shall in a proper case take steps for removing him from undesirable surroundings and for seeing that proper provision is made for his education and training'. The proceedings of the youth court should be less formal than the adult court so that the child or young person fully understands all that is going on.

2.2   THE YOUTH COURT

The lay magistrates who make up the 'youth court panel' are selected from the magistrates in a petty sessional area as having appropriate experience and knowledge of the circumstances of children and young people. They should normally be under the age of 50 when appointed and they receive special training as youth court magistrates.

The public are not admitted to the youth court though the press may report criminal proceedings so long as such reports do not allow the identification of the defendant. Youth courts are under a statutory duty to require a parent or parents to attend court hearings for children and young people between the ages of 10 and 15 unless satisfied that it would be unreasonable to do so. Where the young person is 16 or 17 this duty is relegated to a power. These provisions are set out in section 34A of the Children and Young Persons Act 1933 which also places local authorities in the same position as natural parents where the authority has parental responsibility for the juvenile.

2.3   PRE-TRIAL PROCEEDINGS

A defendant will appear in court either because s/he has been arrested and charged by the police or because s/he has been summoned to appear. If a child or young person has been arrested by the police the Police and Criminal Justice Act 1984 provides special safeguards which control how children and young people may be detained and questioned. An 'appropriate adult', who may be a parent but may also be a social worker, must be contacted by the police and asked to attend at the police station. Questioning of the child or young person cannot begin before the arrival of the appropriate adult who must be present during the questioning. The child or young person is also entitled to have a solicitor present at the police station and during questioning. Children and young people should not be detained in a cell. These are important rights and it may fall to a social worker to make sure that they are adhered to. A knowledge of local legal aid solicitors who are available as police station duty solicitors is useful so that necessary contact can be made and the child or young person's position fully protected.

2.3.1   Bail, remand to local authority accommodation and remands to custody

Defendants who are 17 years old are dealt with in the same way as adult defendants.

Once charged a child or young person should be released on bail by the police. If s/he is detained then they should be transferred to local authority accommodation to await their first appearance in court. Once the child or young person has appeared in court decisions concerning bail will be taken by the court under the provisions of the Bail Act 1976 which establishes a right to bail. Bail may be refused in a number of circumstances including where the court finds that there are substantial grounds for believing that, if granted bail, the defendant would abscond, commit further offences, interfere with witnesses or otherwise interfere with the course of justice.

Where bail is refused the child or young person will be remanded to local authority accommodation and the court has powers to require the young person to comply with conditions that could be imposed under the Bail Act such as a condition of residence or a curfew. The court can also require the local authority not to place the child or young person with a named person.

Section 23 of the Children and Young Persons Act 1969 allows the youth court to remand young people aged 15 or 16 to local authority accommodation with a requirement that they are held in secure accommodation. Such remands can only be made in particular circumstances:

A court shall not impose a security requirement except in respect of a young person who has attained the age of fifteen, and then only if —

a)   he is charged with or has been convicted of a violent or sexual offence, or an offence punishable in the case of an adult with imprisonment for a term of fourteen years or more; or

b)   he has a recent history of absconding while remanded to local authority accommodation, and is charged with or has been convicted of an imprisonable offence alleged or found to have been committed while he was so remanded,

and (in either case) the court is of the opinion that only such a requirement would be adequate to protect the public from serious harm from him.

The power to remand with a security requirement will only be implemented when enough local authority secure accommodation is available. Until that time 15 and 16 year old boys can be remanded to prison accommodation in the same circumstances as for a security requirement.

2.3.2   Legal aid

A child or young person charged with a criminal offence is entitled to legal advice and assistance under the green form scheme and to apply for criminal legal aid for representation in court. If a child or young person is not represented on a first appearance in court s/he may be helped and represented by the court duty solicitor.

2.4   COURT PROCEEDINGS

Proceedings against criminal defendants, including children and young people, are often adjourned several times. This may be necessary in order for the defendant to take legal advice or for the Crown Prosecution Service to give advance disclosure of the prosecution case to the defence where the charge relates to an indictable or either way offence.

Children and young people charged with a criminal offence may plead guilty or not guilty. If there is a plea of guilty the Crown Prosecution Service will outline the facts of the case and the offender and/or their legal representative will be given an opportunity to address the court about the offence and about their personal circumstances before the magistrates decide on sentence. Representations on behalf of the offender may be made by their legal representative though often the magistrates will want to hear from the child or young person directly.

A plea of not guilty will mean that a date for trial has to be fixed so that another adjournment is necessary. At the trial the prosecution will seek to sustain the charge by bringing evidence. Prosecution witnesses may be cross-examined by the defence who will bring their own evidence to refute the charge. The defence is likely to include the evidence of the defendant who, with other defence witnesses, will be open to cross-examination by the prosecution. After all the evidence has been heard and the defence has addressed the magistrates they will retire to reach their decision with the benefit of the legal advice of the court clerk.

The burden of proof is on the prosecution to prove the charge beyond a reasonable doubt. If the defendant is found not guilty then that is the end of the matter but if there is a finding of guilty the decision on sentence may be delayed for up to 4 weeks for the preparation of a pre-sentence report.

2.5   PRE-SENTENCE REPORTS

Very often in the youth court the magistrates will want further information about the child or young person before they decide on sentence and in a number of circumstances reports are required before particular sentences are imposed. This information will be obtained through pre-sentence reports prepared by the social services department or by the probation service, or by a youth justice team comprising of both services; magistrates may also request a school report prepared by teachers and processed by the education welfare service.

Section 7 of the Criminal Justice Act 1991 requires the youth court to obtain and consider a pre-sentence report before it forms an opinion on the suitability of the offender for the more serious community sentences ie probation order with additional requirements, community service, a combination order, or a supervision order which includes requirements imposed under the 1969 Children and Young Persons Act.

The preparation of pre-sentence reports is subject to the National Standards for the Supervision of Offenders in the Community which require the report to address the current offence, to provide relevant information about the offender and a conclusion which may include a proposal for the most suitable community sentence.

2.6   SENTENCING YOUTH OFFENDERS

In many respects the sentences available to the youth court are the same as those which can be made in the adult criminal court, though supervision orders are exclusive to the youth court. The welfare principle contained in section 44(1) of the Children and Young Persons Act 1933 applies to sentencing in the youth court.

Social workers and probation officers preparing pre-sentence reports for the youth court are required to work within the terms of the National Standards but must also take account of the sentencing principles of the Criminal Justice Act identified above and discussed in some detail in Chapter 6. In addition report writers should understand the factors and interests that magistrates regard as important and which therefore influence their sentencing practice. Magistrates welcome concise, coherent reports where they see any proposals as realistic in relation to the offence and the offender. They are also concerned about what they see as their duty to the community; a duty which requires sentences to have some public credibility.

The inclusion of 17 year old offenders within the jurisdiction of the youth court and the recognition of 16 and 17 year old offenders as a category of 'near adults' for sentencing purposes has resulted in a sentencing regime which identifies the 10 to 15 age group as distinct from the 16 and 17 year old offenders.

> Courts will have more flexible sentencing arrangements for them (16 and 17 year old offenders), reflecting that offenders of this age are at a transitional stage between childhood and adulthood. Some will be more developed and independent than others. Bringing all offenders of this age group within the jurisdiction of the youth court, and providing the youth court with a flexible range of disposals for offenders of this age, will enable the penalty given in each case to reflect the individual's development and circumstances.[1]

The principle of 'just deserts' or proportionality requires that

[1] 'Criminal Justice Act 1991. Children and Young Persons'. Guide published by the Home Office, December 1991.

the choice of sentence in the youth court reflects the seriousness of the offence. The continuum of seriousness applies so that sentencers are required to establish that an offence is serious enough for a community sentence and that custody can only be imposed on offenders over 14 when the offence is so serious that only a custodial sentence can be justified or that the offence is a violent or sexual offence and that only custody is adequate to protect the public from serious harm from the offender.

There is one exception to this principle of sentencing thresholds. A supervision order with a requirement of intermediate treatment as an alternative to custody is still available under the new sentencing structure; a community sentence as an alternative to a custodial sentence.

Sections 28 and 29 of the Criminal Justice Act apply to sentencing in the youth court. Section 28 provides that the court can take into account any factors which it considers to be relevant in mitigation of a sentence. Section 29(1) provides that previous offences or a failure to respond to previous sentences do not on their own make a current offence more serious. However, section 29(2) provides that where previous offending discloses aggravating factors relating to the current offence then previous offences may be taken into account when determining the seriousness of the current offence.

2.7   THE RANGE OF SENTENCES

2.7.1   Discharges and fines

An absolute discharge

An absolute discharge is a decision by the youth court that no punishment is necessary.

A conditional discharge

A conditional discharge means that the youth offender is discharged for a period of time (maximum of three years) on condition that s/he does not re-offend during that period. If the child or young person re-offends during the period of the discharge then the court may re-sentence for the original offence as well as for the new offence.

Fines

The Criminal Justice Act 1991 establishes a unit fine system for both the adult magistrates' court and the youth court. This system, which is discussed in detail in Chapter 6 is based on the principle that fines should impact equally on offenders of different means. The seriousness of a particular offence is reflected in the number of units awarded and the level of fine fixed by reference to the unit of seriousness and the offender's disposable weekly income.

In the youth court the court has a duty to require the payment of fines by the parents of 10 to 15 year old offenders unless they cannot be found or it would be unreasonable to order them to pay. In respect of 16 and 17 year old offenders the court has a power rather than a duty to order parents to pay. Where a parent is ordered to pay, the level of the fine will reflect the means of the parent rather than those of the youth offender. Local authorities will be required to pay the fines of those offenders for which it has parental responsibility though the level of the fine is subject to a different financial formula.

Binding over

The youth court may, in addition to sentencing the youth offender, bind over the parents or guardian of the offender. For offenders under the age of 16 the court is under a duty to bind over parents where to do so is in the interests of preventing the commission of further offences by the child or young person. For offenders who are 16 or 17 the court has a power rather than a duty to bind over parents or guardians. The maximum recognisance for such a bind over is £1000. Parents or guardians are required to consent to be bound over and may be fined if they refuse and the court finds the refusal to be unreasonable. Bind overs may be varied or revoked upon application by the parent or guardian where the court concludes that to do so is in the interests of justice.

Compensation order

The youth court can award a compensation order as a sentence in its own right or in addition to another sentence. Parents, guardians and local authorities are responsible for compensation orders in the same circumstances as they are for fines. The level of compensation will reflect the monetary value of the damage caused by the offence and the ability of the parent or guardian to pay.

2.7.2 Community services

Section 6(1) of the Criminal Justice Act specifies the availability of community sentences:

> A court shall not pass on an offender a community sentence . . . unless it is of the opinion that the offence, or the combination of the offence and one other offence associated with it, was serious enough to warrant such a sentence.

Having decided that the seriousness threshold has been passed the youth court is then required by section 6(2) to choose the sentence that is both suitable for the offender and commensurate with the seriousness of the offence.

Supervision orders

This order is exclusive to the youth court and is available for offenders from 10 to 17 years of age. A supervision order, which is made under the Children and Young Persons Act 1969, places the child or young person under the supervision of a social worker or probation officer, for a specified period up to a maximum of three years.

There are a number of varieties of supervision order ranging from the minimum order, with no special requirements, through to the supervision order which includes specified activities as a direct alternative to custody. A number of supervision orders contain a requirement that the child or young person take part in specified activities otherwise known as intermediate treatment. The consent of the offender is required for the imposition of additional requirements by the court.

The Children Act 1989 allows the youth court to include a residence requirement in a supervision order under which an offender is required to live in accommodation provided by or on behalf of a local authority for a period of up to six months. The availability of this requirement is limited to offenders who have committed a serious offence, the commission of the offence was due to a significant extent to the circumstances in which the offender had been living and that when the offence was committed the offender was subject to a supervision order with additional requirements other than those relating to mental treatment or school attendance.

Under section 15(3)(a) of the Children and Young Persons Act 1969 breaches of the terms of the supervision order or of any requirements made under the order can be dealt with by the court by the imposition of a fine or an attendance centre order (see below). Where the supervision order included a specified activities requirement as an alternative to custody its breach can result in the youth offender being re-sentenced for the original offence with custody being a possible new sentence.

> The supervision order has been the cornerstone of developments in relation to juvenile offenders and there is every reason for thinking that this will continue with the advent of the youth court and the new, older age range. Such orders provide a demanding but constructive option for young people, particularly when extra requirements are added.[2]

Attendance centre orders

Youth offenders who have committed an offence for which an adult could be imprisoned may be ordered to attend at an attendance centre for a minimum period of 12 hours; the maximum period is 24 hours for offenders up to 15 years old and 36 hours for offenders aged 16 or 17. If the offender is under 14 the order may be for less than 12 hours where it is thought that a 12 hour order would be excessive. At the centre the offender will be required to take part in activities run by the police in a disciplined environment for two or three hours usually on a Saturday afternoon. If a child or young person fails to comply with the order they can be fined and the order allowed to continue or the order can be revoked and the offender re-sentenced for the original offence.

Community service orders

Community service orders are available for youth offenders aged 16 and 17 who have committed an offence for which an adult could be sent to prison. The offender is interviewed by a community service officer to establish their suitability for unpaid

[2]   Ashworth et al, *The Youth Court* Waterside Press (1992) p 72.

work for the community and s/he must agree to the order being made. The minimum number of hours is 40 and the maximum for a youth offender is 240.

Where the offender has failed to comply with the order breach proceedings may be taken in the youth court. If the breach is established then the court may fine the offender, make a community service order for not more than 60 hours, make an attendance centre order, or revoke the order and re-sentence for the original offence. If the court finds that the offender has wilfully and persistently failed to comply with the order then it may conclude that the young person has failed to give his or her consent to a community sentence; such a finding allows the court to impose a custodial sentence.

Probation

The youth court can make a probation order on an offender aged 16 or 17 for a minimum of 6 months and a maximum of three years. By section 2(1) of the Powers of the Criminal Courts Act 1973 before making such an order the court must be:

... of the opinion that the supervision of the offender by a probation officer is desirable in the interests of —

a) securing the rehabilitation of the offender; or

b) protecting the public from harm from him or preventing the commission by him of further offences, . . .

The offender must consent to the order being made. A number of additional requirements can be included in the order: to live at a particular place such as a bail hostel; to undergo psychiatric treatment for a mental condition; to attend a probation centre; to take part in specified activities or schemes organised by the probation service; to undergo treatment for drug or alcohol dependency or a requirement not to do particular things during a period of time (a 'refraining order').

Breach of a probation order may be dealt with in the same way as the breach of a community service order.

Combination order

This order is available for 16 and 17 year old offenders who have committed an imprisonable offence. Section 11(2) of the Criminal Justice Act 1991 requires the court to be of the opinion that the order is desirable in the interests of:

a) securing the rehabilitation of the offender; or

b) protecting the public from harm from him or preventing the commission by him of further offences.

The order requires the offender to be supervised by a probation officer for a period of one year minimum and three years maximum and to perform between 40 and 100 hours community service. The offender must consent to the order being made. Failure to comply with a combination order has the same implications for the offender as a failure to comply with a probation or community service order.

Curfew order

The youth court may impose a curfew order on offenders aged 16 or 17 in which the offender is required to remain at a specified place for a minimum of two hours and a maximum of twelve hours per day. Before making the order the court must obtain and consider information about the place where the offender will be curfewed and the attitude of people at that place who will be affected by the presence of the curfewed offender. The offender must consent to the order and the order should not, as far as is reasonably practicable, conflict with the offender's religious beliefs, any requirements of another community sentence or with the offender's work or attendance at an educational establishment. The Criminal Justice Act 1991 stipulates that a person must be made responsible for monitoring the order and provides for the electronic monitoring (by 'tagging') of offenders subject to curfew orders.

Failure to comply with curfew orders is dealt with in the same way as for probation, community service and combination orders.

Reports

The 1991 Criminal Justice Act requires the youth court to consider a pre-sentence report before passing the more serious of the community sentences, ie. probation order with additional requirements, community service order, combination order or a supervision order with requirements.[3]

National standards

The preparation and writing of pre-sentence reports and the supervision of community sentences are subject to the National Standards for the Supervision of Offenders in the Community. Published by the Home Office, these required standards of practice for probation services and social services departments in England and Wales identify an expectation that the guidance and requirements contained in them are followed.[4]

2.7.3 Custody

The Criminal Justice Act 1991 sets out the criteria for custodial sentences for all age groups so that the same conditions apply in the adult court and in the youth court. Section 1(2) provides that a court (in this chapter the youth court) shall not pass a custodial sentence in a young offender institution unless it is of the opinion:

a)   that the offence, or the combination of the offence and one other offence associated with it, was so serious that only such a sentence can be justified for the offence; or

b)   where the offence is a violent or sexual offence, that only such a sentence would be adequate to protect the public from serious harm from him.

An associated offence is another offence which the offender is convicted of at the same hearing or another offence which the offender is sentenced for at the same hearing.

The court may also pass a custodial sentence where an offender has refused to consent to a community sentence which requires such a consent.

The minimum age for a custodial sentence is 15. The minimum

---

[3] Detailed discussion of pre-sentence reports appears in Chapter 6.
[4] More detailed reference to the contents of the National Standards appears in the chapter on the criminal justice system.

sentence for a youth offender is two months and the maximum is twelve months.

The seriousness threshold for custody is defined as 'so serious that only a custodial sentence can be justified' and section 29 of the 1991 Act applies so that previous offences or a failure to respond to previous sentences cannot, on their own, make the current offence more serious. However, if the circumstances of previous offences disclose aggravating factors then the previous offences may be taken into account in considering the seriousness of the current offence.

The youth court is required to obtain a pre-sentence report before reaching a conclusion about whether the criteria for a custodial sentence are satisfied or a view on the length of the sentence. The court must consider all information about the circumstances of the offence that is available to it; this will include any aggravating or mitigating factors concerning the offence and section 28 allows the court to take any factors which it considers relevant into account in mitigation of sentence.

In relation to violent or sexual offences the court must take into account information about the circumstances of the offence, including aggravating and mitigating factors, and may take into account any information about the offender when it is considering the protection of the public criterion. For this category of offences it is clear that an offender can receive a custodial sentence even though the offence is not serious enough to justify custody under the provisions of section 1(2)(a).

Under the provisions of section 53 of the Children and Young Persons Act 1933 anyone under 18 convicted of murder will be detained at Her Majesty's Pleasure (the equivalent of a life sentence) and those convicted in the Crown Court of grave crimes (those where an adult offender could be sentenced to 14 years or more) can be sentenced by the Crown Court to a term of imprisonment which may not exceed the maximum term for an adult offender.

2.8   APPEALS

An appeal by a youth offender against conviction and sentence by the youth court may be made to the Crown Court where the case will be re-heard. It is argued that social workers and probation officers have an important role to play in advising children and young people and their parents of rights to appeal against a custodial sentence and in encouraging solicitors to make appeals in such cases.

3   JUVENILE JUSTICE AND SOCIAL WORK PRACTICE: some issues for discussion

3.1   THE CAUTIONING OF YOUTH OFFENDERS

> It is recognised both in theory and in practice that delay in the entry of a young person into the formal criminal justice system may help to prevent his entry into that system altogether.[5]

It is now widely accepted that there is considerable value in reducing the number of children and young people prosecuted in the youth court. The various methods of keeping such offenders out of court are known as 'diversionary schemes or procedures'. Though the police control the exercise of major elements of discretion within diversionary schemes in relation to charge and the preparation of papers for the Crown Prosecution Service, social work has an important role to play in these schemes by influencing the decision making process.

Juvenile bureaux, inter-agency or cautioning panels have been established for some time in a number of areas and these have allowed social services departments to influence, to a greater or lesser extent, the decision of the police in relation to the action to be taken against a child or young person who has come to their notice. As a result of such consultation a caution may be administered as an alternative to prosecution. Police cautioning has become the dominant method of diversion and is in essence a 'serious and strict telling off' and there is widespread agreement that cautioning has been successful in delaying and sometimes preventing the entry of a child or young person into the formal criminal justice system.

Cautions are recorded and in practice are included in an offender's record which is presented in court at any subsequent hearing.

[5]   Home Office Circular to Chief Constables No 14/1985.

Different models of police cautioning have developed over time and those which exclude consultation with other agencies therefore preclude social work influence. So for example an 'instant caution' is administered by the police within a very short time of offending or arrest and is often given without consulting other agencies. Cautioning by letter is increasingly used as a means of saving time and money. More formal cautions may be given after consideration by an inter-agency or multi-agency panel which may include representatives from the police, the probation service, education welfare service, social services, education and the youth service. In such panels there is clearly considerable scope for social work practitioners to influence the decision whether to prosecute a youth offender. In some areas such panels have the benefit of the extra facility of what is termed 'cautioning plus' described by NACRO as 'some form of support or additional activity as an adjunct to a caution. This may include a recommended activity, an apology to the victim or some sort of reparation. It might also include the offer of social work assistance for the young person or the family or some other kind of welfare provision.'[6]

Formally the decision whether to caution a child or young person or to forward the papers to the Crown Prosecution Service for prosecution lies with the police so that the level of influence or control that other agencies have on this decision will depend ultimately on the willingness of individual police forces to cede or delegate such authority to one of the many models of cautioning panel.

Whilst cautioning is generally seen as successful there are a number of reservations which must concern social work practitioners. These include concern over variations between police forces in the rate of cautioning; evidence that white youths are more likely than black youths to receive a caution as an alternative to prosecution; and some evidence that cautioning is sometimes used not as an alternative to prosecution but as an alternative to a more informal warning or 'no further action'.[7] There is also concern that some children and young people may admit an offence to 'get away' with a caution in circumstances

6 'Diverting Juvenile Offenders from Prosecution'. NACRO Juvenile Crime Committee, Policy Paper 2. 1989.
7 'Time for Change: A New Framework for Dealing with Juvenile Crime and Offenders'. NACRO (1987) Chapter 4.

where the evidence is such that the Crown Prosecution Service would not have taken a prosecution. In relation to 'cautioning plus' there are concerns about whether such packages of measures may be disproportionate to the offence and the penalty which a court may have decided on. Also the imposition of quasi-judicial penalties without the benefit of due process available in the youth court is itself problematic.

3.2 THE YOUTH COURT

In some respects the existence of the youth court is a result of both the Children Act 1989 and the Criminal Justice Act 1991. The Children Act established a family proceedings court, within the structure of the magistrates' court, to deal with the civil law aspects of child and family law (including both private and public law matters) thereby taking care proceedings out of the jurisdiction of the old juvenile court. The Criminal Justice Act created the youth court out of the old juvenile court and extended its jurisdiction to 17 year old defendants and offenders. This development has established a youth court with a specifically criminal law jurisdiction thereby ending the sometimes difficult mix of care and criminal jurisdiction administered by the old juvenile court. A number of commentators have expressed the hope that a clearer philosophy of youth justice might emerge from the work of the youth court, though such a hope would not necessarily embrace the 'law and order' rhetoric associated by some with the introduction of the Criminal Justice Act.

It seems though that any emerging philosophy will reflect a number of factors in addition to the principles of the Criminal Justice Act identified in Chapter 6. Such factors include the continuing influence of section 44 of the Children and Young Persons Act 1933, the welfare principle; specific provisions of the Children Act which require local authorities to reduce the need to bring criminal proceedings against children in their area; and the general welfare orientation of the Children Act. Any 'justice' orientation perceived in the 'just deserts' sentencing philosophy of the Criminal Justice Act 1991 must be considered in the light of the 'welfare' provisions just identified. This tension between 'welfare' and 'justice' is reflected in sentencing practice under the Act with the result that, for example, the imposition of a combination order on a 16 year old offender should be understood in terms of the deprivation of liberty and the rehabilitation of the offender.

This discussion of principle and philosophy directly impinges on the youth justice practice of social workers and probation officers. Tensions between 'welfare' and 'justice' must be negotiated in the planning of services and in the every day work of youth justice practice. The authors of pre-sentence reports dealing with community sentences are required to balance the issue of seriousness of the offence with the appropriateness of the order for the offender. Those supervising youth offenders under probation, supervision or combination orders are constantly seeking to fulfill the requirement that such sentences are both demanding of the offender and constructive in the sense that they encourage rehabilitation. Local authority social workers and probation officers are often members of inter-agency or cautioning panels and local authorities are involved in the development of diversionary procedures consequent upon their duties under the Children Act. Schedule 2 of the Act places a number of duties on local authorities to provide support for children and families; one of these duties is the reduction of the need to bring criminal proceedings against children in their area.

3.3 INTER-AGENCY CO-OPERATION

Guidance issued under the Children Act[8] stresses the importance of an inter-agency approach to crime prevention and a Home Office circular[9] also identifies the benefits of inter-agency participation in the cautioning of offenders. It is now assumed that youth justice practice under the Criminal Justice Act will be characterised by inter-agency co-operation between social services departments, probation services and voluntary organisations. In many areas this assumption has seen the establishment of Youth Justice Teams involving social services and probation. For example the Youth Justice Team in the London Borough of Hounslow identifies its reponsibilities as follows:

Provide a Court Duty service.

[8] 'Crime Prevention — The Success of the Partnership Approach' LAC(90)5.
[9] 59/90 'The Cautioning of Offenders'.

Prepare the majority of pre-sentence reports, assessment reports and progress reports for court.

The supervision of supervision orders, probation orders and combination orders.

Ensure arrangements are made for the preparation of community service assessments.

The supervision of young offenders before and after release from Young Offender Institutions.

The team will develop a bail support facility for young people at risk of being remanded to custody (secure accommodation) and local authority accommodation.

Chair the Cautioning Panel.

The team will work in accordance with National Standards . . .

The team will be involved in crime prevention initiatives.

The team will provide an 'appropriate adult' resource to young people detained at the police station where necessary.

This specification identifies the complexity and variety of youth justice practice and provides an example for the development of inter-agency co-operation between social services and probation which is quickly being established as the hallmark of professional practice in the contemporary youth justice system.

3.4   THE USE OF CUSTODY FOR YOUTH DEFENDANTS AND OFFENDERS

In the same way that social work has become involved in schemes which provide alternatives to prosecution so it has also worked to develop alternative to custody schemes most often based on the use of intermediate treatment within the administration of supervision orders. The use of community based initiatives as alternatives to custody was encouraged by the 1983 DHSS intermediate treatment initiative and the monitoring of schemes established under the initiative has provided evidence that the re-offending rates of young persons whilst on such programmes are lower or at least no worse than those sentenced to custody.[10] The development of alternative to custody schemes within community based intermediate treatment initiatives has continued to take place and such schemes are now readily used by youth courts as an alternative to custodial sentences.

That custody should be seen very much as a last resort is confirmed by the strict conditions that must be satisfied before a custodial sentence can be imposed on offenders aged 15 and over. There is no doubt that the restrictions on the use of custody introduced by the Criminal Justice Act 1982 significantly reduced the number of juveniles receiving custodial sentences; between 1980 and 1989 the number of custodial sentences fell from 7716 to 2176, and it is expected that the criteria for custody introduced by the Criminal Justice Act 1991 will continue this trend. In addition the impact of social work and probation work in reducing the use of custodial sentences should not be underestimated; the preparation of effective pre-sentence reports concentrating on the availability of community sentences and the continued development of alternative to custody schemes are two factors having an important impact on non-custodial sentencing decisions in the youth court.

It is to be hoped that the significant reduction in the use of custody achieved in the juvenile court can be sustained in the youth court and that it will extend to the 17 year old offenders who are now dealt with in the youth court.

3.5   RACE AND THE YOUTH JUSTICE SYSTEM

For some time there has been concern that ethnic communities are discriminated against in the administration of virtually all aspects of the criminal justice system.[11] In relation to the youth justice system NACRO has produced evidence to suggest that black youths are discriminated against in the cautioning system, with white youths more likely to receive a caution rather than be prosecuted. They also refer to research carried out by Nottinghamshire Social Services Department and to a study by

[10] 'Phasing Out Prison Department Custody for Juvenile Offenders'. NACRO Juvenile Crime Committee Policy Paper 1. 1989.
[11] Yasmin Alibhai 'Criminal injustice. How the legal system treats blacks'. New Statesman and Society (8.7.88).

the South East London Probation Service both of which suggest that black young people are more likely to be locked up than their white equivalents. If involvement with the official criminal justice system and custody both increase the likelihood of re-offending, as many commentators believe, then it seems that black youths are more likely to be 'processed' and 're-processed' into and within the criminal justice system than white youths.

Social workers practising within the youth justice system and those whose clients are involved with the system should be aware of the racism within it and do all they can to safeguard the interests of their black clients and to develop anti-racist models of practice eg. by the use of non-racist stereotypes and language and the monitoring of sentencing in the youth court.

The Criminal Justice Act 1991 provides important official recognition of this issue; section 95 places a duty on persons involved in the administration of justice 'to avoid discriminating against any person on the ground of race or sex or any other improper ground'.

The National Standards for the Supervision of Offenders in the Community emphasise a commitment to equal opportunities:

> The work of probation services and social services departments must be free of discrimination on the ground of race, gender, age, disability, language ability, literacy, religion, sexual orientation or any other improper ground.

Services must have a stated equal opportunities policy and develop an anti-discriminatory practice. Though the Standards are primarily concerned to identify good practice for probation staff and local authority social workers they are also identified as important statements of principle for all criminal justice agencies including the police and the prison service.

4   CASE STUDIES

These case studies can be used to consolidate work done on the youth justice system.

1.   Ricky Smith is 16 years old. He has been found guilty of

robbery and possession of an offensive weapon, a lock knife. The facts of the case are as follows:

Two boys, one of whom was Ricky, followed a 48 year old Sri Lankan woman along a suburban street and assaulted her stealing a gold chain from around her neck. The chain was worth £500 and in the process of the robbery the woman was cut and bruised around her neck and chest. The two boys ran off but were chased by three building workers who had responded to the shouts of the woman. They challenged the two boys and Ricky pulled the knife. In the ensuing fight Ricky was knocked unconscious by one of the men. The police were called and Ricky was arrested. The other boy escaped and has not been traced.

Ricky pleaded not guilty at his trial but was found guilty of both offences. The court has asked for a pre-sentence report. You have been asked to prepare the report. Ricky is now willing to admit his part in the robbery but does not seem to be concerned about the seriousness of the offence or his position.

The family history is one of a broken home where both Ricky and his mother were physically abused by his father before he left the home. Ricky's younger sister was killed in a road accident 2 years ago and he has been getting into trouble since then. He has two previous convictions; one for possession of an offensive weapon and one for theft. On the first offence he was conditionally discharged and on the second offence he was fined.

a)   Draft a pre-sentence report concentrating on the seriousness of the offence and the range of sentences available to the youth court.

b)   As a youth court magistrate decide on the sentence you would pass and justify your decision.

This is a good case study for role playing. Parts which can be scripted include Ricky, his mother, his lawyer to mitigate on his behalf, the social worker or probation officer who writes the report, the magistrates who make the decision having read the report, and the court clerk who gives the magistrates legal advice on the sentencing options open to them. The role play could take place in different settings and at different times, eg the interview between Ricky and social worker or probation officer;

in the retiring room with the magistrates; and in court when mitigation is given and sentence passed.

2. You are a social worker representing the social services department on an inter-agency or cautioning panel which meets to discuss the cases of children and young people who have come to the notice of the police and in each case decides whether to recommend that the child or young person concerned be prosecuted or receive a 'formal caution' or a 'caution plus'.

In each of the following cases indicate your recommendation and outline the reasons for it:

a) Tim is 11 and has been caught acting as a lookout for his older brother who was stealing a pedal bike from a garden shed. Both boys live with their parents in a large house in a prosperous area of town. Tim's father is a local vicar and is very concerned about any adverse publicity and is keen to do anything to help Tim.

b) Tom is Tim's brother. He has been caught stealing the bike. He is 16 and has been cautioned once before for a similar offence. Tom lives at home and his father's concerns include him as well as Tim.

c) Tracey is 14 and has been caught at the conclusion of a shoplifting 'spree' in the High Street. All the goods stolen were recovered except for a half bottle of vodka which she drank most of before she was caught. Her mother is a single parent living in a council flat and is angry with Tracey for 'being caught'. Tracey has never been in trouble before and her mother refused to come to the police station when she was arrested.

d) Lambert is 16 and has been caught trying to sell a car radio which he stole from a BMW parked at the local tube station. Some £100 damage was done to the car. He was difficult at the police station and has refused to talk to you. The police are very concerned about such crimes which have increased considerably in the area in the last few months.

3. You have been invited by the Clerk to the Justices to talk to the magistrates at the next meeting of the youth court panel about the new 'alternative to custody' scheme you have been

involved in designing and setting up. You have been told that they are sceptical about the whole idea.

What you are going to say to them? Give details of the way the scheme would work for a juvenile offender.

5 ACTIVITIES

1. There is no substitute for seeing the youth court working. It may be possible to gain access as part of a social services or probation placement subject to the approval of the court itself. Students on other placements may be able to get access to the youth court by seeking the permission of the Clerk to the Justices.

A letter of introduction from college or agency asking for permission and giving assurances about protecting the confidentiality of proceedings is normally enough to obtain the necessary authority.

A visit to the youth court can be combined with the preparation of an observation report. Such a report should identify the proceedings observed and provide an outline of the jurisdiction of the court. Observations can also be made on the identity, functions and competence of all those involved in the proceedings. Brief summaries of the cases heard can be provided together with any criticisms of the proceedings themselves. Concluding comments might centre on the 'quality of justice' provided by the youth court.

2. Design a leaflet for defendants and their parents explaining what goes on in criminal proceedings in the youth court.

3. Find out whether there is an 'alternative to custody' scheme operating in your area and get some information on how it works.

4. Where is the attendance centre for your area? Contact the centre and arrange to visit when it is working.

5. What intermediate treatment schemes are operating in your area? How do they work?

6. Talk to a community service officer and find out how community service is organised for youth offenders.

7. What 'diversionary schemes or procedures' operate in your area? Are there any statistics available? Which agencies are involved?

8. Contact the Children's Legal Centre and get a publications list and any free materials they provide.

9. Become a member of NACRO. You will receive mailings of their briefing papers, report summaries, the NACRO News Digest, the annual report and their publications list. NACRO is one of the leading pressure groups in the criminal justice field and provides excellent information.

10. What policy does your social services department and/or probation service have regarding youth offenders? Is it written down? Is it followed in practice? Who monitors youth court appearances and sentences? Is there any ethnic monitoring? Is there a youth justice team; what work does it do?

6   ADDRESSES

Children's Legal Centre,
20 Compton Terrace,
London N1 2UN.
(The Children's Legal Centre
runs a free advice service on
all aspects of the law affecting
children and young people in
England and Wales, by letter
or telephone on 071 359 6251
(2-5pm weekdays).)

National Association for the
Care and Resettlement of
Offenders (NACRO),
169 Clapham Road,
London SW9 0PU.
Phone: 071 582 6500.

National Association of
Probation Officers,
3/4 Chivalry Road,
Battersea,
London SW11 1HT.

7   MATERIALS

7.1   BASIC LEGAL MATERIALS FOR ORDINARY SOCIAL WORK PRACTICE

'A Quick Reference Guide to the Criminal Justice Act 1991' (1992) Home Office.

'National Standards for the Supervision of Offenders in the Community' (1992) Home Office.

NACRO Briefing Papers:

The Children Act — Implications for Young Offenders (1991).

The Criminal Justice Act — Implications for Juvenile and Young Adult Offenders (1991).

Criteria for Custody: Implications for Juvenile and Young Adult Offenders (1991).

The Home Office Circular on the Cautioning of Offenders: Implications for Juvenile Justice (1990).

New Local Authority Duties for Young Offenders and Youth Crime (1991).

Remand Arrangements in the New Youth Court (1992).

The Role of Juvenile Justice Workers in Crime Prevention (1991).

7.2   FURTHER READING

'Diverting Juvenile Offenders from Prosecution' Nacro Juvenile Crime Committee Policy Paper 2 NACRO.

'Race and Criminal Justice: A Way Forward' (1989) NACRO.

Littlechild, B. (Ed.) *Social Work Guidelines to the Police and Criminal Evidence Act 1984* (1987) BASW/Macmillan.

Ashworth et al. *The Youth Court* (1992) Waterside Press.

Morris, A. Giller, H. Croom Helm *Understanding Juvenile Justice* (1987).

King, M. 'Welfare and Justice' in King, M. (Ed.) *Childhood, Welfare and Justice* (1981) Batsford Academic.

Pitts, J. *Working with Young Offenders* (1990) BASW/ MacMillan.

'Young People in the Criminal Justice System: A Practical Guide to Inter-Agency Partnership' (1992) NACRO.

'Youth Crime Prevention: A Co-Ordinated Approach' (1992) NACRO.

CRIMINAL PROCEEDINGS AGAINST CHILDREN AND YOUNG PEOPLE -COURT STRUCTURE

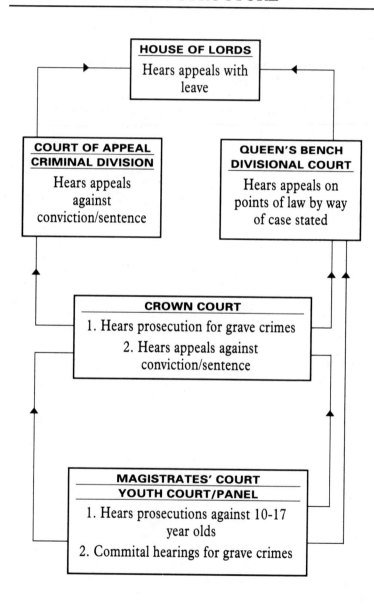

HOUSE OF LORDS

Hears appeals with leave

COURT OF APPEAL CRIMINAL DIVISION

Hears appeals against conviction/sentence

QUEEN'S BENCH DIVISIONAL COURT

Hears appeals on points of law by way of case stated

CROWN COURT

1. Hears prosecution for grave crimes

2. Hears appeals against conviction/sentence

MAGISTRATES' COURT YOUTH COURT/PANEL

1. Hears prosecutions against 10-17 year olds

2. Commital hearings for grave crimes

CHAPTER 8

Mental Health

1 INTRODUCTION

Mental health is one of the major 'professional law' areas of social work practice. The Mental Health Act 1983 allocates to social workers a number of legal rights, powers and duties which partly determine the boundaries and nature of practice with people who have a mental disorder; additionally the Act defines the legal position of patients in relation to their compulsory admission to hospital, their treatment whilst detained, their rights whilst in hospital and their discharge from hospital.

This area of practice is marked out by the law in the sense that a number of these important rights, powers and duties are invested in a social work practitioner called an 'approved social worker' who is required by the Act to have been specially trained and qualified. This post qualification training is required of all those wishing to practise as approved social workers so that they have 'appropriate competence in dealing with persons suffering from mental disorder' — section 114(2).

Social work practice with clients who have a mental disorder extends well beyond the statutory boundaries of the Mental Health Act and may involve other legislation concerning people who are elderly, those who have a chronic illness. a disability, people who are homeless, welfare rights, aspects of community care provision and the criminal justice system. The emphasis of this chapter will be on work within the provisions of the Mental Health Act 1983 though some indication will be given of this wider frame of practice.

The 1983 Act replaced the 1959 Mental Health Act and the 1982 Mental Health (Amendment) Act and was seen partly as a product of pressure group politics in which MIND (the National Association for Mental Health) played a leading role. Their concern was to increase the rights of patients who were compulsorily detained in psychiatric hospital. Other concerns raised in the debate about the reform of the law included those of the health service trade unions who wanted a clearer definition of the legal position of their members working in this area and the desire of other groups to remove people with learning difficulty from the long term detention provisions of the existing legislation. The search for a clearer definition of the legal rights and duties affecting workers and patients was the dominant objective of reform. In many respects this clearer definition has been achieved though views on the nature of the legal rights and duties set out by the Mental Health Act 1983 reflect different professional interests and individual positions on issues such as civil liberties. There are, of course, a number of issues arising from the operation of the current mental health system which are of concern to social work practitioners and others working in the area. Examples include the over representation of women and members of the ethnic communities diagnosed as having a mental disorder and current concern about the regimes within special hospitals.

This chapter provides only a brief outline of the law because those wishing to practise as approved social workers will undergo further post qualification training where the details of the legislation constitute a substantial part of the course. Nonetheless it is necessary to have some knowledge of the main legislative provisions and of the issues they raise for social work practice, and for the rights of patients and social work clients.

2 THE LAW

2.1 THE ACT

The Mental Health Act 1983 specifies procedures for the compulsory admission of patients to hospital; it further defines the position and rights of patients whilst in hospital, the circumstances of their treatment, the procedures for their continued detention and finally for their discharge. Within these specifications the Act details the legal position of patients and of those working within the mental health service. An attempt has been made in this section to identify and discuss areas of the law where social workers have or may have a part to play.

The Act makes provision in relation to people who have a 'mental disorder'; this is a generic concept which is further defined by the Act in terms of four categories: mental illness, severe mental impairment, mental impairment and psychopathic disorder.

There is no minimum age limit for admission to hospital under the provisions of the Mental Health Act though the Code of Practice for the Act sets out the difficult issues raised by the admission of children and young persons to hospital and their treatment whilst in hospital.

> any intervention in the life of a young person, considered necessary by reason of their mental disorder, should be the least restrictive possible and result in the least possible segregation from family, friends, community and school.[1]

2.2 VOLUNTARY PATIENTS

It should be appreciated that the vast majority of patients in psychiatric hospital are voluntary patients and as such they are in substantially the same position as patients in hospital for a physical illness; so for instance they may refuse treatment and may discharge themselves at any time. For psychiatric patients this latter right is subject to short term holding powers exercised by designated doctors and nurses under section 5 of the Act. The doctor in charge of a voluntary patient's treatment has a 72 hour power to detain a patient if s/he reports to the hospital managers that an application for compulsory admission ought be made in respect of the patient. A qualified mental health nurse has a similar holding power for 6 hours if they consider that a patient is suffering from a mental disorder to the extent that it is necessary for their health or safety, or for the protection of others, for the patient to be immediately restrained from leaving the hospital. This power can be exercised only when the doctor treating the patient is not available.

Voluntary patients cannot be treated without their valid consent. It should be noted though that the common law would allow treatment to be administered in cases of necessity. This concept is said to include life saving treatment where the patient is unable

---

[1] Code of Practice, Mental Health Act. Department of Health and Welsh Office. 1990.

to consent and their wishes are not known and it may extend to an emergency intervention to restrain a violent patient where there is a serious and immediate danger to the patient or to others.

2.3   THE WORK OF THE APPROVED SOCIAL WORKER

(Under the Act an approved social worker has legal independence and acts in a personal capacity. The rights, duties and powers of an approved social worker are central to the Act and constitute the statutory boundaries of substantial areas of social work practice in relation to those with a mental disorder. Pre-eminent is the duty to make an application for compulsory admission under section 13.[2]

2.3.1   The application for admission: the preliminaries

Section 13 of the Act places a duty on the approved social worker to make an application for admission to hospital or reception into guardianship in respect of any patient if s/he is satisfied that such an application should be made.

Behind this statutory duty is the important principle that the approved social worker will have an independent professional view as to whether an application for admission is necessary and the section requires the patient to be interviewed before the application is made so that the approved social worker can 'satisfy himself that detention in a hospital is in all the circumstances of the case the most appropriate way of providing the care and medical treatment of which the patient stands in need' — section 13(2). The objective of this requirement is to identify the personal circumstances of the patient and thereby to be able to assess whether there are alternative community based treatment facilities available. The Act is based on the assumption that compulsory admission to hospital should be very much a last resort and one

---

[2] Her Majesty's Stationery Office publish a number of precedent forms to be used in the admission process. Seeing the law as a series of requirements and procedures on a form may help to understand the nature of the law in relation to the application for admission. Form 2 'Application by an approved social worker for admission for assessment'; Form 6 'Emergency application by an approved social worker for admission for assessment'; and Form 9, 'Application by approved social worker for admission for treatment', are included as an appendix at the end of the chapter and may be useful in understanding the requirements of sections 2,4 and 3 respectively.

of the tasks of the approved social worker is to investigate all other treatment and care opportunities.

The section requires the interview to be carried out in a 'suitable manner' and the Act thereby acknowledges that there will be circumstances in which it is impossible to gain the necessary information from a patient. It may even be necessary to use the emergency powers available under section 135 to obtain a warrant to search for and remove a patient so that an attempt can be made to interview the patient.

If a patient's nearest relative[3] so requests a local social services authority must, under section 13(4), direct an approved social worker to consider whether an application for compulsory admission should be made. Again the law requires the formulation of an independent professional opinion by the approved social worker who may decide for or against making an application.

2.3.2 The application

An approved social worker, subject to section 13, has a duty to apply for the compulsory admission of a patient to hospital in three closely defined circumstances specified in Part II of the Act. In all of these circumstances the nearest relative also has the right to apply for admission independently of the approved social worker though provisions in the legislation make it clear that wherever possible the approved social worker and the nearest relative should be in agreement over the necessity to make an application. This agreement is important for an approved social worker is likely to have a continuing relationship with the patient and their family who may be looking after them upon their discharge from hospital. The Code of Practice identifies the approved social worker as the preferred applicant because of their professional training, knowledge of the legislation and of local resources. The Code also raises concern about the relationship between the nearest relative and the patient where the application for admission is made by the patient's nearest relative.

[3] Nearest relatives are defined by section 26 of the Act in descending order of seniority as being: a) husband or wife, b) son or daughter, c) father or mother, d) brother or sister, e) grandparent, f) grandchild, g) uncle or aunt and h) niece or nephew. A cohabitee of more than six months is regarded as a spouse.

The medical recommendation for admission is normally made by an 'approved' doctor; this is a doctor approved by the Secretary of State under section 12(2) of the Act as having special experience in the diagnosis or treatment of mental disorder.

An application for admission is made so that the patient may be compulsorily detained in hospital. The Act envisages that such detention is required in three sets of circumstances: i) in an emergency to protect the patient or to protect others; ii) to allow an assessment of the condition of the patient; and iii) to allow the longer term treatment of a patient. The maximum length of the detention and the rights of the patient vary in each circumstance and these provide a sliding scale of 'seriousness'. Thus the procedures and criteria of admission for treatment are far stricter than for an emergency admission.

2.3.3   Admissions in an emergency

Section 4 provides for an admission in an emergency.

Who by?   An application may be made by an approved social worker or the nearest relative.

Medical support?   The application should be supported by the medical recommendation of a doctor who has previous knowledge of the patient though the recommendation of an authorised doctor is acceptable.

On what criteria?   The diagnostic criteria are a) that the patient is suffering from a mental disorder of a nature or degree which warrants the detention of the patient in a hospital for assessment (or for assessment followed by medical treatment) for at least a limited period; and b) he ought to be so detained in the interests of his own health or safety or with a view to the protection of other persons (section 2(2)).

The additional major criteria for an application for admission in an emergency are the urgent necessity for detention and that going through the requirements for an admission for assessment would cause undesirable delay.

The diagnostic criteria are the same as those for an admission for assessment but the Mental Health Act Code of Practice, published in 1990, distinguishes the two forms of admission by specifying that an emergency situation is evidenced by a significant risk of mental or physical harm to the patient or others, or the danger of serious harm to property or the need for the patient to be physically restrained.

The person making the application must have seen the patient during the 24 hours prior to the application and the admission must take place within 24 hours of the medical examination or the application whichever is the earlier. The patient may be detained for up to 72 hours under this section though it is possible to convert an emergency detention to detention for assessment, or even for treatment, by fulfilling the requirements of section 2 or section 3 respectively.

The Code of Practice stresses that emergency applications should not be made on the basis of convenience in the sense that the procedures for such applications are less rigorous than for an admission for assessment.

2.3.4   Admission for assessment

Section 2 provides for an admission and detention for assessment.

Who by?   Upon the application of an approved social worker *or the nearest relative.

Medical support?   With the support of the medical recommendations of two doctors, one of whom is approved.

On what criteria?   That the patient is suffering from mental disorder of a nature or degree which warrants his detention in a hospital for assessment, or for assessment followed by treatment, for at least a limited period, and he ought to be detained in the interests of his own health or safety or with a view to the protection of others.

The applicant must have seen the patient within the 14 days before the application. The patient may be detained for up to 28 days under this section though again it is possible to convert a detention for assessment to a detention for treatment by satisfying the requirements of section 3. It should be noted that some compulsory treatment of the patient is permitted under this section.

2.3.5   An admission for treatment

Section 3 provides for an admission and detention for treatment.

Who by?   The application may be made by the approved social worker or the nearest relative. Before making an application the approved social worker must, where practicable, seek the agreement of the nearest relative. If this is refused then the approved social worker cannot make the application unless the county court 'displaces' the nearest relative on the grounds that agreement is being unreasonably withheld.

Medical support?   The application must be supported by two medical recommendations with one of the doctors being approved under section 12(2).

On what criteria?   The criteria for admission and detention are:

a)   that the patient is suffering from one of the four categories of mental disorder and that this is of a nature or degree which makes it appropriate for him to receive medical treatment in hospital; and

b)   in the case of psychotic disorder or mental impairment, such treatment is likely to alleviate or prevent a deterioration of his condition; and

c)   it is necessary for the health or safety of the patient or for the protection of others that he should receive such treatment and it cannot be provided unless he is detained under this section.

The applicant must have seen the patient within the 14 days before admission. The patient may be detained for up to six months under this section. There are powers to renew detention for treatment for a further six months and then for periods of one year at a time. Renewal of the order is on the basis of a report from the responsible medical officer to the hospital managers that the original criteria for admission still exist. In addition the 'treatability' condition set out in b) above is satisfied, except that where a patient is suffering from mental illness or severe mental impairment and cannot be treated they may nonetheless be detained where they are unlikely to be able to care for themselves or to obtain the care that they need, or to guard themselves against serious exploitation.

It is important to note that section 1(3) of the Act clearly specifies that a person cannot be classified as mentally disordered 'by reason only of promiscuity, or other immoral conduct, sexual deviancy or dependence on alcohol or drugs'.

The four categories of mental disorder are mental illness, severe mental impairment (both of which are considered to be major disorders), mental impairment and psychopathic disorder (both of which are considered to be minor disorders so that the treatability condition for admission and detention applies to them).

Mental illness is not defined by the Act. The other three categories are defined in section 1(2) in the following terms:

severe mental impairment — 'a state of arrested or incomplete development of mind which includes severe impairment of intelligence and social functioning and is associated with abnormally aggressive or seriously irresponsible conduct';

mental impairment is defined in the same terms except that the word 'significant' is used instead of the word 'severe';

psychopathic disorder — 'a persistent disorder or disability of mind (whether or not including significant impairment of intelligence) which results in abnormally aggressive or seriously irresponsible conduct'.

2.4 GUARDIANSHIP

A patient over 16 may be received into guardianship under section 7 as an alternative to admission to and detention in hospital. The criteria to be established are that the patient is suffering from one of the four forms of mental disorder, and it is of a nature or degree which warrants reception into guardianship, and it is necessary in the interests of the welfare of the patient or for the protection of others that s/he should be so received. The application is by the nearest relative or the approved social worker and must be supported by two medical recommendations. The guardian will be the local social services authority or a person accepted by the authority. The guardian has power to require the patient to live in a specified place and to attend for treatment, occupation, education or training. Patients under a guardianship order have the same common law rights as voluntary patients to refuse treatment.

Guardianship orders are rarely made.

2.5   EMERGENCY POWERS

There are two very important emergency powers under the Act designed to deal with particular situations in which it is necessary to intervene to protect or control someone who has a mental disorder. In both circumstances approved social workers will be working closely with the police.

Section 136 allows a person in a public place to be taken to a place of safety by a police officer where it appears to the officer that the person is 'suffering from mental disorder' and is 'in immediate need of care and control'. This power of detention, which runs for a maximum of 72 hours, is used to allow a medical examination and interview by an approved social worker so that appropriate arrangements for the patient can be made, such as an application for admission to hospital. (A place of safety includes a police station or a hospital.)

Section 135 gives power to an approved social worker to apply to a magistrate for a warrant which allows the police, together with a doctor and the approved social worker, to enter private premises and remove a person to a place of safety. When applying for the warrant the approved social worker must have reasonable cause to believe that the person is suffering from a mental disorder and 'has been, or is being, ill treated, neglected or kept otherwise than under proper control, or is living alone and is unable to care for himself'. This provision allows the person to be removed to a place of safety for up to 72 hours so that the necessary examinations and interviews can take place and appropriate arrangements made if necessary.

2.6   PEOPLE WITH A MENTAL DISORDER AND THE CRIMINAL JUSTICE SYSTEM

The Mental Health Act makes particular provision for people with a mental disorder who have been charged or found guilty of a criminal offence. Again this is a lengthy, complex and therefore specialist area of law and only an outline can be provided here.

There are a small number of special hospitals which are established for patients who have been detained under the Mental Health Act and who require treatment under specially secure conditions because of their 'dangerous, violent or criminal propensities'.

2.6.1   Remands to hospital

Sections 35 and 36 allow people who have been accused of a criminal offence to be remanded to hospital for reports or very occasionally for treatment. The objective of the remand for reports power is to allow a psychiatric medical report to be prepared so that the court can properly decide how to proceed. More often such defendants will be diverted from a remand in custody by the making of a 28 day order for assessment or an order for treatment under sections 2 and 3 respectively.

2.6.2   Hospital orders

The main provision is contained in section 37 and provides the criminal courts with the power to make a hospital order on an offender who is suffering from one of the four categories of mental disorder. The effect of a hospital order is that the offender is admitted to and remains in hospital in circumstances which are similar to those for an admission and detention for treatment under section 3 of the Act. One of the implications of this is that the offender can be discharged, without reference to the courts, by the hospital managers or a Mental Health Review Tribunal, but not by the nearest relative, in the same way as any other patient.

The detention and release of an offender on a hospital order can be controlled by the imposition of a restriction order under section 41. This order is made by the Crown Court on the basis that it is necessary to protect the public from serious harm by restricting the release of the offender either for a specified time or without limit. Such offenders can only be released by the decision of the Home Secretary or a Mental Health Review Tribunal.

2.7   PATIENTS' CIVIL RIGHTS

Although the principle underpinning the Mental Health Act is that compulsorily detained patients should not have their civil rights curtailed there are some important restrictions on the rights of such patients.

Implicit within the discussion of the admission procedures and those relating to emergencies is the principle that such procedures must be administered within the law. Approved social workers have substantial rights and powers the exercise of which may result in the loss of liberty for significant periods of time. The Mental Health Act, section 139 provides a limited protection to anyone acting within the provisions of the Mental Health Act by restricting the access of compulsory patients to the courts. In order to take a civil action a patient must obtain the leave of the High Court by establishing that there are reasonable grounds for their accusation that the person acted in bad faith or without reasonable care. Consent for the bringing of criminal proceedings must be given by the Director of Public Prosecutions.

There are also restrictions on the sending and receiving of correspondence and on voting rights.

Under section 132 detained patients have a specific right to be informed of their rights by the hospital managers. Patients must be informed in writing of their rights in respect of treatment, application to the Mental Health Review Tribunal, correspondence, and of the basis for their detention.

It should also be acknowledged that patients who have spent some time in hospital having been detained because of their mental disorder may well suffer from a long term disadvantage relating to the stigmatisation that surrounds mental illness. Such disadvantage may extend to employment prospects, housing and other aspects of independent living.

2.8 TREATMENT

The treatment of patients with a mental disorder is one of the issues which concerned those arguing for reform of the Mental Health Act 1959. MIND argued that the 1959 Act was never clear as to whether psychiatric treatment could be lawfully administered to compulsorily detained patients without their consent. Nonetheless it was clear that such treatments were administered under the old legislation on the basis that patients could not give the necessary consent because of the nature of their mental disorder.

Voluntary patients are required to give their consent to treatment for their mental disorder in the same way that treatments for physical illness or injury require the consent of the patient. The difficulty centres on whether a patient's mental disorder is such that they are unable to give a consent which is valid in law. The validity of such a consent is based on three elements: i) the provision of sufficient information about the nature and purpose of the treatment including any side effects; ii) the patient must be able to understand what s/he has been told about the treatment and iii) consent must be given voluntarily.

The psychiatric treatment of patients who have been compulsorily detained is closely regulated by a series of statutory safeguards in Part IV of the Act and in particular in sections 57 and 58. The principle is that procedural safeguards must be satisfied before specific treatments can be administered. The more significant the nature of the intervention through treatment the tighter the safeguards.

These safeguards, in relation to psychosurgery and sex hormone implant treatment, require a patient's valid consent and independent certification that the consent is valid and that the treatment is appropriate.

In relation to electro convulsive therapy (or other specified treatments) and a course of medication three months after it is first administered, the patient's valid consent is required and the validity of the consent must be confirmed by the responsible medical officer or an independent doctor appointed by the Mental Health Act Commission. If the patient refuses to consent or is not able to give a valid consent then these treatments can be administered only if a doctor appointed by the Mental Health

Act Commission certifies (after consultation with two others from the care team) that 'the patient is not capable of understanding the nature, purpose and likely effects of that treatment or has not consented to it but that, having regard to the likelihood of its alleviating or preventing a deterioration of his condition, the treatment should be given' (section 58). Social workers may be involved in the consultations required.

Patients admitted in an emergency are not subject to the provisions of Part IV and cannot be treated without their consent except where minimal emergency intervention is necessary to protect the patient or other people.

2.9   DISCHARGE FROM HOSPITAL

There are a number of ways in which patients who have been compulsorily detained in hospital may be discharged from their detention. Subsequently they may remain in hospital as voluntary patients and as such may discharge themselves at any time.

2.9.1   By the hospital

Detained patients may be discharged by the responsible medical officer or the hospital managers at any time and there are no statutory criteria for their discharge. The nearest relative may also discharge a patient who has been admitted and detained for assessment or treatment though they must give the hospital managers 72 hours written notice of their intention. During this period the responsible medical officer can prevent the discharge by certifying to the hospital managers that the patient would be a danger to himself/herself or to others if discharged.

2.9.2   Mental Health Review Tribunals

Mental Health Review Tribunals are responsible for deciding applications for discharge from hospital or guardianship from patients, and in some circumstances from the nearest relative. Applications are normally heard by a three person tribunal comprising a legally qualified chairperson, a doctor and a lay person with relevant knowledge or experience. Cases for hearing may also be referred to the tribunal by the Secretary of State for Health, or the Home Secretary in the case of restricted patients, or through a process of automatic referral. The tribunal has a variety of powers; it may discharge a patient, although this may be subject to a delay to facilitate the arrangement of appropriate after care facilities; grant a leave of absence; or order a transfer to another hospital or into guardianship. Legal aid is available for the representation of patients before tribunal hearings.

2.10   THE MENTAL HEALTH ACT COMMISSION

The Commission, which was established by the 1983 Act, is charged with a general responsibility to protect the rights of detained patients and to keep under review the exercise of the compulsory powers and duties of the Act. The Commission discharges this responsibility by visiting and talking to patients and by the investigation of complaints. It also has important powers to appoint the doctors giving second opinions in relation to compulsory treatment, and to keep under review the continued administration of Part IV treatments.

2.11   THE COURT OF PROTECTION

The Court of Protection has jurisdiction to look after the property and affairs of anyone who has a mental disorder and as a result cannot do so for themselves. Details in relation to the court are contained in Part VII of the Mental Health Act. An application for the court to invoke its jurisdiction can be made by anyone who is interested in the patient so that a social worker may be involved. The court is likely to appoint a receiver to manage the patient's property and affairs over which the court has exclusive powers. Fees and other expenses are recovered from the property which together with any other interests are managed for the benefit of the patient.

2.12   CARE IN THE COMMUNITY

There are a substantial and increasing number of people with a mental disorder who are not being treated or cared for in hospital but who are living and being treated in the community. This is a result of a number of factors including the switch to a policy of community care and the programme of closure of long stay psychiatric hospitals. As a result a significant and increasing element of social work practice with customers who have a mental disorder or learning difficulty takes place outside the psychiatric hospital. Such work, which is not restricted to approved social workers, takes place within the general power of local authorities under section 29 of the National Assistance Act 1948 to promote the welfare of people with a disability and under a number of specific statutory provisions.

a)   The Chronically Sick and Disabled Persons Act 1970, section 2, requires social services departments to arrange for the provision of services to anyone who has a need because of their permanent and substantial handicap. The relevant services are help in the home, recreational facilities in and outside the home, assistance with transport to such facilities, appropriate aids and adaptations to the home, holidays, meals and the installation of telephones.

b)   Under the National Health Service Act 1977 the Secretary of State has a general duty to provide health services and under the same Act a duty has been imposed on local authority social services departments to provide prevention, care and after care services in relation to physical and mental illness.

c)   More specifically the Mental Health Act, section 117, requires a district health authority and the social services department to provide after care facilities for patients who have been discharged from hospital after psychiatric treatment. Additionally social services departments are responsible for providing special residential accommodation for those with an established need relating to their mental disorder.

d)   The Disabled Persons (Services, Consultation and Representation) Act 1986 provides important rights through which the interests of people with a disability can be protected and promoted. The definition of people with a disability includes learning difficulty and those with a mental disorder within the terms of the Mental Health Act 1983. The 1986 Act was designed to provide an assessment of the needs of disabled people by a local authority who must give a written statement of the results of the assessment. The Act provides for the appointment of a person to act as a representative and advocate for the disabled person in the assessment procedure and in the provision of services as a result of the assessment. The representative may well be a guardian appointed under the provisions of the Mental Health Act. The Act is largely designed to secure the provision of local authority services under section 2 of the Chronically Sick and Disabled Persons Act 1970 though the particular sections of the 1986 Act, sections 1, 2 and 3, have never been implemented.

Section 7 of the Disabled Persons (Services, Consultation and Representation) Act 1986 is specifically directed to patients who have been detained in a psychiatric hospital for at least 6 months for treatment and are to be discharged. The section requires the hospital managers to inform the relevant district health authority, local authority and education authority of the patient's date of discharge so that an appropriate assessment of needs may be made. Section 7 has never been implemented.

e) The provisions of the Housing Act 1985 in relation to homelessness are increasingly important for social work practice. The Act specifies that anyone who is vulnerable because of their disability has a priority need for accommodation; it should be accepted that patients who have a mental disorder and are homeless or threatened with homelessness are clearly within such a category of priority need.

f) The community care provisions of the National Health Service and Community Care Act 1990 were implemented in April 1993. The provisions of the Act are imposed on top of legislation already in force and are directed to the provision of care services for people with a disability. The provision of such services is the responsibility of social services authorities, who are the lead authority, though community care plans are to be drawn up in consultation with health authorities, education authorities, housing authorities, voluntary organisations and organisations representing users and carers. People with a mental disorder, including those with learning difficulty, come within the definition of disability and will therefore be assessed and receive care services under the 1990 legislation, including training, attendance at a day centre and domicilary services.

g) Section 17(10) of the Children Act 1989 defines a child in need.

For the purposes of this Part a child shall be taken to be in need if —

a)   he is unlikely to achieve or maintain, or to have the opportunity of achieving or maintaining, a reasonable standard of health or development without the provision for him of services by a local authority under this Part;

b)   his health or development is likely to be significantly impaired, or further impaired, without the provision for him of such services; or

c)   he is disabled,

. . . .

(11)   For the purposes of this Part, a child is disabled if he is blind, deaf or dumb or suffers from mental disorder of any kind or is substantially and permanently handicapped by illness, injury, or congenital deformity or such other disability as may· be prescribed; and in this Part —

'development' means physical, intellectual, emotional, social or behavioural development; and

'health' means physical or mental health.

As a result of this definition children who have a mental disorder or learning difficulty are brought within the provisions of the Act which specify their entitlement to local authority support and services under Part 111 and Schedule 2.

3   MENTAL HEALTH LAW AND SOCIAL WORK PRACTICE: some issues for discussion

Mental health law provides a number of difficult issues for those practising in the area, not least is the possible involvement in the deprivation of a person's liberty. This section will discuss three contemporary problems which are themselves connected. Firstly the way in which the criminal justice system deals with offenders who have a mental disorder; secondly the impact of the policy of community care and hospital closure on people with a mental disorder; and thirdly the limitations of the Mental Health Act in relation to people with learning difficulty. As a reference point during this discussion readers may wish to consider whether and how the issues raised impinge on, or effect social work practice.

3.1 DEFENDANTS AND OFFENDERS WITH A MENTAL DISORDER

Concern about the way in which the criminal justice system deals with people with a mental disorder (both defendants and offenders) has risen as the number of long stay hospital patients being released into the community has increased consequent upon the closure of hospitals and the switch in emphasis to community care. A significant number of people with mental disorders are appearing in the criminal courts and there is concern about whether the procedures and sentencing powers of the criminal justice system are appropriate to their circumstances. It is possible to argue that their offending is evidence more of their mental disorder and of their vulnerability than of their criminality. Those working in the prison service argue that large numbers of prisoners have a mental disorder and should be more suitably treated or cared for outside the prison system. The closure of many long stay psychiatric hospitals and the shift to care in the community makes it more likely that the number of people with a mental disorder appearing in the criminal courts and receiving custodial sentences will continue to rise.

The utility of hospital orders as a response to the commission of a criminal offence by an offender with a mental disorder is limited by the reluctance of hospitals to accept patients with a reputation for violence and criminality. Courts are sometimes forced to adjourn cases and remand such offenders to prison for lengthy periods of time whilst a hospital place is found for them. If no such place can be found the court may be forced to impose a prison sentence thereby increasing the number of offenders with a mental disorder serving custodial sentences. If a hospital place is found the offender/patient, if not subject to a restriction order, may then be discharged on the decision of the responsible medical officer, the hospital managers or a Mental Health Review Tribunal. The likelihood of an early discharge is increased by the policy of hospital closures and the emphasis on community care. Once back in the community the prospect of re-offending will increase if appropriate after care and community care facilities are not available.

The second aspect of what might seem to be an ironic pincer movement is provided by the determination of government to reduce the prison population by the use of non-custodial sentences wherever possible. Here the civil liberties argument imposes difficult principles upon the way in which the system responds to offenders with a mental disorder. It cannot be right that such offenders are sent to prison only because a place in hospital cannot be found. A community based sentencing alternative, whilst preferable, exposes society to the possibility or likelihood of the commission of another offence if appropriate support is not provided by, for example, the probation service. A community based treatment alternative might be appropriate if it provided this group of offenders with the necessary treatment and care the equivalent of which s/he would receive in hospital. These difficulties point to the need for a 'combination' response which provides for both the psychiatric treatment necessary and a sufficient element of 'sentence' to satisfy the objectives of the criminal justice system.

The alternatives currently available to the criminal courts are a probation order with a condition of psychiatric treatment, which might satisfy the 'combination' response outlined above, or the use of a 'criminal' guardianship order under section 37 of the Mental Health Act. The major drawback of both from the point of view of psychiatry is that neither order allows the offender/patient to be treated without their consent. In contrast civil libertarians would argue that if people are thought well enough not to be in hospital then they should be able to decide on their own treatment.

This inability to treat people with a mental disorder living in the community without their consent provides the link with the second issue of law and practice to be discussed.

3.2   HOSPITAL CLOSURES AND THE SWITCH TO COMMUNITY CARE

The consequences of this policy switch have been considerable and have led to calls for reform of the Mental Health Act to allow those with a mental disorder living in the community to be treated compulsorily in the same way that hospital patients admitted and detained for psychiatric treatment under section 3 may be.

The debate begins with the decision to close large numbers of hospital places, a decision which reflected both a liberal desire to move away from the institutionalism of the old psychiatric hospitals to a more humane system of care, and a belief that community care would be cheaper. The failure to adequately fund community care has resulted in large numbers of vulnerable patients with a mental disorder being discharged from hospital into an environment which is hostile to them, and into a system which is unable to adequately care for them. The result has been an increase in the numbers of offenders who have a mental disorder and many of whom are also homeless.

Many people working within the mental health field argue that part of the problem lies in the failure of many patients to continue to take prescribed medication when they are discharged from hospital and living independently in the community. This issue received considerable press coverage consequent upon the Beverley Lewis case and the comments of the coroner about the need to reform the Mental Health Act, and the continuing concern over the substantial numbers of people who are homeless and also have a mental disorder.[4]

A number of commentators have called for the introduction of a community treatment order which would allow patients who have a mental disorder living in the community to be treated compulsorily in the same way that treatment may be administered to patients admitted to hospital for psychiatric treatment. The equivalence between patients in hospital and those in the community is the basis on which such a proposal is made: 'So if it can be done inside hospital, why can't it be done outside?' (Phillips, Guardian 3.11.89.). The objections to such a proposal come from civil liberties advocates who argue that compulsory treatment in the community offends against the civil rights of patients.[5] Others argue that compulsory treatment in the community is a pragmatic response to the failure of the policy of community care, a way of covering up for the inadequacies of the care and treatment available in the community.

In an alternative response to the problems currently facing community care for offenders with a mental disorder and other patients, the Mental Health Act Commission, and others, are

[4] See Phil Fennell 'Blaming the law: lessons of the Beverley Lewis Case'. (3.11.89) Guardian; Melanie Phillips 'A Suitable Case for Treatment'. (3.11.89) Guardian; and David Brindle 'Keep Taking the Tablets'. (3.1.90) Guardian.
[5] See Cavadino, M. 'Community Control?' Journal of Social Welfare Law. No 6 (1991).

arguing for the strengthening of the guardianship order currently available under the Act.[6] It seems that this order has been infrequently used by social services departments since the introduction of the 1983 Act. The guardian does not have the power to force the patient to receive treatment against his/her wishes and any reform to strengthen the guardianship role would be likely to include such a power. If this were the case the well established criticisms of compulsory treatment as 'legalised assault' would be made against such proposals.

3.3   THE MENTAL HEALTH ACT AND LEARNING DIFFICULTY

Comment on the circumstances surrounding the death of Beverley Lewis in November 1988 identified a number of gaps in the legislative framework which should have provided her with appropriate care and protection. This section considers only the problems that relate to the Mental Health Act though the case provides material for considering the various legal provisions which should provide for people with learning difficulty. The problems identified by the case still exist though it is possible to argue that the provisions of the National Health Service and Community Care Act 1990 concerning the assessment of people with a disability and the provision of services to meet their needs are designed to protect and promote the interests of people with learning difficulty among others.

As a result of rubella Beverley Lewis was born blind, deaf and with learning difficulty. She was looked after by her mother all her life but died in squalor as a result of the inadequate care provided by her mother. After Beverley's death her mother was diagnosed as suffering from schizophrenia and was admitted to a psychiatric hospital. Beverley herself had been compulsorily admitted to a psychiatric hospital at the age of 18 for assessment but was released the next day at the request of her mother.

The question raised by these circumstances is why did the Mental Health Act, and those working within its provisions, not provide for the care and treatment needed by a vulnerable person such as Beverley Lewis. Although Beverley Lewis had learning

[6] See also 'Mentally Incapacitated Adults and Decision Making: An Overview' Law Commission Working Paper No. 119.

difficulty it seems that her condition did not bring her within any of the categories of mental disorder provided for by the Act. The Act defines mental disorder as including mental impairment, which is itself defined by section 1(2) as: 'a state of arrested or incomplete development of mind which includes significant impairment of intelligence and social functioning and is associated with abnormally aggressive or seriously irresponsible conduct'. Whilst her learning difficulty would have brought Beverley Lewis within the first criterion of the definition there was no suggestion that she was 'aggressive or seriously irresponsible' in her conduct. It was therefore impossible to admit her to hospital for treatment under section 3 of the Act, an admission which could have provided her with 'nursing, . . . care, habilitation and rehabilitation under medical supervision' all of which are included in the Act's definition of treatment. Because she was not mentally impaired within the terms of the Act a guardianship order was also not available to help and protect her.

Groups representing the interests of people with learning difficulty had argued in the debates leading up to the 1983 Act for the exclusion of people with learning difficulty from the operation of compulsory powers in statute. This argument was partially accepted by the inclusion in the statutory definition of mental impairment and severe mental impairment of the criteria of 'abnormally aggressive or seriously irresponsible conduct'. The unintended consequence has been that vulnerable people such as Beverley Lewis may slip through the Mental Health Act net, a system which might,in the face of obstruction from her mother, have provided her with the care and protection she needed. In her case the other available services provided by doctors, social workers and community health workers were also unable to help. Had sections 1-3 of the Disabled Persons Act 1986, which provide for the independent representation of people with disabilities, been implemented the gaps in the Mental Health Act might have been compensated for by social and health service provision.

4   CASE STUDIES

Here are a number of case studies which can be used to consolidate work done on mental health law. They concentrate on areas of practice in which approved social workers will be involved.

1.   Sam is a heroin addict and has a history of psychiatric illness. He frequently sleeps rough. He has been a client of yours for some time and you have formed the opinion that he needs long term psychiatric treatment for his illness and treatment for his drug dependency. He is very reluctant to enter any psychiatric hospital having been assaulted whilst a voluntary patient last year. He has recently disappeared and you suspect that he is living with a number of other addicts in a local squat which is known to you. You have serious fears about his safety.

What powers are available to you under the Mental Health Act to deal with this situation? You are an approved social worker.

2.   Sonia is 20 and has learning difficulty. She has lived at home all her life and has been cared for by her mother. She attends a day centre but her behaviour has recently become increasingly erratic and aggressive and the workers at the centre have expressed doubts about her being able to continue there. You are an approved social worker and on duty in the area office when you receive a phone call from the centre telling you that Sonia has attacked two of the workers with a pair of scissors and has now locked herself in the toilet and refuses to come out.

In what way, if at all, are your powers under the Mental Health Act relevant to Sonia's condition ?

3.   Ricky, who is 24 and has been a client of yours for a number of years, has a long criminal record for petty theft and burglary. He has been severely depressed since he was 18 and has been in the local psychiatric hospital on a number of occasions as a voluntary patient but has always discharged himself after a few days. Yesterday Ricky was arrested by the police and has been charged with yet another burglary. He came to see you this morning having been released on bail by the police and says that he wants to go into hospital and get himself 'properly sorted out for once and for all'. He has said this before and you know that the hospital will not accept him as a voluntary patient again. You have just received a phone call from Ricky's solicitor who says that her client is going to plead guilty and that he may well receive a custodial sentence unless something can be done to persuade the court to keep him out of prison.

Discuss how you, as an approved social worker, might tackle Ricky's case both in the short and longer term.

4. You receive a phone call from Dr. Majors, a local GP, who tells you that a patient of his needs to be compulsorily admitted to psychiatric hospital. The doctor describes to you a 45 year old woman patient whose marriage has just broken up and who has tried to commit suicide by taking an overdose of sleeping pills. The attempt was frustrated by the woman's son who seized the sleeping pills after she had taken three and then called the GP. When you attend the woman's home you find that she is quite calm and lucid and her son tells you that he is willing and able to care for her during the next week. Dr. Majors is quite convinced of the need for admission and argues strongly that the woman should be 'sectioned straight away so that she can't do it again'.

What are your powers and duties as an approved social worker under the Mental Health Act? What are you going to do?

5 ACTIVITIES

Here are a number of activities which are suggested to increase knowledge and experience of social work practice within the context of mental health law. The information collected can be used to expand any existing collection of materials.

1. Get hold of a copy of the Mental Health Act Code of Practice published by the Department of Health and the Welsh Office in 1990.

2. Write to MIND (National Association for Mental Health) for a copy of their publications list and any other materials they distribute.

3. A series of free leaflets are available from the Court of Protection giving information about its work.

4. Within the context of community care mental health services are provided by a partnership of health authorities, local authority social services and housing departments, and by the voluntary sector. Get hold of a copy of the Community Care Plan published by your local authority.

The local voluntary sector may include a local MIND association and the local MENCAP.

5.   Obtain copies of the forms used by the local authority for applications for admission to psychiatric hospital. These will help in understanding the process and the procedures that must be gone through before someone can be admitted to hospital compulsorily.

6.   Design a 'flow chart' or other diagram to explain the admissions process and the role of the approved social worker in it.

7.   Design a leaflet or a series of leaflets which could be given to customers to explain their rights under mental health law. As an example one could deal with the admissions process, one with rights whilst an in-patient, one about treatment and another about being discharged from hospital.

8.   Keep up to date with the experience and evaluation of the community care aspects of the National Health Service and Community Care Act 1990 during its first years in force.

6   ADDRESSES

MENCAP,
123 Golden Lane,
London EC1Y 0RT.
Phone: 071 253 9433.

MIND. National Association for Mental Health,
22 Harley Street,
London W1N 2ED.
Phone: 071 637 0741.

The Mental Health Act Commission,
2nd Floor,
Maid Marion House,
56 Houndsgate,
Nottingham, NG1 6BG.
Phone: 0602 504040.

The Court of Protection,
The Public Trust Office,
Protection Division,
Stewart House,
24 Kingsway,
London WC2B 6JX.
Phone: 071 269 7000.
Fax: 071 831 0060.

7 MATERIALS

7.1 BASIC LEGAL MATERIALS FOR ORDINARY SOCIAL WORK PRACTICE

Gostin, L. *A Practical Guide to Mental Health Law* (1983) MIND.

Grimshaw, C. *A-Z of Welfare Benefits for People with a Mental Illness* (1990) MIND.

'Mental Health Act Code of Practice. Department of Health and the Welsh Office' (1990).

MIND Rights Guides 1-4. Civil Admission and Discharge. Patients Involved in Criminal Proceedings. Your Rights in Hospital. Mental Health Review Tribunals.

'The Mental Health Act 1983 — An Outline Guide' MIND.

7.2 FURTHER READING

Whelton, M., Mann, G. *Mental Handicap and the Law (1989)* MENCAP.

Jones, R. *Mental Health Act Manual* (3rd edn 1991) Sweet and Maxwell.

Hoggett, B. *Mental Health Law* (3rd edn 1990) Sweet and Maxwell.

Cohen, J. Ramon, S. *Social Work and the Mental Health Act 1983* (1990) BASW.

Sheppard, M. 'The Role of the Approved Social Worker' (1990) Joint Unit for Social Services.

Form 2

Mental Health Act 1983
Section 2

Application by an approved social worker for admission for assessment

To the Managers of

(name and address of hospital or mental nursing home)

(your full name)   I

(your office address)   of

hereby apply for the admission of

(full name of patient)

of

(address of patient)

SPECIMEN

for assessment in accordance with Part II of the Mental Health Act 1983.

(name of local social services authority)   I am an officer of

appointed to act as an approved social worker for the purposes of the Act.

Complete the following section if nearest relative known

(a) To the best of my knowledge and belief

(name and address)

is the patient's nearest relative within the meaning of the Act.
OR
(b) I understand that

(name and address)

has been authorised by

delete the phrase which
does not apply
     a county court
     the patient's nearest relative

to exercise the functions under the Act of the patient's nearest relative.

delete the phrase which
does not apply
     I have
     I have not yet

informed that person that this application is to be made and of his power to order the discharge of the patient.

Please turn over

Complete the following section if nearest relative not known

delete the phrase
which does not
apply

(a) I have been unable to ascertain who is this patient's nearest relative within in meaning of the Act.

OR

(b) To the best of my knowledge and belief this patient has no nearest relative within the meaning of the Act.

The following section must be completed in all cases

(date)   I last saw the patient on

I have interviewed the patient and I am satisfied that detention in a hospital is in all the circumstances of the case the most appropriate way of providing the care and medical treatment of which the patient stands in need.

This application is founded on two medical recommendations in the prescribed form.

If neither of the medical practitioners knew the patient before making their recommendations, please explain why you could not get a recommendation from a medical practitioner who did know the patient:-

SPECIMEN

Signed _____   Date _____

8821025/75M/8.84/45292

Application by approved social worker for admission for treatment

To the Managers of

(name and address of hospital or mental nursing home)

(your full name) I

(your office address) of

hereby apply for the admission of

(full name of patient)

(address of patient) of

SPECIMEN

for treatment in accordance with Part II of the Mental Health Act 1983 as a person suffering from:

mental illness, mental impairment, severe mental impairment, psychopathic disorder

(enter whichever of these is appropriate)

I am an officer of

(name of local social services authority)

appointed to act as an approved social worker for the purposes of the Act.

The following section should be deleted if no consultation has taken place.

Complete (a) or (b)

(name and address) **(a)** I have consulted

who to the best of my knowledge and belief is the patient's nearest relative within the meaning of the Act

Please turn over

OR

(name and address)   (b) I have consulted

who I understand has been authorised by

Delete the phrase
which does not
apply

a county court

the patient's nearest relative

to exercise the functions under the Act of the patient's nearest relative.

That person has not notified me or the local social services authority by whom I am
appointed that he/she objects to this application being made.

The following section should be deleted if consultation has taken place.

Delete whichever
do not apply

(a) I have been unable to ascertain who is this patient's nearest relative within the meaning
of the Act.

OR

(b) To the best of my knowledge and belief this patient has no nearest relative within the
meaning of the Act.

OR

(name and address)   (c) I understand that

is

delete either
(i) or (ii)

(i) this patient's nearest relative within the meaning of the Act

(ii) authorised to exercise the functions of this patient's nearest relative under the Act

AND in my opinion it is not reasonably practicable or would involve unreasonable delay
to consult that person before making this application.

The following section must be completed in all cases

(date)   I last saw the patient on

I have interviewed the patient and I am satisfied that detention in a hospital is in all the
circumstances of the case the most appropriate way of providing the care and medical
treatment of which the patient stands in need.

This application is founded on two medical recommendations in the prescribed form.

Continued

If neither of the medical practitioners knew the patient before making their recommendations, please explain why you could not get a recommendation from a medical practitioner who did know the patient:-

_____

_____

_____

_____

_____

_____

_____

Signed _____   Date _____

SPECIMEN

Printed in the UK for HMSO Dd.8816354 11/83 100m 20355

Emergency application by an approved social worker for admission for assessment

This form is to be used only for an emergency application

To the Managers of

(name and address of hospital or mental nursing home)

(your full name) I

(your office address) of

hereby apply for the admission of

(full name of patient)

(address of patient) of

for assessment in accordance with Part II of the Mental Health Act 1983.

I am an officer of

(name of local social services authority)

appointed to act as an approved social worker for the purposes of the Act.

(date) I last saw the patient on

(time) at

I have interviewed the patient and I am satisfied that detention in a hospital is in all the circumstances of the case the most appropriate way of providing the care and medical treatment of which the patient stands in need.

In my opinion it is of urgent necessity for the patient to be admitted and detained under section 2 of the Act. Compliance with the provisions of Part II of the Act relating to applications under that section would involve undesirable delay.

This application is founded on one medical recommendation in the prescribed form.

Please turn over

If the medical practitioner did not know the patient before making his recommendation, please explain why you could not get a recommendation from a medical practitioner who did know the patient:-

_____

_____

_____

_____

_____

_____

_____

Signed _____   Date _____

                                            Time _____

SPECIMEN

Printed in the UK for HMSO 30m Dd8919749 9/85 24145

CHAPTER 9

Adoption and Fostering

1 INTRODUCTION

The law, by means of adoption and fostering, provides a series of 'alternative family' structures within which children can be afforded care and upbringing on a short or long term basis in the case of fostering, or permanently in the case of adoption. In many respects the law in this area has adapted to changes in child care practice and in particular to the tenor of what is known as the 'permanency debate'. A significant amount of child care practice in recent years has been based on the objective of establishing permanent arrangements for the care and upbringing of children.

Fostering is a 'child care arrangement' which confers no legal rights, in respect to the child, on the foster carers, though the arrangement is subject to statutory regulation. Fostering is an important part of local authority child care practice and it provides for the care of some 40% of children being looked after by local authorities. Prior to the Children Act 1989 the ambiguous legal position of foster carers had caused some concern; the availability of 'section 8 orders'[1] under the Act now provides an avenue through which foster parents who wish to do so may be able to legally formalise an existing relationship with the child(ren) they are fostering.

Much of social work practice in these areas of child care work is regulated by the law which places a number of specific duties on local authorities. Local authorities themselves act as adoption agencies so that a number of local authority social workers will undertake specialist adoption work and other adoption agencies will employ their own social workers. In adoption proceedings the law requires the preparation of reports by reporting officers

[1] See chapter on the Children Act 1989.

and guardians ad litem and these functions will be undertaken by practitioners with a social work qualification and background.

Despite the specialist nature of adoption work the child care basis of adoption and fostering means that all social work students must have some basic understanding of the relevant law.

2 THE LAW

2.1 FOSTERING

Children who are being looked after by a local authority, whether in care or not, may be placed with foster carers. This arrangement may be for a short or long period of time and is subject to the Children Act 1989 and regulations made under it. Such placements are regulated by the provisions of sections 20–24 of the Act, by Part II of Schedule 2 to the Act and by the Foster Placement (Children) Regulations 1991.

Section 20 of the Act requires local authorities, so far as is reasonably practicable, to ascertain a child's wishes before placing him or her with foster carers and to give due consideration to those wishes. Section 22 sets out the general duty of local authorities to safeguard and promote the welfare of all children being looked after by them. The same section provides that foster carers should be consulted before decisions are made about children they are looking after where the authority considers their wishes and feelings to be relevant. Section 23 provides for children who are being looked after to be placed with foster carers and that where reasonably practicable and consistent with the child's welfare such accommodation should be near the child's own home and that siblings should be placed together. Section 24 provides that children who are fostered by a local authority should receive advice and assistance so that their welfare is promoted when they cease to be looked after by the authority.

Part II of Schedule 2 to the Act specifies the matters to be covered by regulations concerning children placed with foster carers by a local authority. The Foster Placement (Children) Regulations 1991 provide for the detailed control of foster placements. The regulations cover such things as the approval of foster carers and the supervision of foster placements by local authorities.

Authorities are required to satisfy themselves that a particular placement is the most suitable and that it is the most suitable way of providing for the child's welfare.

Foster carers acquire no legal rights over the children placed with them from the fact of fostering alone though they may apply for a 'section 8' order under the provisions of the Children Act. A foster carer is entitled to apply, without leave of the court, for a residence order or a contact order if the child has been living with them for at least three years or they have the consent of those with parental responsibility for the child. If either of these conditions is not present then foster carers may seek leave of the court to apply for a 'section 8' order. This ability to seek the leave of the court to make an application for a section 8 order is subject to the consent of the local authority or the foster carer applicant being a relative of the child or the child having lived with the applicant for at least three years. These limitations are established to make sure that the foster carers of a child who has only been placed with them for a short time will need the consent of the authority and the court before being able to make an application for a 'section 8' order.

2.2 PRIVATE FOSTERING

A large number of children are fostered as a consequence of arrangements between private individuals. Private fostering is in turn regulated by Part IX of the Children Act 1989, by Schedule 8 to the Act and by the Children (Private Arrangements for Fostering) Regulations 1991, made under the Act.

Volume 8 of 'The Children Act 1989 Guidance and Regulations, Private Fostering and Miscellaneous', deals with the local authority role in respect of private foster arrangements:

> Private fostering is the arrangement made between usually the parent and the private foster parent, who becomes responsible for caring for the child in such a way as to promote and safeguard his welfare. The role of local authorities is to satisfy themselves that the arrangements are satisfactory and that the foster parents are suitable. They do not approve or register private foster parents.

Section 67 of the Act deals with the welfare of privately fostered children and a general duty is placed on local authorities to satisfy themselves that the welfare of such children is safeguarded and promoted. This duty is further detailed in the regulations which require authorities to visit private foster children and inspect the premises where the child(ren) is accommodated. Sections 68 and 69 set out circumstances in which people may be disqualified or prohibited by a local authority from privately fostering children. Section 70 specifies a number of criminal offences in relation to private fostering.

2.3   ADOPTION

Adoption is a legal procedure by which the parental responsibilities of a child's natural parents are extinguished and replaced by a set of legal relations between the child and his or her adoptive parents and their family. In virtually every aspect these are the same as existed between the child and the natural parents.

The relevant law is currently contained in the Adoption Act 1976, the Adoption Rules 1984 and the Adoption Agency Regulations 1983. Since the passing of the Children Act 1989 a review of adoption law has taken place and a consultation document, 'Review of Adoption Law, Report to Ministers of an Interdepartmental Working Group' was published in October 1992. It is expected that the government will come forward with legislative proposals in 1993. The current law is described in this part of the chapter and the proposals for reform will be identified in the Law and Social Work Practice section.

2.3.1   The structure of adoption services

Under the 1976 Adoption Act many local authorities maintain an adoption service through their social services departments. There are also a number of voluntary adoption agencies approved by the Secretary of State under the Act. The services to be provided by 'adoption agencies' include making assessments of children and of those who wish to adopt, and the placing of children for adoption. The work and duties of adoption agencies are further specified by the Adoption Agencies Regulations 1983.

The arrangement of private adoptions is severely limited by the

1976 Act to those where the proposed adopter is a relative of the child or is acting under a High Court order.

Adoption, as a legal jurisdiction, is exercised by the county court and the magistrates' courts (family proceedings court) and in certain circumstances by the High Court.

When adoption agencies and the courts are making any decision in relation to the adoption of a child they are under a duty to:

> . . . have regard to all the circumstances, the first consideration being given to the need to safeguard and promote the welfare of the child throughout his childhood; and shall so far as is practicable ascertain the wishes and feelings of the child regarding the decision and give due consideration to them, having regard to his age and understanding. (Section 6)

2.3.2 The process leading to adoption

A number of stages in the adoption process can be identified and described but it should be understood that the order of description does not imply a strict sequence of events.

Identification of potential adopters

Couples who wish to adopt will register with an adoption agency who will in turn assess the suitability of applicants as potential adopters.

Identification of a child suitable for adoption

Such an identification may take place in a number of circumstances including:

— the natural parents may decide to have their child adopted and approach an adoption agency with such a proposition;

— a local authority may decide as part of its child care work in relation to a child it is looking after to work toward that child's adoption;

— local authority foster carers may decide to seek to adopt a child in their long term care and seek local authority support for such a proposition.

The consent of natural parents to the adoption of their child

No adoption can be made unless the child's parents (or guardians) consent. Such a consent is given in relation to a specific adoption application and must be given freely and unconditionally and with a full understanding of the situation. It may be withdrawn at any time up to the making of the adoption order.

A mother cannot give an effective agreement until 6 weeks after her child's birth.

Freeing for adoption

Natural parents can agree to give a general consent to the adoption of their child. In this situation an adoption agency, with the consent of the child's parents, applies to the court for an order 'freeing the child for adoption'. If parents will not consent to a freeing order an application to the court for such an order may be combined with an application to dispense with the parents' consent. The effect of a freeing order is that parental responsibility in relation to the child is vested in the adoption agency and the issue of parental consent to adoption is settled (subject to the limited circumstances in which a freeing order can be revoked).

Dispensing with parental consent

The necessity for parental consent can be dispensed with by the court in certain specified circumstances set out in section 16(2) of the 1976 Act:

a)   that the parent or guardian cannot be found or is incapable of giving agreement;

b)   that the parent or guardian is withholding his agreement unreasonably;

c)   that the parent or guardian has persistently failed without reasonable cause to discharge the parental duties in relation to the child;

d)   that the parent or guardian has abandoned or neglected the child;

e)   that the parent or guardian has persistently ill-treated the child;

f)   that the parent or guardian has seriously ill-treated the child. (This last ground does not apply unless the rehabilitation of the child and parent or guardian is unlikely.)

Recommendations of the adoption panel

The decision by an adoption agency to place a child with prospective adopters prior to adoption must first be verified by an 'adoption panel'. The task of the panel, whose membership is specified by the Adoption Agency Regulations, is to make recommendations to the agency in relation to the suitability of the prospective adopters, on whether the adoption would be in the best interests of the child and on the best way of proceeding to adoption. No placement can take place until the panel's recommendations have been made.

Placement of the child

When a child is placed by an agency with the prospective adopters the Adoption Agency Regulations impose a number of duties on the agency including the necessity to monitor the placement by visits and reports and to review the placement if no application to adopt is made within three months. The position of the adopters and the child is very uncertain at this stage in the sense that the child may be removed from the placement by those who have parental responsibility at any time, and by the agency with notice. This uncertainty is reduced substantially by the application for adoption where the parents have consented to the adoption, or by an application to free the child for adoption as a result of the fact that removal of the child from the person who has care without their permission or by court order is an offence.

The Act also gives protection to long term foster parents who have applied to adopt the child in their care by preventing the removal of a child who has been living with them for five years by the parents or the local authority which has legal care of the child without permission of the court.

Where the placement is arranged by an adoption agency an adoption order cannot be made unless the child is at least 19 weeks' old and has had his or her home with the applicants for at least the preceding 13 weeks.

The application to adopt

The Act, in sections 14 and 15, specifies those who may adopt though it must be recognised that the policy of adoption agencies in their choice of suitable prospective adopters may vary considerably and may be very different from the statutory criteria. Adoption proceedings are 'family proceedings' under the Children Act 1989 so that a court may grant a residence order, or other 'section 8' order, in proceedings which were started by an application to adopt. The choice of order will be determined by the welfare principle contained in section 1 of the Children Act.

Reports for the court

The application to adopt is made by the prospective adopters and may be made to the High Court, the county court or the magistrates' court. If the child has been placed by an adoption agency the application to adopt triggers the preparation of a report by the agency to the court. The contents of the report are specified by Schedule 2 of the Adoption Rules but generally must deal with the suitability of the prospective adopters and the desirability of the adoption in relation to the welfare of the child.

If the applicants want the court to dispense with the parents' consent to adoption then the grounds for that dispensation must be contained in the application. In such applications the court will appoint a guardian ad litem to protect the child's interests and the guardian will investigate the circumstances and report on them to the court. A guardian may also be appointed at any time by the court where it considers that there are special circumstances warranting such an appointment.

If the child's parents consent to the adoption the court will appoint a reporting officer to investigate the issue of consent and report to the court that it has been given freely, unconditionally and with full understanding of the situation and the implications.[2]

---

[2] Guardians ad litem and reporting officers are appointed from panels administered by local authorities. They will hold a CQSW or Diploma in Social Work and have experience of work with children and families.

The hearing

The court hearing is held in private and the court must make sure that all the necessary requirements have been satisfied. In making the order the court is bound by section 6 of the Act to have regard to all the circumstances and give first consideration to the need to safeguard and promote the welfare of the child throughout his or her childhood. It is also required to ascertain the wishes and feelings of the child and to give appropriate weight to them having regard to the age and understanding of the child.

The order

If the court is satisfied that all the necessary requirements have been complied with and that adoption is appropriate in relation to the welfare of the child then the adoption order may be made. The order vests parental responsibility in the adoptive parents and extinguishes those responsibilities in the natural parents.

The court may, as an alternative, make an interim order which gives parental responsibility to the applicants for a probationary period of two years or it may refuse to make an order and the child will be returned to the agency which placed the child.

As a further alternative the court may make a Children Act, section 8 order.

2.3.3 The origins of adopted children

All adoptions are registered in the Adopted Children Register and on reaching their eighteenth birthday an adopted person is entitled to a copy of their original birth certificate. The Adoption Contact Register was established by the Children Act for the purpose of enabling adopted people to contact birth parents and other relatives who have registered their details on the Register.

3 THE LAW AND SOCIAL WORK PRACTICE: some issues for discussion

3.2 ADOPTION AND THE PERMANENCY DEBATE

'Permanency' is seen to be of fundamental importance in child care planning in social work. For many social workers and local authorities 'permanency' is synonymous with adoption and so the search for permanency often leads to a decision to place a child for adoption. Adoption is a permanent and irrevocable step and the process leading up to the making of the order involves decisions of fundamental significance, such as those concerning placement and the suitability of prospective adopters, which require high levels of social work skill. Often, under current law, the court will not be involved until it hears the adoption application and at such a hearing it will rely heavily on the reports it receives. The guardian ad litem is appointed to safeguard the child's interests and in his/her report s/he is expected to test the agency's case for adoption.

In a discussion of the 'permanency debate' June Thoburn has drawn attention to the alternatives to adoption as permanency, including custodianship (now abolished) and long term fostering, and urged guardians ad litem to: 'exercise your independence by refusing to accept on behalf of the children for whom you are appointed to speak, narrow definitions of permanence, and of ways of achieving it.'[3] The guardian's report may be the most significant check on what must sometimes seem to be the inexorable progress of a permanency decision involving the placement of a child for adoption through to a successful adoption application. The responsibility on the guardian is considerable and if the court is to make the 'right' decision in respect of the child's welfare it is to be hoped that all permanency solutions are adequately canvassed before an adoption order is made.

As a result of the implementation of the Children Act those solutions now include a residence order made under the provisions of Part II of the Act. The granting of a residence order has the effect of establishing parental responsibility in the person granted the residence order, though it does not extinguish the parental responsibility of others. This provision allows the legal status of non parents such as foster carers to be recognised. It is likely that in time this order will establish itself as a permanency option and thus as an alternative to adoption.

[3] Thoburn, J. 'The Permanency Debate: Its Impact on Decisions About Children' in 'Guardians — The First Three Years. A Success?' Papers Prepared for a Day Conference (16.10.87). Inner and North London Panel of Guardians Ad Litem and Reporting Officers.

Though the objective of permanency is seen as good practice recent years have seen a distinct push toward 'open adoption' within which contact between the child and his or her birth parents is facilitated prior to and after adoption. This openness may be achieved in a number of ways, for example by allowing the birth parents to express a view on the choice of adoptive parents, by the making of a contact order under the Children Act and by requiring information about the adopted child to be given to the birth parents. These developments are themselves problematic; they challenge the 'legal transplant' model of adoption and in some circumstances the objective of openness may become dominant to the detriment of the welfare of the child.

3.3 THE REFORM OF ADOPTION LAW

An inter-departmental working group, set up in 1989, has reviewed the law of adoption and its report was published as a consultation document in October 1992. The need for review of the law is related to a number of developments identified in the introduction to the consultation document. These include:

— a fall in the number of children needing adoption;

— an increasing emphasis on placing older children, children in care and children with special needs;

— a recognition of the need to involve birth parents in the process of adoption;

— the need of some adopted people to have information concerning their birth families;

— the importance of race and cultural background to the needs of an adopted child;

— the need to seek adoptive families from the ethnic communities;

— the implementation of the Children Act with its emphasis on the welfare of the child through the section 1 principles, the welfare checklist and the process of consultation with children so that their wishes can be taken into account;

— the growth of inter-country adoptions and the difficulties generated by this growth.

The consultation document makes a number of recommendations in response to these issues with the prospect of legislation in 1993.

The document recommends that adoption remain an irrevocable order within which a child's legal links with his or her birth family are severed and parental responsibility is transferred to the adoptive parents. It is recognised, however, that the nature of the order should not preclude the possibility of contact being maintained with a child's birth family nor should it preclude the prevention of contact where such an order is necessary. In consequence the document recommends that a new adoption law should re-affirm the courts' power to make a contact order as part of the adoption order and that conversely there should also be a power to make a non-molestation order in conjunction with an adoption order.

It is recommended that principles equivalent to those in section 1 of the Children Act 1989 be incorporated in new adoption legislation so that there would be a welfare checklist, a recognition that delay is likely to be prejudicial to the welfare of the child and a requirement that the court should make no order unless it considers that doing so would be better for the child than making no order at all.

It is recommended that an adoption order for a child of 12 or over should not be granted without the consent of the child unless the child is incapable of giving its consent.

Freeing for adoption should be abolished. Placements for adoption should be the subject of a placement order granted by the court. If the granting of the order, or any associated matter, is contested the order should not be granted without a hearing. A placement order would give parental responsibility to the prospective adopters but not take it away from anyone else.

The grounds for dispensing with parental consent should be limited to three: i) that the parent cannot be found or is incapable of giving consent; ii) that the advantages to the child of becoming part of a new family are so significantly greater than the advantages of any alternative option as to justify overriding the wishes of a parent; iii) where a parent having agreed to a placement withdraws that agreement and there have been no significant changes since the parent agreed to the placement.

Other recommendations include the appointment of a guardian ad litem in all adoption proceedings, the placing of duties on adoption agencies to ascertain the wishes and feelings of all those concerned in a particular adoption application, and the ability of parents and other relatives to register a wish on the Adoption Contact Register that they do not wish to be contacted.

There are specific recommendations to facilitate inter-country adoptions where it is in the interests of the child, but also to safeguard the welfare of the child and to eliminate corrupt practices. Consequently admission to the UK would be subject to authorisation by the Department of Health or local authorities and adoption agencies delegated to do so by the Department.

It is expected that changes in adoption law will be introduced independently of any consideration of the effects of the implementation of the Children Act and of the acceptance of the Hague Conference draft convention on inter-country adoption. This decision to move to new adoption legislation without first waiting to assess the impact of the availability of residence orders under the Children Act may be seen by some people as unnecessarily hasty. Doubts about a precipitate reform of adoption law may be seen as well placed particularly in the light of developments in other countries. In Sweden, for example, parental responsibility for children is irrevocable and only transnational adoptions are possible.

4 CASE STUDIES

1. Sandy is seventeen, single and six months' pregnant. The father of the child is an ex boyfriend who has made it clear that he wants nothing to do with the baby. She has been rejected by her parents and has referred herself to the social services. She is currently living with her grandmother who is happy to support her. She has indicated to you that she is thinking of having the baby adopted when it is born but knows nothing about how to go about it or what is involved.

How are you going to answer her questions?

2.   Kylie is six months old and has been looked after by the local authority for four months, initially on an emergency protection order, and latterly since a care order was made by the family proceedings court as a result of proceedings brought on the basis that she had been abused by her parents. Kylie is currently living with foster carers. The authority have facilitated contact for the parents since Kylie has been in their care but they have taken only a sporadic interest in Kylie and have not appeared for the last three contact visits.

The authority has decided to work towards Kylie's adoption and when the idea is put to the parents they are both adamant in their refusal to agree to such a move. An ideal placement has been found for Kylie with prospective adopters and the authority wishes to move toward adoption as soon as possible.

What rights do the parents have to object to the proposed adoption and how may the local authority move forward with its plans despite the parents' refusal to consent?

How will the court decide the issue of consent and what reports will it need before it can decide on any adoption application?

5   ACTIVITIES

1.   It may be possible for students on a social services or adoption agency placement to get some experience of adoption work as part of their placement work.

2.   If direct experience is not possible then local authorities, as adoption agencies, will provide information about all aspects of adoption in their area. Contact can be made through the social services department. Other adoption agencies will be listed in the phone book and information can also be obtained from them. Some addresses are listed below.

3.   British Agencies for Adoption and Fostering provide a service mainly for those working in adoption. They provide a useful publications list which can be obtained by sending a stamped addressed envelope. (Address below.)

4. Keep a check on changes in law and practice in the area particularly with the prospect of a major reform to adoption law. Adoption and Fostering is a specialist journal for this area of practice and copies should be available in college libraries or through the inter-library loan service.

Other journals worth looking at are: Community Care, Family Law, Journal of Social Welfare Law, and Social Work Today.

5. Write to the National Foster Care Association (address below) for a publications list and their 'student's pack on fostering'.

6 ADDRESSES

Barnado's Homefinding Project,
Barnado House,
Tanners Lane, Barkingside,
Ilford,
Essex IG6 1QG.
Phone: 081 551 0011.

British Agencies for Adoption and Fostering (BAAF),
11 Southwark Street,
London SE1 1RQ.
Phone: 071 407 8800.

National Children's Home,
Highfield,
Ambrose Lane,
Harpenden,
Herts AL5 4BX.
Phone: Harpenden
(05827) 4688/9.

Catholic Children's Society,
73 St Charles Square,
London W10 6EJ.
Phone: 081 969 5305.

Church of England Children's Society,
Edward Rudolf House,
69–85 Margery Street,
London WC1X 0JL.
Phone: 071 837 4299.

National Foster Care Association,
Francis House,
Francis Street,
London SW1P 1DE.

7 MATERIALS

These recommendations cover general materials and some that are of more specialist interest. Practitioners working in the adoption area will require additional specialist materials.

1.   Specialist Family Law texts provide detailed information on adoption, and fostering. For an accessible discussion see:

Dewar, J. *Law and the Family* (2nd edn, 1992) Butterworths, chs 10 and 11.

2.   The Children Act 1989 Guidance and Regulations:

'Volume 2: Family Placements'.

'Volume 8: Private Fostering and Miscellaneous'.

3.   'Review of Adoption Law. Report to Ministers of an Interdepartmental Working Group. A Consultation Document. (1992) Department of Health'.

4.   BAAF produces two short leaflets:

'Adoption: some questions answered' (1985).

'Fostering: some questions answered' (1988). This leaflet is also available in Urdu, Hindi and Punjabi.

5.   BAAF also produces a series of Practice Notes which are designed to update workers on law and practice. See in particular:

'Accommodating Children' (1990).

'Schedule 2 Reports under the Adoption Rules 1984' (1989).

CHAPTER 10

Social work, education and the law

1 INTRODUCTION

The responsibility for the provision of public education rests largely with local education authorities though central government, through the Department of Education, is responsible for financing an increasingly large grant maintained sector. Statutory responsibilities for social work agencies and practitioners in this area of work lie principally under the Education Acts 1944 and the Children Act 1989 and are discharged by specialist practitioners known as education welfare officers. In addition social workers employed by social services departments may be involved with clients who, as parents and children, are concerned with other aspects of the education system such as the assessment of 'special needs' and dealing with the consequences of school exclusions.

This chapter considers three areas in which social workers and education welfare officers are involved: school attendance, the assessment and statementing procedures for children who have special educational needs, and the exclusion of children from school following the exercise of school disciplinary procedures.

This chapter identifies, in the same way as the other chapters have done, how social workers can become involved in an area of practice at a number of levels and in a variety of ways. For the education welfare officer the law relating to education is of primary importance and such practitioners will need a working knowledge of the statutory framework dealing with attendance, special needs and exclusions. Additionally, because the immediate consumers of education provision are children, they will also need to know and understand the implications of the appropriate sections and schedules of the Children Act 1989 dealing with the education supervision order introduced for the first time by the Act. Other social workers will need to understand this same statutory framework because their existing clients, be they

259

children and/or parents, may be subject to the statutory provisions identified above. As an example it is possible that in preparing a pre-sentence report on a young offender in the expectation that the youth court will impose a community sentence, the social worker becomes concerned that the young person has considerable learning difficulties which have hitherto gone unassessed, and also discovers a disciplinary record at school which has meant that the young person has been excluded from school on a number of occasions in the past year. In such circumstances, and in many others, practitioners working for social services departments will need to liaise with and possibly work with education welfare officers, educational psychologists and the school in addition to working with the young person and their family. Such work will have a number of objectives and will involve a variety of agencies and practitioners including a consideration of whether the young person is a 'child in need' under the definitions of the Children Act.

The example above identifies, once again, why it is that social work practitioners require a broad knowledge of the law beyond any detailed understanding of how it relates to their area of particular practice. The example encompasses a number of 'legal regimes', ie the youth justice system and the provisions of the Criminal Justice Act 1991, the 'special needs' provisions of the 1981 and 1988 Education Acts, the school disciplinary provisions of the Education (No.2) Act 1986, Part III of the Children Act 1989 dealing with local authority support for children and families and possibly Part IV of the same Act which, by section 36, provides for education supervision orders.

2   THE LAW

2.1   SCHOOL ATTENDANCE

The Education Act 1944 sets out basic rights to education but also imposes duties on parents, by section 36, to ensure their child's attendance at school. If parents fail in this duty the education authority has the power under section 37 to serve a school attendance order on the parents identifying the school to be attended by the child. Failure to adhere to the terms of the order render the child's parents liable to a criminal prosecution in the magistrates' court.

Parallel provisions directed to a child who is not attending school are set out in section 36 of the Children Act 1989. This section provides for the making of an education supervision order on a child upon the application of a local education authority. The grounds for making such an order are set out in section 36(3):

> . . . that the child is of compulsory school age and is not being properly educated.

Section 36(5) of the Children Act makes it clear that failure to comply with a school attendance order or a failure to attend regularly at a child's registered school will constitute the criteria required for the order unless the contrary can be proved.

An education supervision order may not be made on a child who is in the care of a local authority.

Part III of Schedule 3 to the Children Act sets out the details of education supervision orders. The order requires the supervisor, invariably an education welfare officer, to advise, assist and befriend the child and also empowers the supervisor to give directions to a child and his or her parents which address the objective of ensuring the child's proper education. The supervisor is required to consult the child and parents and to give appropriate consideration to their wishes and feelings.

While the order is in force it supersedes the statutory duties of parents under the Education Act 1944, and any school attendance order will be terminated by the making of an education supervision order.

Such orders run for one year but may be extended for a period up to three years but will end when the child concerned reaches school leaving age. The order can be discharged by the court on the application of the local education authority, the parents or the child. Parents who persistently fail to comply with directions made under an education supervision order commit an offence and persistent failure by the child requires the local education authority to notify the appropriate local authority who must then investigate the child's circumstances.

2.2   SPECIAL EDUCATIONAL NEEDS

The Education Act 1981 provides the current structure for the education of children with special educational needs. The present law is due to be partially reformed by the provisions of the Education Bill 1992 which is due to be enacted in 1993, though the basic assessment and statementing process will remain.

Under the Act a child has a learning difficulty if he or she has 'significantly greater difficulty in learning than the majority of children of his age' or the child 'has a disability which prevents him from making use of educational facilities of a kind generally provided in school, within the area of the education authority concerned, for children of his age'.

If the learning difficulty requires a special educational provision to be made then the child is said to have special educational needs. If this provision is at such a level that it requires determination and provision by a local education authority then a formal assessment under the Act should take place. As a consequence it should be noted that many children with special needs are not formally assessed under the Act because the education authority is able, or believes it is able, to provide for their special educational needs without recourse to the assessment and statementing procedures provided by the 1981 Act. Many difficulties and disputes arise from this rather loose legal regulation and much criticism of the legislation comes from parents who are concerned that their child's learning difficulties are not properly understood nor provided for.

The assessment of a child, who it is believed has special educational needs, can take place on the initiative of the local education authority or in response to a request by the child's parents made under section 9 of the Education Act 1981. Commentators in this field recommend that such a request be substantiated by an expert report normally compiled by an educational psychologist.[1] The local education authority is normally bound to accede to such a request unless it considers the request for assessment to be unreasonable in the sense that there are no grounds for such a request.

[1] See Children with Special Needs. Assessment, Law and Practice — Caught in the Act (1991) Chasty and Friel Chapter 6.

The process of assessment is governed by section 5 of the Act and by subsequent regulations and is designed to identify the needs of the child and the provision that is required to meet them. Within the assessment process the education authority must seek a wide variety of advice including educational, medical and psychological information concerning the child and must consult with the child's parents and take into account information received from any district health authority and/or social services authority.

The Education Reform Act 1988 allows children with statements of special educational needs to be excluded from the provisions of the national curriculum. As a result any assessment must now include reference to this issue.

The assessment process is lengthy and should normally take any time between six months and a year. If as a result of the assessment the education authority decides that a statement is necessary it must serve a draft statement on the child's parents who in turn have the right to make representations on the statement and to a meeting with the authority. This process of consultation may cause the draft to be amended or the authority to decide not to make a statement. The final statement must be notified to parents who must also be informed of their right to appeal against the determination of special educational needs and/or the educational provision specified in the statement; such appeals are made to a tribunal known as an Education Committee. If the education authority decides, as a result of the assessment, that a statement is not necessary then the parents can appeal to the Secretary of State.

The operation of this complex legal regime means that children with special educational needs may be educated in a variety of environments. Basically there are two categories of 'special needs' children: i) those children who have special educational needs but who are provided for within an ordinary school without having been assessed or statemented under the Act; ii) those children who have been assessed and for whom a statement of provision has been made under the provisions of the Act. This latter group may in turn be divided into those children who are educated in an ordinary school and those educated in a special school.

The ability of the Act to appropriately provide for the special educational needs of children has been severely criticised and a number of these criticisms have been discussed in the government's White Paper 'Choice and Diversity' and the Audit Commission's report 'Getting in on the Act'. The Education Bill 1992 introduced in Parliament in November addresses a number of issues and proposes to improve the involvement of parents in the statementing process, to increase rights of appeal and to promote the ability of parents with a child who has special educational needs to have their child educated at a school of their choice, subject to a place being available.

2.3   SCHOOL DISCIPLINE AND EXCLUSIONS

Discipline within schools is the responsibility of head teachers. Under section 22 of the Education (No 2) Act 1986 head teachers are responsible for measures which are aimed at four objectives:

i) promoting, among pupils, self discipline and proper regard for authority;

ii) encouraging good behaviour on the part of pupils;

iii) securing that the standard of behaviour of pupils is acceptable;

iv) otherwise regulating the conduct of pupils.

These day to day responsibilities are subject to general policy laid down by governors and to any particular guidance provided by the governing body.

It is under these provisions that school pupils are given detentions and are excluded from school. Under section 22 of the Act the power to exclude a child from school is reserved to the head teacher and sections 23–27 set out procedures within which any exclusion must take place. If a child is excluded the child's parents must be informed of the exclusion without delay, told of reasons for the exclusion and of their right to make representations to the governing body and the local education authority. In grant maintained schools representations are made to the disciplinary committee of the governing body. If the exclusion is for more than five days in any one term or it means that the excluded child will not be able to take a public examination then the head teacher must also inform the governing body and the education authority (the disciplinary committee in the case of a grant maintained school) of the period of the exclusion and the reasons for it.

Where the head teacher has excluded a pupil for an indefinite period the education authority must, after consulting the governers, set a date for the pupil to be re-instated if the governors have not already done so. The governors may appeal to a local appeal committee against a re-instatement direction by the education authority. In grant maintained schools directions concerning re-instatement are made by the disciplinary committee of the governors.

Head teachers can decide to exclude a pupil permanently thereby expelling them from school. Such a decison gives parents the right to appeal to the local appeal committee against the expulsion; the decisions of the committee are binding on the education authority, governors and the head teacher. The committee will also hear appeals by governors against a direction of the education authority to re-instate an expelled pupil.

Pupils who have been permanently excluded or expelled have their names removed from the school roll but the education authority remains under a duty to provide them with appropriate education either at another school or by other means. The parents of an expelled pupil have the right to choose an alternative school which must provide a place unless it is full.

3 THE LAW AND SOCIAL WORK PRACTICE: some issues for discussion

3.1 SPECIAL NEEDS EDUCATION

Mary Warnock headed the committee whose report led to the establishment of the current system of special needs education introduced by the Education Act 1981. Writing in a special Schools Report for the Observer newspaper she now concludes that the system is failing thousands of children and is in need of substantial reform.[2] Her concerns about the special needs education system are reflected in similar criticisms made in the Audit Commission's report 'Getting in on the Act', in the government's White Paper 'Choice and Diversity' and by pressure groups working in the area such as the Royal Association for Disability and Rehabilitation (RADAR) and the Advisory Centre for Education (ACE). Their criticisms centre on a number of issues including the integration of children with special educational needs in ordinary schools, problems with the assessment process, difficulties in the drafting and agreement of statements and the actual provision by education authorities for established special educational needs. It seems that social workers may often find themselves acting as a broker between the needs and demands of customers and an education authority unable or unwilling to provide the necessary support.

The Warnock Report was based on the assumption that most children with special educational needs would be educated in ordinary schools. Such has been the case since the implementation of the Act though a recent report published by the Centre for Studies on Integration in Education has identified that there are a significant number of parents who cannot find places in ordinary schools for their children who have a statemented special educational need. There is also some concern that the introduction of the National Curriculum, with league tables of examination results, and school budgetary control through the local management of schools, has had the impact of making some schools reluctant to accept children with special educational needs. It is to be hoped that provisions in the Education Bill 1992, which are designed to prevent public sector schools refusing to accept a child with a statement of special educational need, will mean that the integration of education provision for such children, assumed by Warnock, will continue with renewed commitment.

There is little doubt that education authorities are experiencing a significant squeeze on their resources and there is some evidence that money is being saved by education authorities slowing down the assessment and statementing process. Writing in the Observer's Schools Report[3] Julia Hagedorn argues that the recent

[2] Mary Warnock 'Special case in need of reform' (18.10.92) Observer Schools Report.
[3] Ibid. page 4.

Audit Commission Report revealed the assessment and statementing system to be 'in chaos: many LEA's were evading their
responsibilities and children were waiting an averge of 15 months
for assessment. In the worst cases, they had to wait up to three
years'. She also refers to a recent survey by the Spastics Society
which confirms the findings of the Audit Commission's Report.
The survey, 'A Hard Act to Follow', comments on the distinction
between the presumption in the 1981 Act that a statement will
be produced within 6 months of assessment and the experience
of many families who have waited considerably longer.

> For 64% of families the initial assessment of their child's needs took
> more than six months.

> Only 10.7% of cases met the six months deadline for a child's statement.
> In over half the cases the process took over two years.

> Some 42% of parents were not even told of their right to have their
> child's needs assessed — or were told in such a way that they were
> unsure of whether they had been informed or not.[4]

The government intends to introduce provisions to ensure that
the assessment and statementing process takes place within
specified timescales though bodies representing local government
and education authorities argue, with some justification, that
time limits cannot be adhered to where the collection of
information for the assessment process is often beyond their
control and where adequate funding for the system is denied.

The drafting of statements by local education authorities is also
the subject of considerable criticism. Statements are often vague;
indeed Her Majesty's Inspectors have found that such drafing
can be deliberate in an attempt to avoid an open ended funding
commitment. Other education authorities draft statements which
reinforce their education policies and provision rather than in
response to a child's individual needs. However, a recent Court
of Appeal decision has now specified the required form of
statements of special educational need.[5] The Court of Appeal
agreed with the High Court's analogy in which a statement of
special educational need was compared to a medical diagnosis

---

[4] 'Report Shows Education Act is Failing Disabled Children'. RADAR Bulletin.
October 1992.
[5] *R v Secretary of State for Education and Science, ex p E* 'Schools Report
Special Needs Issue' (1991) Observer.

of needs and to a prescription for the diagnosed special educational needs. The Court ruled that a statement must set out all the child's special educational needs and specify the special educational provision that should be made for every one of these needs. It is to be hoped that education authorities heed the clear message of the Court of Appeal decision and provide clear and comprehensive statements of a child's special educational needs and of the provision to be made to meet them.

Superimposed on these specific problems is the wider problem inherent within the system established by the 1981 Act, namely that the local authority is under a duty to assess and provide only for children whose special educational needs are such that they require determination and special provision. The Warnock Report was based on the belief in a continuum of ability and disability so that only those at the end of the continuum will be identified by a statement. Mary Warnock is herself now critical of this belief.

> The whole concept of 'statementing' for only a few children, with the rest supposedly having their needs met according to what individual schools can provide, must be radically rethought.[6]

The Education Bill 1992 continues to utilise this continuum of ability and disability with the result that Mary Warnock is critical of proposals to improve and open up the process of statementing.

> But the drawback with such amendments is that they will be introduced against the background of the old ill-drawn line between those who do and those who do not merit statements. What happens to those whose needs still exist, but for whom the education authority has no statutory duty remains untouched. The suspicion must be that these children will be increasingly pushed to one side.[7]

3.2   SCHOOL EXCLUSIONS

The incidence and circumstances of permanent exclusions from public sector schools under the provisions of the Education (No 2) Act 1986 have been monitored over a two year period through the National Exclusions Reporting System. The Department of

---

[6] Mary Warnock 'Special case in need of reform' (18.10.92) Observer Schools Report

[7] Ibid, page 3.

Education published a discussion paper in November 1992, 1 month before the 2 year period ended. A summary at the beginning of the paper clearly identifies the Department's concerns:

> Too many children are excluded from school, either permanently or temporarily. There is evidence that some exclusions go on too long, and that the alternative educational provision made for many excluded pupils is subject to unacceptable variations in both quality and quantity.[8]

Information identified through the Reporting System provides specific evidence concerning permanent exclusions which will be of concern to many people including education welfare officers and social workers who will be working with a significant number of the children excluded and with their families.

* In the first year of the monitoring exercise there were approximately 3000 permanent exclusions reported.

* About 12.5% of those excluded were children with statements of special educational needs.

* Afro-Caribbean pupils appeared to be disproportionately represented within the excluded pupil population (8.1% of the overall total).

The variation in the number of exclusions between individual schools seemed to be too great to be explained by the socio-economic nature of the schools' catchment areas.

It seems that returns to the Reporting System did not always include information concerning alternative educational provision for excluded pupils. From the information that was provided it appears that 44% of excluded pupils were receiving home tuition, 29% were at another mainstream school, 22% were in special units and 5% had gone to a special school or changed special schools.

The Discussion Paper draws a number of preliminary conclusions from these and from other findings. Principally, the paper asserts that the number and level of exclusions is too high and that often alternative educational provision for excluded pupils is

[8] 'Exclusions. A Discussion Paper'. Department of Education. November 1992.

inadequate. The principle which underpins departmental policy is to reduce exclusions by encouraging schools to deal with difficult pupils without recourse to exclusion.

For schools pupils who cause severe disciplinary problems are expensive to cope with in terms of staff and other resources. Permanent exclusions are often seen by schools as a cost effective and permanent solution to the problem. This is recognised in the discussion paper which suggests using financial incentives to discourage schools from excluding pupils and encouraging schools to take on pupils excluded from other schools.

Children who are excluded from school may often spend some time on suspension before exclusion and further time awaiting the arrangement of alternative educational provision. During this period they and their families may well need the services of an education welfare officer or social worker. This need for social work intervention becomes a high priority when the circumstances of the child are such that he or she is properly to be regarded as a child in need under the provisions of the Children Act 1989.

The implications of an exclusion for a child are often serious. Where alternative educational provision is inadequate or inappropriate the child will not receive a proper education.

> Without it these children may not be able to benefit fully from a subsequent return to mainstream education and the opportunities of the National Curriculum; their personal happiness, fulfilment and job prospects as adults may also be adversely affected and some of them may drift into crime.[9]

If this rather pessimistic scenario is accurate it will often be a practitioner with a social work training who seeks to help the child pick up the pieces. Fieldwork social workers, education welfare officers and probation officers may all be involved with those children who, for whatever reason, are excluded from the mainstream education system.

---

[9] Ibid, page 4.

4 CASE STUDIES

1. Damian is eleven years' old and is in the first year of secondary school. He has had an appalling attendance record ever since he started in September and the school has now referred the matter to the education welfare service.

How might the matter proceed following this reference?

2. Dawn is 14 and lives at home with her mother and elder sister. Dawn is subject to a school attendance order and her mother has been successfully prosecuted for not ensuring her attendance at school. Her attendance continues to be poor and her school teachers are concerned that she may have become involved in drugs. Dawn's elder sister has been convicted of selling cannabis from their house.

You are a social worker employed by the local authority. The family is well known to social services and you have been asked to take over the file as the key worker has recently left. How are you going to deal with this matter?

3. Samantha is a four and a half year old child with cerebral palsy. Her parents want her to go to the primary school at the top of her road. The local education authority have offered her a place at a special school four miles away. Her parents do not want her to go to a special school and have asked you for help in getting a place at the local primary school. You are a local authority social worker employed by the social services department; you have been working with the family since Samantha was a year old. What can you do in these circumstances?

4. Ricky is ten years' old and cannot read with any fluency; his writing and spelling are very poor. His parents are very concerned about his lack of progress at school and think that he may be dyslexic. They have asked the head teacher whether Ricky can be assessed but have been told that he is a slow learner and that they should wait a year to see if things get better. You are an education welfare officer and Ricky's parents have rung your office to find out what their rights are. What advice are you able to give them?

5. Tracey is 14 years' old and has been suspended from school for four weeks for attacking a first year pupil and demanding

money. Tracey's parents are both working and do not want her at home all day; they are therefore concerned to try and get the suspension reversed. What can they do?

In the meantime the parents of the first year pupil have rung the head teacher demanding that the police become involved and that Tracey is charged.

Discuss the legal implications of this scenario.

6. Lee is 15 and has been permanently excluded from school for assaulting a female student teacher. He is currently being educated at a tuition centre for eight hours per week. His parents think that this is hopelessly inadequate particularly as he has been entered for GCSEs in seven subjects. They would like him to go to another school and have asked for your advice. What are you able to tell them? Lee is due to appear in the youth court next week on a charge of assault following the attack on the student teacher.

5 ACTIVITIES

1. Get hold of publication lists from pressure groups working in this area; for example contact:

Advisory Centre for Education.

Campaign for the Advancement of State Education.

Centre for Studies on Integration in Education.

Royal Association for Disability and Rehabilitation (RADAR). Contact the Policy Officer for Education.

2. Make contact with your local education welfare service and discuss their work and the policies that underpin it.

3. Keep track of the Education Bill 1992 as it goes through Parliament. What changes will it make to the special educational needs system? When will it be implemented?

4. See if you can arrange to visit local schools to see how children

with statements of special educational need are integrated into the education provision of the school. Try to visit a local special school.

6 ADDRESSES

Advisory Centre for Education,
1b Aberdeen Studios,
22 Highbury Grove,
London N5 2EA.
Phone: 071 354 8321.

Campaign for the Advancement of State Education,
4 Hill Road,
Carshalton,
Surrey SM5 3RJ.
Phone: 081 669 5929.

Centre for Studies on Integration in Education,
415 Edgware Road,
London NW2 2EH.
Phone: 081 452 8642.

Children's Legal Centre,
20 Compton Terrace,
London N1 2UN.
Phone: 071 359 6251/2.

RADAR,
25 Mortimer Street,
London W1N 8AB.
Phone: 071 637 5400.

Voluntary Council for Handicapped Children,
c/o The National Children's Bureau,
8 Wakley Street,
London EC1V 7QE.
Phone: 071 278 9441.

7 MATERIALS

7.1 BASIC MATERIALS for ordinary social work practice (not sufficient for specialist education welfare officers)

Chasty, H., Friel, J. *Children with Special Needs. Assessment, Law and Practice — Caught in the Act* (1991) Jessica Kingsley Publications.

Education Rights Handbook (1987) Children's Legal Centre.

RADAR Factsheets:

1. 'The Education Act 1981'.

2. 'Assessment Under The Education Act 1981' (Section 5).

3. 'Appealing Under The Education Act 1981'.

RADAR Briefing Note: 'Education Reform Act 1988'.

Newell, P. 'Special Educational Handbook — the new law on children with special needs' (5th edn 1992) Advisory Centre for Education.

7.2   FURTHER READING

'Exclusions. A Discussion Paper' (1992) Department for Education.

Lawson, B. *Pupil Discipline and Exclusion in Schools* (1991) Longman.

'Schools Report. Special Needs Issue' (18.10.92) Observer.

Liell, P., Saunders, J. *The Law of Education* (1990) Butterworths.

'The Report of the Committee of Enquiry into the Education of Handicapped Children and Young People' (The Warnock Report) (1978) HMSO.

CHAPTER 11

Social security benefits

1 INTRODUCTION

1.1 SOCIAL WORK AND THE SOCIAL SECURITY SYSTEM

The importance of ensuring that social work clients are receiving all that they are entitled to by way of social security benefits cannot be over emphasised. Consequently benefit entitlement can be understood as an issue that links social work practice across the band of different client groups. For some clients social security benefits will constitute their only source of income and though the level of benefits means that this income is often at subsistence level only, for such clients the importance of securing their maximum entitlement is crucial.

A number of benefits are specifically designed for particular groups of claimants. Included in this category are benefits for claimants who are ill or have a disability, for elderly people and for single parents, and it is no coincidence that these groups of claimants represent a substantial proportion of social work clients. It is quite legitimate to speculate about the link between the status and character of social security claimants and social work clients and though such a discussion is beyond the boundaries of this book it is not difficult to assert that the lack of adequate financial resources available through the benefit system forces a number of claimants to seek social work support.

If the importance of social security benefits to social work clients is accepted then it is necessary to identify how social work practice might relate to the social security system. Social workers have no statutory rights or duties in this area of work and so any involvement will be determined by individual and perhaps agency definitions of good practice. For local authority social workers much will depend upon whether an individual practitioner's employing authority has a welfare rights team or adviser. For social workers in such a fortunate position the 'social security burden' is much reduced in the sense that specialist advisers can give advice and other help to individual practitioners and their customers. Nonetheless social workers will still need to know their way around the system so that clients can be given preliminary advice and assistance and so that complex and difficult problems can be recognised for what they are and referred on for specialist help.

For local authority social workers who do not have such a facility and particularly for those working in the voluntary sector or doing residential work the problem is more acute. Decisions will need to be made about the extent to which social work practice involves 'social security practice'. Such a decision will depend on a number of factors including the availability of and access to expert social security knowledge and skills through, for example, a law centre, citizens' advice bureau or other advice agency.

Some discussion of the extent to which social work practice might involve 'social security practice' will allow an identification of the skills and knowledge involved in this area of work and some assessment of how far social work can and should become involved. A number of questions can be posed:

— Should social workers merely offer basic social security information and advice to clients?

— Should help be provided in the actual claiming of benefits eg by completing claim forms, accompanying clients to the Department of Social Security or Department of Employment; by contacting the department on behalf of the client by letter or telephone?[1]

— Should social workers be involved in appeals against the department either as witness, accompanying friend or as advocate/representative?

Behind these questions are concerns about the relationship between social worker and client; social worker as advocate, as facilitator, as enabler. Probation officers are required to advise,

---

[1] The Social Security Benefits Agency is technically responsible for the delivery and administration of social security benefits.

assist and befriend their clients made subject to a probation order; what is the proper relationship between social worker and a client who is also a claimant; what knowledge and skills in relation to the social security system does a social worker require?

1.2 MATERIALS

The complexity of the social security system is legendary and a basic text on social work and the law can only provide an introduction to the system and the various benefits. Social workers, be they students or practitioners, will need to know this basic information so that they can make use of the specialist materials that are available and it is recommended that a basic 'reference library' is compiled and updated. Fortunately this is both easy and relatively inexpensive and can be accomplished by the purchase of three 'claimant's guides' each of which is published as a new edition in April each year. These guides are:

1. *Disability Rights Handbook*. Published annually by the Disability Alliance Educational and Research Association.

2. *National Welfare Benefits Handbook*. Published annually by the Child Poverty Action Group (CPAG).

3. *Rights Guide to Non-Means Tested Benefits*. Published annually by CPAG.

This chapter will deal only with benefits administered by central government departments. Housing benefit, which is administered by local government, is considered in the chapter on housing rights.

Benefit rates are updated each year and any rates identified in this chapter are those that apply for the year April 1993 to April 1994.

2 THE LAW

Before identifying and describing the individual benefits it is important to understand some of the major concepts that are used as part of the language and culture of the social security system.

2.1 CONTRIBUTORY AND NON-CONTRIBUTORY BENEFITS

Much of the social security system is financed by the national insurance contributions paid by employers and employees and topped up by the government. As well as providing the income from which many benefits are paid contributions are also used as a qualification for benefit entitlement. This 'insurance' principle works on the basis that entitlement to some benefits, called contributory benefits, is partly dependent on the claimant having paid sufficient and appropriate contributions. Unemployment benefit is a contributory benefit so that an unemployed claimant will not be entitled to it unless they have a sufficient and appropriate contribution record.

2.2 MEANS-TESTED AND NON-MEANS-TESTED BENEFITS

Another division that is frequently made in the social security system is that which distinguishes between means-tested benefits and non-means-tested benefits. Entitlement to a means-tested benefit depends, among other things, on an examination of the financial circumstances of the claimant and a decision that they fall below a particular figure. Income support and family credit are means-tested benefits.

The financial resources of the claimant are irrelevant to the question of entitlement to non-means-tested benefits. Unemployment benefit is non-means tested.

2.3 BENEFITS WHICH ACT AS PASSPORTS TO OTHER BENEFITS

Entitlement to some benefits acts as a passport to entitlement to others. A claimant who is receiving income support is also entitled to free school meals for his or her children, free dental treatment, free prescriptions etc. Claimants receiving disability living allowance are entitled to disability premiums where they are receiving income support.

2.4 INDUSTRIAL AND NON-INDUSTRIAL BENEFITS

A number of benefits are available only to claimants who have a work related injury or who have contracted an industrial disease.

2.5 SOCIAL SECURITY LAW

Social security law is found in a series of Acts of Parliament and in numerous complex regulations made by the government under powers given to them in the Acts. This statutory law is sometimes interpreted by specialist Social Security Commissioners and the courts and these decisions constitute legal precedents which are themselves legally binding.

2.6 THE ADJUDICATION STRUCTURE

Benefit claims are decided upon by an independent adjudication officer working within the Department of Social Security or, for certain benefits, the Department of Employment. The majority of decisions made by adjudication officers can be appealed against to a Social Security Appeal Tribunal (SSAT). It may be possible 'with leave' to appeal against the decision of a SSAT to the Social Security Commissioners. There is the possibility, again with leave, to appeal against the decision of the Commissioners to the Court of Appeal. Legal aid is not available for claimants to be represented before SSATs or the Commissioners.

A number of decisions are made on behalf of the Secretary of State by authorised officers known as Secretary of State's Representatives; these decisions cannot be appealed against to a SSAT.

2.7 TIME LIMITS FOR CLAIMS

Benefits have time limits in which claims must be made. Late claims may be allowed if the claimant can establish 'good cause'; entitlement can be 'backdated' if there is good cause for a late claim.

2.8   THE BENEFITS

This section will be divided into four:

i)   non-means tested benefits;

ii)   means tested benefits;

iii)   disability benefits;

iv)   industrial injury benefits.

This section will provide a basic outline only of each benefit. Detailed information can be obtained from the appropriate claimant's guide.

2.9   NON-MEANS TESTED BENEFITS

2.9.1   Unemployment benefit

This benefit is paid for days of unemployment in a period of interruption of employment. Though the benefit is normally paid at a weekly rate it is calculated on a six times daily basis per week. Complex rules allow claimants who have an irregular work pattern to claim for days of unemployment.

Claimants must be available for work and actively seeking work to be entitled to unemployment benefit. The law specifies a number of circumstances in which the claimant is said to be 'voluntarily unemployed' and where, as a result, they can be disqualified from benefit for up to a maximum of 26 weeks. These circumstances include dismissal for misconduct and voluntarily leaving employment without just cause. Disqualification for voluntary unemployment will also be reflected in a reduction of the claimant's entitlement to income support.

Unemployment benefit is paid for up to a year, technically for 312 days or 52 six day weeks. Dependency additions in respect of adult and child dependants are payable in specified circumstances. Unemployment benefit is taxable and claimants must satisfy the appropriate contribution requirements.

The level of unemployment benefit means that most claimants who have a family will also have to claim income support as a 'top up' to bring their income up to the subsistence level represented by the income support personal allowances.

2.9.2 Short term sickness and disability benefits.

Statutory sick pay (SSP) is paid to employees who are incapable of work because of some mental or physical incapacity. SSP is paid by employers though a number of employees are excluded from entitlement. SSP is paid at one of two levels depending on the level of the claimant's normal weekly pay. SSP is treated in the same way as wages or a salary and so is subject to deductions for tax and national insurance contributions. SSP is the minimum that must be paid to employees; they may also be entitled to sick pay under any occupational scheme provided by their employers.

The method by which an employee must notify his or her employer of their sickness will be determined by the employer, hopefully by agreement, but is circumscribed by regulation.

Sickness benefit is paid to those who are not in employment and have an incapacity for work or to those who are not entitled to SSP. Claimants must satisfy the required contribution conditions or be entitled through an industrial injury or disease. Sickness benefit is paid with adult and child dependency additions where appropriate and claimants may be disqualified in specified circumstances which can be described as approximating to a concept of 'voluntary incapacity'.

SSP and sickness benefit normally run out after 28 weeks of entitlement and may be replaced by long term sickness and disability benefits constituted by invalidity benefit or possibly severe disablement allowance.

2.9.3 Non-means tested maternity benefits

Statutory maternity pay (SMP) is the equivalent of statutory sick pay for women during maternity leave and is paid by employers as a minimum entitlement to those women who are entitled. The maximum period for which SMP can be paid is 18 weeks though many women will not be entitled to SMP for the full period. SMP is paid at two rates depending upon the length of time the claimant has been employed by the employer. It is subject to tax and deductions in respect of national insurance contributions.

Maternity allowance (MA) may be payable to women who are not entitled to SMP but who have been employed for 26 out of the previous 52 weeks and have an appropriate contribution record. MA is paid for 18 weeks.

2.9.4 Child benefit

Child benefit is one of the most important benefits for claimants with families. It is a universal benefit in the sense that it is non-contributory, non-means tested and tax free and is paid to all families with children unless the child is in the care of a local authority and living away from home. Entitlement normally ceases when a child reaches 16 but is extended if the child continues in full time secondary education. Priority is given to a wife as the claimant.

Single parents are entitled to child benefit and may also be entitled to *one parent benefit*, which is paid as an addition to child benefit, in respect of a child living with the claimant. The claimant must not be living together with the parent of the child, or with their spouse or living with a partner as husband and wife.

Where a person is looking after a child who is effectively orphaned and is entitled to child benefit in respect of that child they may also be entitled to *guardian's Allowance*.

2.9.5 Widows' benefits

There are a number of non-means tested benefits to which a widow (a woman married to a man at the time of his death) may be entitled. Widow's payment, the widowed mother's allowance and the widow's pension are contributory benefits in the sense that entitlement will depend, among other matters, on the widow's late husband having fulfilled the required contribution conditions.

The *widow's payment* is a lump sum of £1000 paid where the

widow is under 60 when her husband dies, or if the widow is older her husband was not getting a retirement pension.

The *widowed mother's allowance* is paid to widows who are also mothers of children for whom they are entitled to receive child benefit.

The *widow's pension* is paid to widows who are under 65 and over 40 when their husbands die or when they cease to be entitled to widowed mother's allowance.

There are non-contributory equivalents to widowed mother's allowance and widow's pension for widows whose husbands had not adequately complied with the contribution requirements for the contributory benefits.

2.9.6 Retirement pensions

There are two main contributory retirement pensions; *category A pensions* which are paid on the basis of the claimant's own contribution record, and *category B pensions* which are paid to married women, widows and some widowers and are based on the contribution record of the claimant's spouse.

Retirement pensions are paid to those who have reached pensionable age (60 for women and 65 for men).

Category A pensions are paid to claimants on the basis of their own contribution records and there are a number of additions which may be added to the basic pension including a benefit to reflect graduated contributions paid between 1961 and 1975 and an additional pension based on any SERPS (state earnings related pension scheme) contributions.

Category B pensions are paid on the basis of the claimant's spouse's contributions and are paid to a married woman, a widow or a widower over pensionable age. Again category B pensions can be increased by additional payments including those in respect of graduated contributions and SERPS contributions.

State Earnings Related Pension Scheme (SERPS).

This scheme provides an earnings related pension for employees whose employers have not 'contracted out' of the scheme. Where the employer has contracted out an additional occupational pension will be paid via the employer. Employees may choose to join a personal pension scheme as an alternative.

2.10 MEANS-TESTED-BENEFITS

This category of benefits is dominated by income support and the social fund. The social fund, a largely discretionary based benefit, is designed to provide for exceptional circumstances and expenses by a series of grants and loans. The discretionary basis of the scheme has been heavily criticised and many social workers have refused to become involved with its administration. Nonetheless there are circumstances in which recourse to the social fund may be necessary as a final resort for customers.

Family credit provides a means tested benefit for low paid families and is best understood as a supplement to the weekly income of a family with children trying to live on low wages.

2.10.1 Family credit

Family credit is paid to couples or single parents with children who are in low paid work. There are a number of conditions which must be satisfied for entitlement to family credit:

— residence in Great Britain;

— the claimant or partner must usually work for more than 16 hours per week;

— the claimant or partner must be responsible for a child who is a member of their household;

— the family's capital must not exceed £8000;

— weekly income must be below a certain level which will depend upon the size of the family and the age of the children.

Working out the amount of family credit is done on the basis of a complicated arithmetical formula involving a comparison between the family income (for family credit purposes) and the 'applicable amount'.

The 'applicable amount' is set by the government and is increased each year; the current figure is £69. If the family income is below the applicable amount then the family credit entitlement will be the maximum for the particular family calculated by reference to a set of scale rates.

If the family income is above the applicable amount then the family credit entitlement will be the maximum family credit amount reduced by 70% of the excess of income over the applicable amount.

There are complex rules concerning the calculation of income.

Family credit is normally paid for 26 weeks and a change of circumstances during that period will not usually alter entitlement.

2.10.2 Income support

Income support is the benefit which provides the safety net for the social security system. It is designed to provide a subsistence level of weekly income for those whose financial resources are not sufficient to meet their needs. The majority of claimants are drawn from three categories: pensioners, single parent families and the long term unemployed.

The law of income support is contained in the Social Security Act 1986, as amended by the Social Security Acts 1988 to 1990, and in a series of complex regulations contained in statutory instruments. The legislation is subject to interpretation by the Social Security Commissioners and very infrequently by the Court of Appeal or even the House of Lords.

Basic conditions for entitlement to income support

— claimant must be in Great Britain;

— generally aged 18 or above (there is limited entitlement for 16–17 year olds);

— not in full time advanced education;

— claimant (or partner) must not be working for 16 hours or more a week;

— must be available for work and actively seeking work;

— capital must not be in excess of £8000.

For most claimants income support acts as a top up benefit in the sense that it fills the gap between the total of other benefits paid to the claimant together with any other income, and the weekly level of income which the government has fixed as being appropriate for a person in the claimant's circumstances. This latter figure, which is called the 'applicable amount', is supposed to provide for normal weekly needs and is made up of three elements: personal allowances, premiums for regular additional expenses, and housing costs.

So income support can be understood as:

APPLICABLE AMOUNT - INCOME = INCOME SUPPORT PAID.

The 'applicable amount is made up of personal allowances, premium payments and allowable housing costs.

Personal allowances for the claimant and his or her dependants are fixed by government each year and represent an official definition of the subsistence costs of living. They differ by reference to age and marital status.

Premiums are weekly additions to personal allowances and are paid to take account of the additional costs incurred because the claimant has children or is a single parent, or because the claimant or a dependant is a pensioner, or because of the disability of the claimant or another person in the household.

The *housing costs* of claimants who are paying rent will normally be met through the housing benefit scheme administered by local authorities. Claimants living in bed and breakfast accommodation will also have their housing costs paid through housing benefit. Special rules apply for those living in registered care homes and nursing homes. Claimants paying a mortgage may have the interest met through income support as a housing cost.

Income is a generic term that includes both capital and income.

Capital is not defined by law but includes savings, lump sum payments and some property. There is sometimes difficulty in deciding whether an item is a capital asset and if so how to treat it for income support purposes. Some capital is taken wholly into account in the calculation of entitlement to income support, other items are partially disregarded in the calculation and others are wholly disregarded.

Claimants who have capital assets of over £8000 are not entitled to income support. Capital of over £3000 but under £8000 is taken to produce a weekly income of £1 for every £250 of capital.

Income can take a number of forms including earnings, other benefit payments and maintenance.

Earnings from part-time work will be taken into account in the calculation of income subject to a £5 disregard; a number of claimants, including those receiving premiums based on sickness and disability, may be entitled to a £15 disregard on their income.

Most benefits paid to income support claimants are counted as income though some, such as disability living allowance, are ignored in the calculation of income.

Most maintenance payments are counted as income and are taken into account in the calculation of income.

The rules in relation to income calculation for income support purposes are extremely complex and further reference can be made to the CPAG *National Welfare Benefits Handbook* for comprehensive information.

2.10.3 Particular aspects of income support

Social workers with clients who are claiming income support will come across a number of common problems which therefore warrant some consideration.

Aggregation and cohabitation

A principle of aggregation operates within income support, by which the income and capital of the claimant is taken to include the resources of his or her spouse or cohabitee.

There is a legal obligation on spouses to maintain each other and their children but no such obligation exists between cohabitees. A single mother who is claiming income support for herself and her child(ren) may have her benefit withdrawn if she enters into a relationship with a man which the Department of Social Security considers to be 'living as man and wife'. In such circumstances the man may claim benefit for the whole 'family' but if he is working full time then neither he nor the woman is entitled to benefit. This situation is compounded by the fact that the woman has no right to be maintained by her new partner at a time when she has lost her independent right to benefit.

Maintenance and child support

The right of a spouse to be maintained can be enforced through the law but the difficulties of securing adequate maintenance through the courts are such that many women with children who have been deserted are forced to claim income support. When such a claim is made the Child Support Agency, established by the Child Support Act 1991, is responsible for assessing the level of child maintenance to be paid by parents who are not discharging their legal obligation to maintain their children and for collecting and enforcing assessments.

Premiums

It is important for social workers to do all they can to ensure that clients are receiving any appropriate premiums to which they are entitled. Entitlement to the family premium, the lone parent premium and the pensioner premium should not be difficult to establish and entitlement to other premiums, though sometimes complex, is specified by regulation.

Entitlement to the disability premium flows from receipt of other disability benefits such as disability living allowance, invalidity pension and severe disability allowance, and also from being registered blind. There are other avenues of entitlement and it is important that social workers check that clients who are disabled are receiving their full entitlement to income support.

The general rule is that a claimant may receive only one premium though they may qualify for more than one. If there is 'multiple' qualification the most valuable premium will be paid. This general rule applies to the disability premium, the pensioner premium, the higher pensioner premium, and the lone parent premium. The family premium will be paid in addition to any of these and the disabled child premium is paid in addition to any other premium. Claimants and/or partners receiving the disability premium or the higher pensioner premium may also qualify for the severe disability premium in strictly defined circumstances.

2.10.4 The social fund

The social fund, which was legislated for in the Social Security Act 1986, is divided into two quite separate parts. The statutory social fund provides legal entitlement to a maternity payment, to funeral expenses and cold weather payments. Claims are decided by an adjudication officer and appeals can be made to a SSAT. The discretionary social fund provides for claimants faced with exceptional expenses; this part of the social fund makes community care grants, budgeting loans and crisis loans on a discretionary basis only. There is no legal entitlement to such benefits so that claimants are forced to rely on the discretionary decision making of a social fund officer. These officers are required by the 1986 Act to decide any claim or other social fund matter, 'in accordance with any general directions issued by the Secretary of State and in determining any such question shall take account of any general guidance issued by him'.[2]

The directions are binding on social fund officers but they do not constitute a legal entitlement for claimants. They tell an officer what s/he may award and what cannot be awarded. Such discretion is itself circumscribed by the cash limited budget of the social fund so that if the budget of an office has been exhausted no social fund payments will be made.

There are three types of discretionary payment which may be made by the fund:

[2] Social Security Act 1986, section 33(10).

Community care grants

These payments are made by way of grants and are designed to facilitate community care rather than institutional care. They can be paid so as to keep someone out of care or to help someone coming out of institutional care. Grants can also be made to help a family cope with an exceptional pressure or stress.

Claimants for a community care grant must be on income support and there is a capital limit of £500 so that any capital above that amount must be used to meet the need.

Budgeting loans

These are loans from the social fund to income support claimants for special expenses which they are unable to meet from their normal weekly budget. Income support must have been in receipt for at least 26 weeks and the same £500 capital rule applies. The maximum loan is £1000 and all loans are repaid by deductions from weekly income support.

Crisis loans

These are loans made to pay for costs arising from an emergency or disaster. Anyone may make an application provided they have no savings and no other way of meeting the need. The loan must be the only way to prevent serious risk to the health or safety of any member of the family.

The outlines of these three types of social fund payment tend to hide the difficulties associated with claiming them. In addition to the limited budgets for grants and loans the social fund directions frequently exclude categories of payment and categories of claimant from receiving grants and loans. These directions are binding on social fund officers and social workers advising clients about the possibility of a claim on the social fund should be aware of the directions relating to each of the three social fund 'benefits'. These directions, which are published in the *Social Fund Manual*, are reproduced in the *Disability Rights Handbook* and they are essential, if depressing, reading for any social worker dealing with the social fund.

Directions and Guidance

Many of the directions tell social fund officers what they cannot do and this negative aspect of the social fund is often reinforced by the guidance which officers must take account of. The guidance states that:

> The overriding principle upon which the budgetary system is based is that the total cost of payments made by any local office in a financial year must not exceed its budget allocation for that financial year.

In order to facilitate the application of a fixed budget the guidance states a series of priorities for social fund payments so that a hierarchy of needs and claimants is established. Despite the fact that the guidance is not binding on social fund officers there is little doubt that they stick very closely to the priorities listed and that claimants whose needs have a relatively low priority are unlikely to be successful in their application for a grant or loan.

Challenging a social fund decision

Because the discretionary part of the social fund is not based on legal entitlement there are no rights of appeal to a SSAT. There is, however, a right to have a review of social fund decisions including those concerning the refusal of a loan or grant, the amount awarded and the award of a loan rather than a grant. It is also possible to complain about the details concerning the repayment of a loan.

A review is carried out by a social fund officer by reference to the law and all the circumstances of the case and will include a review of the way in which the decision was reached and whether the social fund officer exercised his or her discretion fairly.

If the review does not go wholly in favour of the claimant then the claimant must be invited for an interview at which the decision will be explained and the claimant will be able to put his or her case.

If the case is not decided in the claimant's favour after interview it is referred to a senior social fund officer for decision. This decision, which is given in writing, may be further reviewed by a social fund inspector.

2.11   INDUSTRIAL INJURIES BENEFITS

There is a specific set of benefits available to employed claimants who have received an industrial injury or contracted an industrial disease. In some cases the character of the benefit and the level at which it is paid compares favourably with the non-industrial equivalent.

2.11.1   General conditions

An industrial injury is a personal injury which has been caused by an accident which has arisen out of and in the course of employment. If the different elements of this definition are established the claimant may be entitled to one or more of the industrial injury benefits.

An industrial disease is a disease which has been identified by law as having a clear occupational cause. A number of occupations are prescribed in relation to such diseases and in specified circumstances a claimant who is employed in a particular occupation and who is suffering from a disease prescribed for that occupation is accepted as suffering from an industrial disease and again may be entitled to one or more of the industrial injuries benefits.

2.11.2   The benefits

A short term, temporary incapacity for work caused by an industrial injury or disease is provided for under the statutory sick pay scheme.

Disablement benefit

This is paid where the claimant has suffered a long term disability resulting from loss of mental or physical faculty which has been assessed at 14% or more.

The amount of the benefit depends on the extent of the disablement.

Two benefits are paid as increases to disablement benefit:

1. Constant attendance allowance which is the industrial equivalent to attendance allowance, is paid to claimants who are entitled to disablement benefit at the 100% rate and who require constant attendance because of their loss of faculty.

2. Exceptionally severe disablement allowance will be paid to claimants who are receiving more than the normal maximum constant attendance allowance.

2.12 DISABILITY BENEFITS

Some time is spent in the chapter on the law of community care to identify the benefits that are available to claimants in respect of their short term and long term sickness and disability. An outline of each of the different benefits is provided in that chapter and so the information will not be duplicated here.

2.12.1 Disability premiums in income support

Many claimants with a disability rely upon the extra income provided by the disability premiums paid in addition to their basic income support.

The disability premium is paid in respect of someone who is under 60 and where the claimant satisfies the 'incapacity condition' or the claimant or their partner passes the 'disability condition'. (For those over 60 the disability premium is replaced by the higher pensioner premium.)

The 'incapacity condition' requires the claimant to have had an incapacity for work for a 28 week qualifying period. The 'disability condition' can be satisfied by the claimant or their partner being registered as blind, or receiving attendance allowance (or constant attendance allowance), disability living allowance, disability working allowance, invalidity benefit, or severe disablement allowance.

Severe disability premium can be awarded in addition to the disability premium for a claimant who lives on their own and who receives attendance allowance (or constant attendance allowance) or disability living allowance care component at the middle or higher rate and where no one receives invalid care allowance in respect of them. For a claimant who is one of a couple qualification for the severe disability premium depends upon both the claimant and partner receiving the above benefits. Where both are being cared for by someone who is receiving invalid care allowance the premium will not be paid.

2.12.2 The character of disability benefits

There is little doubt that the complexity of the benefit system for people who have a disability disadvantages a number of claimants. Currently the system is based on a number of individual benefits each designed to provide for a specific need. Some are contributory benefits, most are non-contributory. Income support and its disability premiums are means tested; other disability benefits are non-means tested. Invalid care allowance is paid to a carer whilst attendance allowance or disabled living allowance is paid to the disabled person. Entitlement to some benefits acts as a passport to others so that a claimant for invalid care allowance must be caring for someone who is receiving attendance allowance, constant attendance allowance or disability living allowance care component at the middle or higher rate; entitlement to the income support disability premiums depends, among other factors, on receipt of a 'qualifying benefit' which includes attendance allowance, disability living allowance and severe disablement allowance.

For many people who have a disability social security benefits provide their only source of income and it is argued by many commentators in the field that the current system of disability benefits is not the best means of providing adequate financial support for this group of claimants. It must also be remembered that the benefit system provides only financial support, other forms of support are available through the community care system.

Pressure groups working on behalf of people who have a disability have for some time been calling for a radical reform of the benefit system and specifically for the introduction of a unified and comprehensive disability benefit to be paid at a level which relates directly to a claimant's needs. These calls continue despite the introduction in 1992 of the disability living allowance and the disability working allowance.

3   THE LAW AND SOCIAL WORK PRACTICE: some issues for discussion

3.1   SOCIAL WORK AND THE SOCIAL FUND

There is no doubt that the introduction of income support and the social fund in 1988 has had a profound impact on the ability of many social work clients to 'make ends meet'.[3] Income support only provides a subsistence level of income and claimants faced with an extra item of expenditure, such as a new cooker, are forced to seek help from the social fund. The basis of a claim on the discretionary social fund is essentially a request for help; there is no legal entitlement. The nature of that help, if it is forthcoming, is likely to be in the form of a loan which must be repaid by deductions from weekly income support. If there is no money left in the budget or the claim is of a low priority then no loan will be made. If it is decided that the claimant cannot afford to pay the loan back then no loan will be made notwithstanding the degree of necessity for the item in question.

In such circumstances it is not surprising that a number of social work clients are turning to social services departments for claims that in the era of supplementary benefit and the single payments system, were obtainable by legal right from the Department of Social Security.

This tendency towards a shift of responsibility from state benefit to social services has been seen by a number of commentators as a quite deliberate policy decision by government. There is no doubt that the implications of the social fund for local authority social services departments were envisaged by government. Guidance to social fund officers refers specifically to the need to create close links with other agencies, particularly with social services departments. The guidance identifies issues for discussion between social fund officers and social workers, and others:

—   establishing priorities for awards after exchanging views with social workers about the relative priorities for grants and loans in the local area;

[3]   See 'The Social Fund: What's Wrong With It?' (1990) CPAG.

— identifying the responsibilities and priorities of social services departments;

— arranging contacts with social services departments;

— consulting social services departments about social fund applications, subject to the rules about confidentiality of both agencies. The guidance envisages joint visits and case conferences where appropriate;

— co-operation where social and financial problems are linked;

— discussing the system for the review of decisions.

The guidance makes it clear that the last three issues may also be discussed with other welfare rights and voluntary agencies involved with social fund claimants.

The social fund has been subject to substantial criticism from social services departments, and groups representing social workers see the establishment of the social fund as an attempt to transfer responsibility for a large number of poorer families and individuals from the Department of Social Security to social services; from central government to local government. As a result many social workers have seen co-operation with the fund as no part of their business.

Nonetheless the nature of the social fund and the position of many of those who are forced to seek help from it means that the availability of help in claiming or challenging a decision may be important. The British Association of Social Workers argues for a policy of determined advocacy which is designed to ensure that individual claimants are properly equipped to deal with the social fund and thereby maximise their claim on the fund.

The Disability Alliance has identified the need for claimants to be fully informed:

Different organisations may have some difference in emphasis, or in their philosophy, and may call their policy by different names, such as 'determined', or 'aggressive' advocacy, or the 'rights' approach. The central idea is that you (the claimant) must have the right to decide for yourself what course you wish to take. And to do that,

you need fully informed advice and information about the social
fund. Advisors who take this approach will not take on the role
of social fund officers and so will not make judgments or get drawn
into discussions about relative priorities between their clients.[4]

The seventeenth edition of their Handbook provides some
strategic advice to claimants:

* ask for all the help you need; an advisor should be ready
  to help you fill in the application form so that you can present
  your case in the most effective way;

* ask for a grant rather than a loan;

* if you are awarded a loan, try and negotiate the longest
  repayment period possible . . .;

* check to see if your need is specifically excluded from help
  in the directions, or if your situation excludes you from help;
  if you are not sure, go ahead and ask for help in any case;

* if you are refused help, 'appeal' through the review procedure;

* if you still don't get help, seek further advice.

Many social workers are increasingly finding that the social fund
fails to meet the needs of their customers and they are being
forced to turn to charities for help. In turn the Charity
Commissioners have issued a set of guidelines concerning the
social fund to the trustees of charities. The essence of the
guidelines is that whilst charities might properly supplement
help from the social fund charitable funds should not replace
such help. The Commissioners stress that those in need should
look to the social fund first for grants and/or loans before
approaching charities for help and that social fund officers should
only refer a claimant onto a charity for help having first sought
the advice of the charity. Charities should expect to help where
grants cannot be made and the social fund directions list those
things for which a loan or grant cannot be made. These include
an educational or training need (including clothing and tools),
the cost of respite care, medical, surgical, optical, aural or dental

---

[4] The Disability Alliance ERA 'Advice About the Social Fund' *Disability Rights
Handbook* (14th edn).

items or services and anything for which an application was made in the previous 26 weeks unless the circumstances have changed.

The discretionary nature of the social fund denies claimants any legal entitlement to a grant or loan. It also means that the decisions of social fund officers can only be reviewed, there is no right to appeal to an independent appeal body such as a Social Security Appeal Tribunal.

Because the social fund is cash limited the size of the annual budget is fundamental to the ability of the fund to meet the needs of claimants. Each local office is allocated a budget for grants and a budget for loans, and there is, in theory, some ability to transfer funds between offices and to supplement an office budget from a small contingency fund. In 1992/93 the budget was £302 million made up of £211 million for loans and £91 million for grants. In relation to grants, funds that are under spent in any one year will only go to reducing the exchequer contribution for the next year. Social fund officers are not allowed to make payments which exceed the office budget and they must have regard to the size of the budget when deciding to make a loan or grant.

In practice it seems that social fund officers are discouraged by budgetary limitations from making grants and loans. No application can be considered in isolation from its financial implications for the budget. Every grant or loan made reduces the budget for other grants and loans. Such a system encourages, indeed it is based on, parsimony with the result that claims, which social work and other voluntary agencies would understand as perfectly legitimate, are denied.

3.2   ENFORCING SOCIAL SECURITY RIGHTS

Entitlement to social security benefits (excluding the social fund) is based on the existence of legal rights provided for in statute and regulations. The decision of an adjudication officer can be appealed against to an independent Social Security Appeal Tribunal (SSAT).

Unfortunately the positive character of these statements is somewhat undermined by the complexity of most social security law and the unavailability of legal aid for representation before a SSAT or the Social Security Commissioners. Many claimants are discouraged from appealing because of the intimidating nature of the appeal process and those that do exercise their rights of appeal are often not able to make the best use of a tribunal hearing.

There are a number of possible practical responses to this situation for a social worker with a client who has had a claim denied or limited. It is to be hoped that social workers will have enough knowledge of the social security system to be able to 'spot a potential appeal' and if necessary refer the client to specialist advice and assistance. This may be available through a law centre or welfare rights agency or could be provided by a lawyer under the 'green form scheme'.

The legal aid scheme does not cover representation before Social Security Appeal Tribunals so that a social work client will be left very much to their own knowledge and skills unless a representative can be provided by one of the welfare or rights agencies, or by Citizens' Advice Bureaux. Advocacy before tribunals by social workers on behalf of their clients was often very effective in establishing an exceptional need or the risk of serious harm or serious damage to health in an appeal involving supplementary benefit and single payments. These issues are now dealt with (or not) by the social fund and there is less scope for effective advocacy based on establishing such characteristics. Nonetheless the experienced and knowledgeable social worker can provide important help and support for a client who is appearing in an income support appeal before a SSAT or a review with a social fund officer. The greater the social worker's knowledge and experience of the social security system the greater the help and support they can provide clients seeking to establish their legal right to social security benefits or the legitimacy of their request for a social fund grant or loan.

4   CASE STUDIES

The case studies in this section are designed to provide an introduction to working with a variety of benefit systems. As such they are relatively simple; however the methods needed are common to more complicated circumstances. It will be necessary to refer to current benefit rates, which are updated in April each year, and to one of the social security rights guides. Where appropriate an opportunity has been taken to include circumstances which require consideration of aspects of social work practice not concerned with social security benefits but which are of relevance for the claimants/clients portrayed in the problem.

1. Erica, who is 25, is a single mother with two children aged 4 and 8; they live in local authority accommodation. She has no savings and relies entirely on state benefits for her income.

What is her entitlement to income support ?

Explain how this figure was worked out.

2. Lloyd and Loretta are married and have two children aged 9 and 14. They live in local authority accommodation. Lloyd has been unemployed for 2 months and is claiming unemployment benefit. Loretta has a part-time job (12 hours per week) earning £35 net per week. Lloyd was paid £4500 in redundancy money when he became unemployed and this figure is in a building society account.

What is the family's entitlement to income support ?

Explain how this figure was worked out.

3. What benefits would the family be entitled to if Loretta were working full time earning £85 per week (net)?

4. George and Ethel are both 72 and receive the basic state pension. They have no savings. They live in a local authority house. Ethel has very bad arthritis and is unable to get up stairs to the bathroom any more or to walk to the shops which are at the end of the road. Their cooker is not working and they cannot afford to get it repaired or to replace it.

As a local authority social worker what steps would you take to provide them with suitable facilities in the flat?

What social security benefits are they entitled to?

5. Bill and Mary have been married for ten years and have two

children Andrew (7) and Michael (5). Andrew has severe learning difficulty; he has epilepsy and needs constant nursing and care. Bill works as a lorry driver and earns £120 per week (net). Mary does not work.

What social security benefits are the family entitled to ?

5a. What benefits would the family be entitled to if Bill had been involved in an accident while he was driving his lorry and had been off work for ten weeks?

5b. What benefits would the family be entitled to if Mary were a single mother?

5c. How would you, as a local authority social worker, respond to a request for help from the family?

What are the statutory responsibilities of the local authority in respect of this family, and what services and other help can be offered through the medium of social work?

5 ACTIVITIES

1. It is important to build up a good package of reference materials. The three major guides are the basic materials:

— *Disability Rights Handbook*. (Published by the Disability Alliance Educational and Research Association.)

— *Rights Guide to Non-Means Tested Benefits*. (Published by the Child Poverty Action Group (CPAG).)

— *National Welfare Benefits Handbook*. (Published by CPAG.)

Each of these guides is updated annually by the publication of a new edition in April. It is important to have the current edition.

Benefit rates are updated in April each year.

2. To supplement these basic materials it is worth identifying specialist social security advice for particular client groups. As

an example Age Concern publishes a number of fact sheets and briefing papers dealing with social security for older people.

See in particular:

Income Support.

The Social Fund.

Help with Heating.

3. Publication lists can be obtained from Age Concern, The Disability Alliance, CPAG and from other groups concerned with social security issues.

4. The Department of Employment and the Department of Social Security publish explanatory leaflets for all benefits. Many of these can be obtained free from post offices. For full publication lists write to the department concerned.

5. The Department of Social Security runs a freephone service which provides general benefits advice and information.

For England, Scotland and Wales the number is 0800 666 555.

For Northern Ireland the number is 0800 616757.

Advice in Urdu — 0800 289188;

Advice in Punjabi — 0800 521360;

Advice in Welsh — 0800 289011;

Advice in Cantonese — 0800 252451.

There is also a Benefits Enquiry Line for advice and a claim form completion service:

0800 882200.

6. It is important to know of local advice centres and other agencies who can provide social work clients with help on social security matters. This information can be investigated and

compiled in the form of a local directory which can be made available to clients and others.

The *Disability Rights Handbook* has an excellent section at the back of its guide which contains the names, addresses and phone numbers of pressure groups, law centres, advice centres, tribunal representation units and other agencies working in the social security field.

6 ADDRESSES

Child Poverty Action Group.
4th Floor,
1-5 Bath Street,
London EC1V 9PY.
Phone 071 253 3406.

Department of Employment,
Caxton House,
Tothill Street,
London SW1H 9NF.
Phone 071 273 6969.

Department of Social
Security,
Alexander Fleming House,
Elephant and Castle,
London SE1 6BY.
Phone 071 407 5522.

Department of Social
Security,
Leaflets Unit,
PO Box 21,
Stanmore,
Middlesex, HA7 1AY.

Disability Alliance
Educational and Research
Association,
Universal House,
88-94 Wentworth Street,
London E1 7SA.
Phone 071 247 8776.

7 MATERIALS

7.1 BASIC MATERIALS FOR ORDINARY SOCIAL WORK PRACTICE

Disability Rights Handbook (New edition each April.) Disability Alliance Educational and Research Association.

National Welfare Benefits Handbook (New edition each April.)
Child Poverty Action Group.

Rights Guide to Non-Means Tested Benefits (New edition each
April.) Child Poverty Action Group.

'Social Security benefit rates'. Leaflet NI 196. Department of
Social Security.

'Which benefit? A guide to the social security and NHS benefits
you can claim'. Leaflet FB 2. Department of Social Security.

Keeping up to date on social security matters is a major problem.
The following are bulletins which are published regularly and
aim to provide up dated information:

'Welfare Rights Bulletin'. Published bi-monthly by the Child
Poverty Action Group's Citizens' Rights Office.

'Disability Rights Bulletin'. Published 4 times a year by the
Disability Alliance.

'The Adviser'. Published by Wolverhampton — NACAB
Specialist Support Unit (63 Waterloo Road, Wolverhampton,
WV1 4QU. Phone 0902 310568.)

7.2   FURTHER READING

Mesher, J. *Income Support, The Social Fund and Family Credit:
The Legislation* Sweet and Maxwell (Annual editions and
supplements).

Bonner, D., Hooker, I., Smith, P., White, R. *Non-Means Tested
Benefits: The Legislation* Sweet and Maxwell (Annual editions
and supplements).

Ogus, A. I., Barendt, E. M. *The Law of Social Security* (3rd
edn 1988) Butterworths.

APRIL 1993 UPRATING

MEANS-TESTED BENEFITS

Income Support

Personal Allowances
Single

under age 18*	£26.45/£34.80
aged 18-24	£34.80
aged 25 and over	44.00

lone parent

under age 18*	£26.45/£34.80
aged 18 and over	£44.00

couple

both under age 18*	£52.40
at least one aged 18 or over*	£69.00

dependent children

Under age 11	£15.50
aged 11-15	£22.15
aged 16-17*	£26.45
aged 18	£34.80

Premiums

family	£9.65
lone parent	£4.90

pensioner

single	£17.30
couple	£26.25

enhanced pensioner

single	£19.30
couple	£29.00

higher pensioner

single	£23.55
couple	£33.70

disability

single	£18.45
couple	£26.45

severe disability

single	£33.70
couple (one qualifies)	£33.70
couple (both qualify)	£67.40

disabled child	£18.45
carer	£11.95

* for eligibility of under-18s and calculating amounts, see CPAG's *National Welfare Benefits Handbook*.

Housing costs — deductions for non-dependants

aged 18, or over, and in remunerative work

gross income: £70 to £104.99	£8.00
gross income: £105 to £134.99	£12.00
gross income: £135 or more	£21.00

others, aged 18 or over and not in work or earning less than £70, or on income support and over 25	£4.00
aged 16-17, or 18-24 and single and on IS, in receipt of YT allowance	nil

Allowances for personal expenses

residential and nursing homes	£12.65

dependent children

under age 11	£5.20
aged 11-15	£7.60
aged 16-17	£8.80
aged 18	£12.65

local authority — Part III accommodation	£11.20

hospital

higher rate	£14.05
lower rate	£11.20

Maximum board and lodging allowances

residential care homes

old age	£185.00
very dependent elderly	£215.00
mental illness	£195.00
drug/alcohol dependence	195.00
mental handicap	£225.00

physical disablement

under pension age	£255.00
over pension age	£185.00
other	£185.00

Greater London maximum increase	£25.00
nursing homes	
mental illness	£280.00
drug/alcohol dependence	£280.00
mental handicap	£285.00
terminal illness	£280.00
physical disablement	
under pension age	£315.00
over pension age	£280.00
other	£280.00
Greater London maximum increase	£35.00

Deductions for child maintenance £2.20

Deductions for arrears of Community Charge

single	£2.20
couple	£3.45

Deductions for arrears of Council Tax £2.20

Deductions for direct payment of fuel debt

5% rate £2.20

Deductions for direct payment of housing

costs arrears £2.20

Deductions for direct payment of water rates arrears £2.20

Deductions for recovery of fines £2.20

Deduction in benefit for strikers £23.50

Disregards

standard earnings	£5.00
higher earnings	£15.00
war pensions	£10.00
voluntary and charitable payments	£10.00

student loan	£10.00
student's covenanted income	£5.00
income from boarders	£20.00
	(plus 5% of the balance of the charge)

Expenses for sub-tenants

furnished or unfurnished	£4.00
where heating is included	£8.60

Capital limit

disregarded	£3,000
tariff income on capital between £3,000 and £8,000 — £1 for every £250 or part thereof	
upper limit	£8,000
child's limit	£3,000
Maternity expenses payment	£100

Housing benefit

Applicable amounts, ie, personal allowances and premiums as for income support except

single person aged 16-24	£34.80
lone parent under 18	£34.80
lone parent premium	£10.95

Amenity deductions

heating	£8.60
hot water	£1.05
lighting	£0.70
cooking	£1.05
all fuel	£11.40

Meals deductions

full board	
each person aged 16 or over	£15.75
each child under 16	£7.95
half board	
each person aged 16 or over	£10.45
each child over 16	£5.25

breakfast only
each person (including
children) £1.90

Non-dependant deductions As for IS
housing costs

Earnings disregard

where disability premium
awarded £15.00

specified employments £15.00

lone parent — not in receipt
of IS £25.00

where the claimant has a
partner £10.00

single claimant £5.00

where carer premium
awarded £15.00

Other income disregards

maintenance £15.00

charitable or voluntary
payments £10.00

war pensions £10.00

student loan £10.00

student's covenanted income £5.00

income from boarders £20.00
(plus 50% of the
balance of the charge)

Expenses for sub-tenants As for IS

Capital limit

disregarded £3,000

tariff income on capital
between £3,000 and £16,000
— £1 for every £250 or part
thereof
upper limit £16,000
child's limit £3,000

Council tax benefit

Personal allowances and premiums

As for HB except that
personal allowances are not
payable for young people
aged 16 and 17

Non-dependant deductions

aged 18 or over, and in
remunerative work
gross income: less than
£105 £1.00
gross income: £105 or
more £2.00
others, aged 18 or over £1.00

Alternative maximum council tax benefit

second adult on IS 25%
second adult's gross income
up to £105 15%
£105.01 to £135 7.5%

Capital disregards and tariff income As for HB

Earnings and other disregards As for HB

Family credit

adult credit £42.50
child credit
under age 11 £10.75
age 11–15 £17.85
age 16–17 £22.20
age 18 £31.00

Capital and tariff income As for IS

Disregards

As for HB, except no
earnings disregards

Expenses for sub-tenants   As for IS

**Applicable amount (ie, taper
threshold level)**   £69.00

Disability working allowance

Adult allowance

Single people   £43.95

couples/lone parents   £60.95

**Applicable amount (ie, taper
threshold)**

single people   £41.40

couples/lone parents   £69.00

Capital and tariff income

As for FC, except
    upper limit   £16,000

**Child allowances and
disregards**   As for FC

APRIL 1993 UPRATING

NON-MEANS-TESTED BENEFITS

Attendance allowance

higher rate	£44.90
lower rate	£30.00

Child addition to widow's, invalidity and retirement pensions, widowed mother's allowance, invalid care allowance and severe disablement allowance and unemployment and sickness benefits where claimant is over pension age £10.95*

Child benefit

only, elder or eldest child	£10.00
each subsequent child	£8.10

Disability living allowance

care component

higher	£44.90
middle	£30.00
lower	£11.95

mobility component

higher	£31.40
lower	£11.95

Earnings rules

Invalid care allowance	£50.00
Unemployment benefit (daily rate)	£2.00
Therapeutic earnings limit	£42.00

Guardian's allowance/child's special allowance £10.95*

Industrial injuries benefits:

Disablement benefit (100% assessment)	£91.50
Reduced earnings allowance (maximum)	£36.64

* This is reduced by £1.15 for any child for whom you receive the higher rate of child benefit.

Invalid care allowance	£33.70
increase of invalid care allowance for adult dependant	£20.15

Invalidity benefit

standard rate of invalidity pension	£56.10
adult dependant	£33.70

Invalidity allowance

higher rate	£11.95
middle rate	£7.50
lower rate	£3.75

Maternity allowance	£43.75
One parent benefit	£6.05

Retirement and widow's pension and widowed mother's allowance

single person	£56.10
wife or adult dependant	£33.70

Severe disablement allowance	£33.70
adult dependant	£20.15

age-related addition

higher rate	£11.95
middle rate	£7.50
lower rate	£3.75

Sickness benefit

Beneficiary under pension age

single person	£42.70
wife or other adult dependant	£26.40

Beneficiary over pension age

single person	£53.80
wife or other adult dependant	£32.30

Statutory maternity pay
(standard rate)   £47.95

Statutory sick pay

lower rate (earnings £56 to
£194.99 a week)   £46.95

standard rate (earnings
more than £195 a week, no
change)   £52.50

Unemployment benefit

Beneficiary under pension
age
   single person   £44.65
   wife or other adult
   dependant   £27.55

Beneficiary over pension
age
   single person   £56.10
   wife or other adult
   dependant   £33.70

CHAPTER 12

Race

1 INTRODUCTION

Social workers have to confront the issue of race in many different ways. At the personal level Afro-Caribbean and Asian social workers will come to their practice with personal experiences of life in a society which discriminates against them. White social workers will have Afro-Caribbean and Asian clients and must be sensitive to the differences in life experience and expectations that are determined in part by race and ethnicity.

A number of institutions and agencies dealing with social work clients including social services departments, the police, the probation service, the criminal justice system, and local government housing departments have been accused of incidents of racism. Indeed some commentators have accused both the police and the criminal justice system of being institutionally racist.

Government has provided legislative statements which are 'anti racist' in their language and an agency, the Commission for Racial Equality (CRE), which is responsible for improving race relations and taking action against racial discrimination. Despite this official response to racism many social workers and many of their clients experience aspects of society as racist. The Policy Studies Institute in its third survey 'Black and White Britain', published in 1984, found that people who are Afro-Caribbean and Asian disproportionately live in bad housing, have low paid jobs, receive poor health care and inadequate education, are more heavily policed and are over-represented in the prison population. Subsequent research and comment has done nothing to counteract the results of this survey. Indeed the CRE has recently called for a strengthening and extention of the Race Relations Act 1976 to improve its effectiveness in combating racism and its effects.

Additionally the nationality laws and the administration of the immigration service seem to those who experience them, and to many commentators, to be designed to discriminate against non-white immigrants and in particular against applicants from the Indian subcontinent.[1]

Social workers have to practise within such a structure and environment and though the law has a poor record in the battle against racism and in responding to individual incidents of discrimination, some understanding of its basis and character and an assessment of its utility will be useful to all social workers.

The concern of social work about the issue of race includes the important aspects of how discrimination is experienced by ordinary members of society, as well as the experience specifically as a social work client, for example an offender sentenced to a probation order.

The law of race relations concerns itself with the incidence of discrimination and racial hatred in the population as a whole and as a result it contains no statutory duties or provisions which specifically determine social work practice. However, other legislation is beginning to impose statutory duties which have an impact on social work practice; section 95 of the Criminal Justice Act 1991 requires those involved in the administration of criminal justice to avoid discrimination. Such issues are now also covered in official guidance such as the National Standards for the Supervision of Offenders in the Community which specifies the need for anti-discriminatory practice.

This chapter will provide only a very brief outline of the law. However in recognition of the impact of discrimination experienced by many social work clients there will be a longer discussion in the social work law and practice section.

---

[1] See the following publications by the Runnymede Trust: Gordon, P. and Klug, F. *British Immigration Control: A Brief Guide* (1985); Sondhi, R. *Divided Families: British Immigration Control in the Indian Subcontinent* (1987); Gordon, P. Fortress Europe? The meaning of 1992. (1989).

2 THE LAW

2.1 THE STRUCTURE

The Race Relations Act 1976 established the Commission for
Racial Equality (which replaced the Race Relations Board and
the Community Relations Commission) and charged it with the
objective of working towards the elimination of racial
discrimination, promoting equality of opportunity and keeping
the working of the equality laws under review.

The Act also defined a criminal offence of incitement to racial
hatred, with a variety of offences now being contained in the
Public Order Act 1986.

A definition of racial discrimination was provided by the Race
Relations Act to cover both direct and indirect discrimination.
Direct discrimination has been defined as 'treating one person
less favourably than another on grounds of colour, race, ethnic
or natural origin, in the provision of goods, facilities and services,
employment, housing, and advertising'. Indirect discrimination
can be understood as discrimination by the imposition of certain
conditions which can be met by more people of one colour, race,
ethnic or natural origin than another so long as it is unjustifiable.

A person who has been discriminated against can take an
individual civil action against the discriminator in the
appropriate forum. In employment matters this will be an
industrial tribunal; for discrimination in other circumstances a
county court action is available.

The Commission also has investigative and enforcement powers
which can be used against discriminators.

2.2 LOCAL AUTHORITY DUTIES

Section 71 of the Act requires local authorities:

... to make appropriate arrangements with a view to securing
that their various functions are carried out with due regard to the
need —

a) to eliminate unlawful racial discrimination; and

b)   to promote equality of opportunity, and good relations, between persons of different racial groups.

2.3   THE CRIMINAL LAW

The law in relation to the generic criminal offence of incitement to racial hatred is now contained in six offences specified by the Public Order Act 1986. The two major offences are established in sections 18 and 19.

Under section 18 (use of words and gestures) a person is guilty of an offence if:

a)   he uses threatening, abusive or insulting words or behaviour, or

b)   he displays any written material which is threatening, abusive or insulting, and

c)   either he intends thereby to stir up racial hatred, or

d)   having regard to all the circumstances racial hatred is likely to be stirred up thereby, and he intended his words or behaviour or the written material to be, or was aware that they might be, threatening, abusive or insulting.

Under section 19 (publishing or distributing written material) a person is guilty of an offence if:

a)   he publishes or distributes written material, and

b)   the written material is threatening, abusive or insulting, and

c)   either he intends thereby to stir up racial hatred or having regard to all the circumstances racial hatred is likely to be stirred up thereby.

'Racial hatred' is defined by section 17 to mean 'hatred against a group of persons in Great Britain defined by reference to colour, race, nationality (including citizenship) or ethnic or national origins'.[2]

---

[2] For further discussion on this definition and generally on the racial hatred offences see Thornton, P. *Public Order Law* Chapter 4 (Financial Training). 1987.

The other criminal offences cover stirring up racial hatred by the public performance of a play, through sound or visual recordings, broadcasting, and the possession of racially inflammatory material.

The utility of the criminal law as a weapon against racial hatred is severely limited by the requirement that the Attorney-General consent to a criminal prosecution. Between 1965 and 1973 (under the old law) only seven prosecutions against fifteen people were brought. It seems that successive Attorneys-General have taken the view that such prosecutions do nothing to improve race relations and there is no evidence that under the 1986 Act this view has changed.[3]

2.4   CIVIL ACTIONS BASED ON ALLEGATIONS OF RACIAL DISCRIMINATION

Direct and indirect discrimination in the fields of housing, employment, education and in the provision of goods, services and facilities to the public is unlawful.

In employment matters the person who is alleging discrimination may make a complaint to an industrial tribunal which may award compensation in the same way that a civil court may award damages. Complaints about racial discrimination in other areas can be taken by way of a civil action for damages in the county court.

By definition complaints by an individual to an industrial tribunal or a civil action for damages are taken largely to secure compensation and prevent the continuation of discrimination against an individual. Where discrimination operates to disadvantage a large group of people such individual actions may not be an effective response unless taken as a test case.

2.5   THE POWERS OF THE COMMISSION FOR RACIAL EQUALITY TO COMBAT RACIAL DISCRIMINATION

The Commission has powers under the Race Relations Act to conduct formal investigations and to issue non-discrimination

[3] See Dexter Dias, J. 'A Licence to Hate: Incitement to Racial Hatred and the Public Order Act 1986' (1987/88) 4 Socialist Lawyer (winter).

notices. Such notices, which may be served where the Commission thinks that the Race Relations Act is being broken, can be enforced if necessary through an application by the Commission to the courts for an injunction.

A number of court decisions have led some commentators to conclude that the courts are hostile to the powers granted to the Commission for carrying out formal investigations. Some judicial decisions have tended to emphasise the rights of the person or body under investigation rather than the objectives of the Race Relations Act and the duties of the Commission.[4]

The restrictions imposed by the courts on formal investigations highlight the limitations of the individual response to discrimination outlined above. Though the Commission can give assistance to an individual taking legal action, and can provide conciliation services, the individuality of such actions restricts their impact on established discriminatory practices and on institutional racism.

Despite these problems the Commission has continued to undertake formal investigations, sometimes with the voluntary co-operation of the body concerned and in its annual reports the Commission has highlighted how such investigations can help in identifying indirect discrimination in particular and how they can initiate a positive response from the body concerned such as happened in Hackney and Liverpool after investigations into the allocation of council housing.

3 SOCIAL WORK LAW AND PRACTICE: some issues for discussion

3.1 RACIAL DISCRIMINATION IN THE ALLOCATION OF COUNCIL HOUSING AND THE PROVISION OF ACCOMMODATION FOR THE HOMELESS

There is concern that the system operated by some local authorities for the allocation of council housing works to

[4] For a discussion of the decisions in the House of Lords and in general on anti-discriminatory legislation see Carty, H. 'Formal Investigations and the Efficacy of Anti-discriminatory Legislation' (July 1986) Journal of Social Welfare Law 207–214.

discriminate against people who are Afro-Caribbean or Asian. Similar criticisms are made of the way some local authorities undertake their duties to the homeless under Part III of the Housing Act 1985. These criticisms are of particular concern to social work because many Afro-Caribbean and Asian customers are either on local authority housing lists or are homeless or threatened with homelessness.

One London borough has been criticised by the Commission for Racial Equality in the report of its investigation into its housing policy as it affected the Bangladeshi community.[5] The report considered the council's housing allocation policy and the way in which it interpreted the criteria of intentional homelessness to include a person who had left family and accommodation in Bangladesh, when deciding on an application for accommodation under the homelessness legislation.

The Commission has produced evidence to support the claim that in the allocation of council accommodation Afro-Caribbean and Asian people are discriminated against and that accommodation made available to them is often of a very low standard and often on problem estates.[6] Many social workers will know that racism is well established on some council estates and that Asian and Afro-Caribbean tenants are subjected to abuse and other forms of racial hatred.[7]

A number of local authorities have included anti-harassment clauses in their tenancy agreements so that the council may seek a possession order against tenants who have been involved in racist behaviour against other ethnic community tenants on the basis that they have breached their tenancy agreement. One of the grounds for possession under the Housing Act 1985 is that the tenant is 'guilty' of conduct which is a nuisance or annoyance to neighbours and a number of local authorities have sought to evict tenants who have racially abused or harassed Afro-Caribbean and Asian tenants on this ground.

Local authorities who use these provisions to evict racist tenants

5 'Homelessness and Discrimination. Tower Hamlets'. Commission for Racial Equality CRE.
6 See 'Out of Order: Report of a formal investigation into the London Borough of Southwark'. (1990) CRE.
7 See 'Living in Terror', a report of racial violence and harassment in housing (1987) CRE.

may well experience something of a 'Catch 22' situation. Tenants evicted on such grounds are themselves homeless and though they may be considered to be intentionally homeless the council may well have to provide them with temporary accommodation if they have a priority need. If such a need is based on the family having children the authority also has other statutory duties in relation to the children under the Children Act 1989. These duties may include the provision of services for families with children in need and are not discharged only by providing the family with bed and breakfast accommodation or other council accommodation.

Social workers working for the social services department of a local authority which appears to be operating racist housing policies are in a difficult personal and professional dilemma which it is not easy to resolve. It is probably not the place of the individual social worker to tackle the issue by exposing the racism of the council's housing policies, indeed such a course of action may constitute a breach of their obligations as an employee. Working within such policies to the benefit of their own clients whilst identifying and complaining about racism in housing policy through the established hierarchy and procedures of the social services department may be the only way forward. Clients are of course free to take the issue up with the Commission or articulate complaints through other independent channels.

3.2 A RACIST CRIMINAL JUSTICE SYSTEM?

> We know that all British institutions operate in a racist way and it is no surprise to find that the criminal justice system does so also. If you examine this context you would immediately see why you have the gross disparity in the number of black people in the prison population and the treatment meted out to them in the courts. (Vivien Stern, Director of the National Association for the Care and Resettlement of Offenders.)

There are a number of stages or divisions within the criminal justice system and it is possible to establish for each stage how the system may discriminate against Afro-Caribbean and Asian people. The stages can be identified as:

— policing policy;

— individual discretion;

— arrest, charge and bail;

— in court;

— sentencing, including probation and prison.

Some analysis of the ethnic origins of the magistracy and the judiciary is also necessary.

3.2.1 Policing policy

There is little doubt that the police have developed particular policing policies for different events, areas and communities. The impact of such policies can be considerable and it has been suggested that the policing methods for areas and communities defined by the police as sensitive or difficult may be part of a complex 'chain of causation' leading to civil disorder such as occurred in Brixton and on the Broadwater Farm estate in North London.

3.2.2 Individual police discretion

Individual police officers have a substantial amount of discretion in how they react to the situations and circumstances they face 'on the street'. The decision to stop and question; to warn rather than arrest are, in practice, within the discretion of individual police officers. The choices they make can be influenced and possibly determined by racial stereotyping and other assumptions concerning race and ethnicity.

NACRO claims that 'There is some evidence to suggest that a disproportionate number of young black males are stopped by the police, and that black juveniles are less likely to be cautioned and more likely to be prosecuted than comparable white juveniles.'[8]

[8] 'Some Facts and Findings About Black People in the Criminal Justice System'. NACRO Briefing Paper No 77. May 1989.

3.2.3   Arrest, charge and bail

The evidence gathered by NACRO supports the assertion that black people are more likely to be arrested and charged with criminal offences than whites. This is particularly the case in respect of the decision to caution rather than charge. The Home Office Statistical Bulletin 6/89 reveals that black defendants are more likely to be refused bail by the courts and remanded in custody than white defendants.

From Home Office figures NACRO is also able to conclude in their Bulletin No 77 that 'A higher proportion of the black defendants remanded in custody are subsequently acquitted than white defendants, suggesting that black people may be more likely to be inappropriately remanded in custody.'

The Home Office publication 'Race and the Criminal Justice System', published in 1992 under the provisons of section 95 of the Criminal Justice Act, confirms many of the conclusions drawn by NACRO in particular that 'Afro-Caribbeans are significantly more likely than whites to be stopped by the police'.[9]

3.2.4   The courts

There are conflicting research findings concerning the experience of black defendants in the criminal courts, but any observer of the magistrates' courts or of the Crown Courts will appreciate that the criminal court is an overwhelmingly 'white institution' and experience.

NACRO, in its Bulletin No 77, refers to two studies reported in the early 1980s which found no evidence of systematic bias on racial grounds in the Crown Courts. However, studies in Hackney by the Commission for Racial Equality and in Croydon by the South East London Probation Service show quite different results. White defendants were more likely to be acquitted when pleading not guilty and black young people were nearly twice as likely to receive a custodial sentence and were grossly over represented in youth custody centres (now young offender institutions). 'Race and the Criminal Justice System' (Home Office 1992) identifies the fact that Afro-Carribeans are more likely than whites to be remanded in custody.

[9] See Skogan, W. 'British Crime Survey'. (1990).

The percentage of magistrates who are Black or Asian is around 2% though the Lord Chancellor's Department has acknowledged the importance of recruiting more Black and Asian magistrates. The number of judges who are Black or Asian is negligible.

3.2.5 Sentencing

There is very little evidence available about the racial pattern of non-custodial sentencing. Statistical information mainly relates to custodial sentencing.

> Between 1986 and 1990 the proportion of sentenced prisoners who came from ethnic minorities rose every year. However it fell slightly in 1991. Afro-Caribbeans in particular are very heavily over represented in prison. In 1986 they made up 8% of sentenced male prisoners and 12% of sentenced female prisoners. By 1990 these figures had increased to 10% for males and 24% for females. This apparently dramatic rise for women may be accounted for by an increase in those convicted of drug smuggling, many of whom are foreign nationals.[10]

Recent research undertaken by Dr Roger Hood, for the Commission for Racial Equality, investigated the sentencing of Crown Court judges in the West Midlands. The report identifies that black males had a 17% greater chance of going to jail than whites, while Asians were 18% less likely to be imprisoned.[11]

Research carried out by the West Yorkshire Probation Service has found that Afro-Caribbean and Asian offenders are more likely to receive custodial sentences or fines and are less likely to be placed on probation or given a community service order than white offenders. Such a finding provides some evidence for the contention that ethnic minority offenders are discriminated against by a reluctance of the courts to use supervisory sentences for them. This reluctance may of course stem from the nature of recommendations in social inquiry reports (now proposals in pre-sentence reports) on offenders who are Afro-Caribbean or Asian.

The NACRO report 'Black People and the Criminal Justice System' found indications that probation officers are less likely

[10] 'Race and the Criminal Justice System' (Home Office 1992).
[11] 'A Question of Judgement' (1993) CRE.

to recommend supervision in the community in social inquiry reports on black offenders. This makes it more likely that black offenders will receive a custodial sentence. The report puts this down to individual officers having a lack of confidence in their ability to carry out successful probation supervision. This may reflect the poor recruitment figures for black officers in the probation service. Only about 2% of officers are black.

The disproportionate number of black prisoners is also commented on in the NACRO report which goes on to commend the prison service for its commitment to good race relations. 'The framework, structures and commitment exist to ensure the provision of a fair and non-discriminatory regime to the large numbers of prisoners for which the prison system is responsible.' However the report goes on to make it clear that such commitment must be translated through individual prison officers into the every day experience of black prisoners.

3.2.6   The Criminal Justice Act 1991

Section 95(1)(b) of the Act provides:

(1)   The Secretary of State shall in each year publish such information as he considers expedient for the purpose of —

b)   facilitating the performance by such persons of their duty to avoid discriminating against any persons on the ground of race or sex or any other improper ground.

'Race and the Criminal Justice System', Home Office, 1992, is one of the first publications under this section and in his foreword the Home Secretary, Kenneth Clarke, states 'It is vital that management practices and criminal justice processes are, and are seen to be, devoid of any improper discrimination.'

Social work and probation practitioners working in the criminal justice system now have a clear statutory duty to work within an anti-discriminatory model of practice. Equally important is the impact of this duty on the other agencies of the criminal justice system; all are now accountable to this standard. It is to be hoped that, despite the absence of specific enforcement powers, this duty becomes more than statutory rhetoric.

3.2.7 National Standards

The National Standards for the Supervision of Offenders in the Community, issued by the Home Office, have a clear equal opportunities statement in their introduction.

> The work of probation services and social services departments must be free of discrimination on the ground of race, gender, age, disability, language ability, literacy, religion, sexual orientation or any other improper ground ... effective anti-discriminatory practice is essential to avoid further disadvantaging those already most disillusioned and disadvantaged in society.

This statement is backed up by particular specifications:

> All services must have a stated equal opportunities policy and ensure that this is effectively monitored and reviewed. Effective action to prevent discrimination (anti-discriminatory practice) requires significantly more than a willingness to accept all offenders equally or to invest an equal amount of time and effort in different cases. The origin, nature and extent of differences in circumstances and need must be properly understood and actively addressed by all concerned — for example, by staff training, by monitoring and review and by making an extra effort to understand and work most effectively with an offender from a different cultural background.

3.2.8 The Judiciary

The Judicial Studies Board has established an Ethnic Minorities' Advisory Board to take forward judicial training in the area of race relations. In the introduction to its first report the Committee outlines familiar demographic material that discloses discrimination against the Asian and Afro-Caribbean communities in this country. It acknowledges allegations of bias and racism and comments that these 'co-exist unhappily with a judiciary and a magistracy which maintain that they are doing everything possible to be fair and to deal evenly with all who come before the criminal courts'.

The Committee outlines its training objectives and describes a prime objective in the following terms:

> The prime objective of this training is to raise the awareness of all who sit in any form of judicial capacity in courts or tribunals of

the need to demonstrate that the judicial system must be culturally and racially neutral, and to show them how injustice may result from culturally based errors or misconceptions or misunderstandings.

4 CASE STUDIES

This chapter provides only a brief introduction to the law in respect of racial discrimination and as a result the case studies do not address the complexity of the law as it is encountered in, for example, employment or housing disputes. (Clients involved in such disputes should be advised to seek specialist legal help, possibly through the offices of the CRE.) Consequently these case studies provide no more than a starting point for a discussion of some of the issues raised in this chapter.

1.   Hassan is unemployed and sees an advert in the paper for a job as a packer. He rings the phone number and when he gives them his name he is told that the job is filled. He knows that the company needs lots of packers and so he gets his friend Alan to ring. Alan is asked to attend for an interview and is offered a job.

What can Hassan do?

2.   Michael and Chantelle are a black couple who have recently moved onto a local authority housing estate. Ever since they moved into the house their neighbours have been rude and abusive towards them. Recently this abuse has become racist and their garden fence has also been daubed with obscene and racist slogans.

Chantelle is frightened and wants to know how she can stop it.

3.   Sharmina is a staff nurse in the local hospital. She is very well qualified and has been on a number of training courses. Her annual assessments are always good and she is well thought of in her hospital. She has applied for promotion on a number of occasions but has never been shortlisted or interviewed. A number of more junior nurses have recently been promoted over her and Sharmina has noticed that they are all white. When she asked the personnel officer why she wasn't considered she

was told that she wasn't sufficiently well qualified or experienced for promotion.

How would you advise Sharmina?

4.   Hanif has been arrested on a theft charge. While he was being questioned at the police station he was racially insulted by two police officers. He was kept in custody overnight and when he appeared in court the next morning he asked the magistrates whether he could see the duty solicitor. The chairman of the bench refused and when Hanif asked for bail the chairman said 'oh no; not for your sort.'

You are the probation officer on court duty and you saw what went on in the court. You speak to Hanif in the cells who tells you about his experiences in the police station. What are you going to do?

5.   Robinson, who was born in Barbados but came to Britain at the age of three, has just graduated with a very good English degree. He wants to be a journalist and he sees an advert in his local paper for trainee journalists. The advert asks for graduates in English but also specifies that applicants must be 'native born English speakers'.

Robinson applies for an interview and states on his form that he was born in Barbados. He receives a letter 3 weeks later which tells him that the post has been filled.

What can he do?

5   ACTIVITIES

1.   Get hold of the CRE's extensive publications list. They produce a large number of free booklets and leaflets some of which are of particular interest to social workers and can be used to build up a good set of appropriate materials and references.

2.   Publications lists are also available from pressure groups working in the area of race relations including the Civil Liberties

Trust, the Institute of Race Relations and the Runnymede Trust. (See the addresses section.)

3.   Try to establish how particular social work agencies are dealing with the race relations context of their work. What systems are in place to promote racial equality in the provision of social work services and within the agency itself?

4.   This information will be particularly important in respect of local authority housing departments. As an example: will the local authority take possession proceedings against tenants on the basis that they are involved in racially abusing or harassing other tenants?

5.   If a client needs advice concerning race relations where can they go for specialist help? Identify the agencies who can help, eg the law centre, the CRE, race relations advisors, trade unions.

6.   Is race relations information available for clients in other languages? If not who can help with interviewing, form filling, translations and interpreting?

7.   Try to establish what training is available for social workers in the field of race relations.

8.   Do the local police have a community relations section? Find out what sort of work they are involved in.

9.   For information and advice on all aspects of immigration and nationality contact the Joint Council for the Welfare of Immigrants (see addresses section).

10.   Advice on the employment aspects of race relations legislation can be obtained from the CRE and the Advisory, Conciliation and Arbitration Service (ACAS) (see addresses section), and the Race Relations Employment Advisory Service of the Department of Employment.

11.   Get hold of the list of local Community Relations Councils from the CRE and get in touch with your local council.

6 ADDRESSES

Advisory, Conciliation and
Arbitration Service,
Clifton House,
83-117 Euston Road,
London NW1 2RB.
Phone 071 388 5100.

Commission for Racial
Equality,
Elliot House,
10/12 Allington Street,
London SW1E 5EH.
Phone 071 828 7022.
The Commission has regional
offices in Birmingham (phone
021 632 4544), Manchester
(phone 061 831 7782/8),
Leicester (phone 0533 517852)
and Leeds (phone 0532 434413).

Civil Liberties Trust,
21 Tabard Street,
London SE1 4LA.
Phone 071 403 3888.

Institute of Race Relations,
2/6 Leeke Street,
London WC1X 9HS.
Phone 071 837 0041.

Joint Council for the Welfare
of Immigrants,
115 Old Street,
London EC1 9JR.
Phone 071 251 8706.

Runnymede Trust,
11 Princelet Street,
London E1 6QH.
Phone 071 375 1496.

7 MATERIALS

7.1 BASIC MATERIALS FOR ORDINARY SOCIAL WORK PRACTICE

Gordon, P. Wright, J. Hewitt, P. *Race Relations Rights* (1985)
National Council for Civil Liberties.

'Racial Discrimination: A Guide to the Race Relations Act, 1976'
Home Office HMSO.

'Race and Criminal Justice. Briefing Paper' NACRO (January
1991.)

'The Public Order Act' Liberty Briefing (1987).

'Working with Black Youth' CRE.

'Your Rights to Equal Treatment under the Race Relations Act

1976'. A series of leaflets on employment, housing, education and service provision; and a general guide. CRE.

7.2   FURTHER READING

Dominelli, L. *Anti-Racist Social Work: A Challenge for White Practitioners and Educators* (1988) BASW Practical Social Work Series, Macmillan Education.

'A Question of Judgement' (1993) Commission for Racial Equality.

'Black Communities and the Probation Service: Working Together for Change' (1991) NACRO.

'Black People, Mental Health and the Courts' (1991) NACRO.

Shallice, A. Gordon, P. *Black People, White Justice? Race and the Criminal Justice System* (1990) Runnymede Trust.

'Children in Care' (1983) CRE's Submission to the House of Commons Social Services Select Committee Inquiry into Children in Care.

'Code of Practice in Rented Housing: For the elimination of racial discrimination and the promotion of equal opportunities' (1991) CRE.

'Race and the Criminal Justice System' (1992) Home Office.

Racial and Ethnic Relations in Britain: Past, Present and Future 'New Community' Vol 14, No 1/2 (Autumn 1987) CRE.

'Tackling Racial Violence and Harassment in Local Authority Housing: A Guide to good practice for local authorities' (1989) HMSO.

CHAPTER 13

Housing rights

1 INTRODUCTION

Problems with housing affect a large number of social work clients and though housing law is a specialist area of legal practice an understanding of the basic principles and provisions will help social workers in their efforts to see that clients' housing rights are protected and enforced where necessary.

Though social workers have no statutory rights or duties in the housing field their involvement with housing problems on behalf of clients is often considerable and for the purposes of this chapter can be identified as including the following issues:

— homelessness;

— repairs to dwellings;

— security of tenure;

— harassment and eviction;

— housing benefit.

1.1 HOMELESSNESS

Homelessness is an increasing problem and local authorities have statutory duties under the Housing Act 1985 and the Children Act 1989 to provide, in particular circumstances, accommodation for people who are homeless. This duty is undertaken by housing authorities and a number of local authorities have specialist social workers based in homeless persons units. Social work case loads may include families who are homeless and living in bed and breakfast accommodation; such clients may need social work support and it may be that the problems faced by clients with children living in such circumstances warrant help and support under Part III and Schedule 2 of the Children Act 1989.

1.2   REPAIRS

The condition of much of both public and private rented housing accommodation is poor and tenants often need help in encouraging and persuading landlords to meet their obligations in respect of repairs. The social worker who has a basic understanding of the relevant legal rights of their clients in this area will be able to identify when the law can be used to secure appropriate housing rights and be able if necessary to refer a client to specialist legal help.

1.3   SECURITY OF TENURE AND PREVENTING HARASSMENT AND UNLAWFUL EVICTIONS

For a number of social work clients security of tenure is an important aspect of their housing rights. Again this is a specialist area of housing law expertise but the ability to recognise a problem and provide elementary but informed advice and support to a client is a valuable practice skill. This is also the case in helping clients protect themselves from a landlord who is harassing them or attempting to evict them unlawfully.

1.4   HOUSING BENEFIT

Entitlement to housing benefit is of crucial importance to large numbers of social work clients. In the same way that social security entitlement is an area of specialist expertise so also is housing benefit entitlement, so that social workers should have an understanding of the principles of the system rather than a comprehensive working knowledge. The availability of specialist housing benefits advisers or rights agencies will reduce the burden on individual social workers but a familiarity with the principles of the housing benefit scheme will again allow social workers to provide preliminary informed advice and support to clients seeking to claim the benefit or challenge the decisions of the local authorities who administer them.

1.5   CONTENT

In the same way that the chapter on social security benefits seeks to provide a basic understanding of the social security system so will this chapter offer basic information on a range of housing law issues which have a particular impact on social work clients. Together these issues can be viewed as a package of housing rights which can be enforced, through the law if necessary, to the benefit of clients.

1.6   THE SOCIAL WORK ROLE

The role of the social worker, in relation to 'housing rights' will be determined by a number of factors which include the nature of their employment (eg social services, voluntary sector, residential work, probation officer), the availability, or otherwise, of specialist housing rights advice and expertise, the willingness of local authorities to comply with their legal duties in the field of housing rights, and importantly, their own ability in terms of housing rights knowledge and skills. As a minimum social workers should have a basic understanding of the provisions and principles in the field of housing rights so that they are able to 'identify a problem', ensure that a client does not act to their own detriment and refer a client on to specialist help where that is necessary, whilst all the time being able to offer informed basic advice and support.

2   THE LAW

2.1   HOMELESSNESS

The Housing (Homeless Persons) Act 1977 placed important duties on local government housing authorities in respect of people who are homeless. These duties are now contained in Part III of the Housing Act 1985 and though they do not amount to a right to a home for people who are homeless they do provide a route for some people to secure accommodation. The law gives local authorities a significant amount of discretion in the way they exercise their duties though the Act is supported by a Code of Guidance which indicates to local authorities how the provisions of the Act should be put into practice. Authorities are required by the 1985 Act to have regard to the Code but it is not legally enforceable so that the attitude of individual authorities to people who are homeless will vary considerably. Though most local authorities, especially in the big cities, are very short of housing stock, some authorities are sympathetic to people who are homeless whilst others are conspicuous in their determination to avoid all but their basic duties under the Act.

It is perhaps easiest to see the provisions of Part III of the Housing Act as establishing a number of conditions which need to be fulfilled by the person who is homeless in their application for accommodation.

2.1.1 Is the applicant homeless or threatened with homelessness?

The law specifies situations in which people will be considered as being homeless or being threatened with homelessness:

— there is no accommodation which they are legally entitled to occupy;

— they have accommodation but there is a danger of violence if they live there;

— they are living in emergency or crisis accommodation, eg a refuge;

— they have accommodation which does not provide for the family unit which is split up because they have nowhere to live together;

— they have accommodation but it is not reasonable for them to stay in it because of eg overcrowding or the standard of the accommodation (this criterion is relative in the sense that the accommodation is subject to comparison with prevailing accommodation conditions in the area);

— they have accommodation but cannot secure entry to it eg because of illegal eviction.

Being threatened with homelessness is defined as having accommodation but likely to be homeless within 28 days.

If the housing authority has reason to believe that an applicant is a person who is homeless or threatened with homelessness they must make inquiries to ascertain the circumstances.

So the first step is to get the housing authority to accept (after their inquiries if necessary) that the applicant for accommodation is a person who is homeless or threatened with homelessness.

2.1.2   Is there a priority need?

Section 59 defines four categories of people with a priority need:

— a person with dependent children living with them or who might reasonably be expected to live with them;

— a person who is homeless through flood, fire or disaster;

— a person, and anyone who might reasonably be expected to live with them, who is especially vulnerable because of age, disability or other special reasons;

— a woman who is pregnant or the woman with whom the person is living or might reasonably be expected to live is pregnant.

Two categories of priority need are of particular interest to social work. The applicant with children is treated as a 'family' even though their children may be being looked after by a local authority or have gone to live elsewhere when the family was made homeless. By treating such an applicant as a 'family' a priority need is established so that accommodation should be provided for the applicant and children to live together as a family. This is intended to prevent homelessness being the cause of a family breaking up and the children being accommodated by a local authority on a long term basis.

A number of social work clients may be considered as 'vulnerable' so that they have a priority need under the terms of the Act. The definition of 'vulnerable' is clearly important and the Code of Guidance identifies people with a mental disorder or learning disability and people with a physical disability and people who are blind, deaf or dumb as vulnerable. Housing authorities are also told by the Code to consider as vulnerable those who are above the normal retirement age and those who are approaching retirement age and are particularly frail or in poor health. Some housing authorities are prepared to accept women without children who have been assaulted by their partner and young people at risk as vulnerable. It should be noted that the vulnerability must be established, it is not assumed automatically because of disability etc. Social workers clearly have some space for persuading housing authorities that a client is vulnerable and thereby getting them accepted as having a priority need.

2.1.3   Is the applicant intentionally homeless?

Section 60 defines intentional homelessness in terms of the applicant deliberately doing or failing to do something the result of which is that they have ceased to occupy accommodation which is available for their occupation and which it is reasonable for them to occupy. Examples are leaving accommodation or being evicted because of non-payment of rent.

It is up to the housing authority to establish the intentionality of an applicant's homelessness and they may take past events into account in reaching their decision. Decisions on intentionality must take all relevant matters into account and they must be reasonable. It is not surprising therefore that there has been a considerable amount of case law on what amounts to intentional homelessness.

2.1.4   Does the applicant have a local connection?

By section 61 housing authorities can avoid their statutory responsibilities to make accommodation available where they do not accept that the applicant, and anyone who might reasonably be expected to live with them, has a local connection with their authority AND where they do have a local connection with another authority in England, Wales or Scotland.

Local connections might be established by residence in the authority's area for six months out of the last year or three years out of the last five or by employment in the area or by having close family in the area for at least five years or by any other special connections with the area.

If the applicant is entitled to permanent accommodation under the other three conditions then that responsibility can be transferred to the authority to which the applicant does have a local connection.

2.1.5   What is the applicant entitled to?

a)   An applicant who has satisfied the three conditions of i) being homeless, ii) having a priority need and iii) not being intentionally homeless, is entitled to have suitable accommodation made available for them and those who might reasonably be expected to live with them, by the housing authority.

b)   Applicants who are homeless and have a priority need BUT who are also intentionally homeless are only entitled under the Act to advice and help with finding accommodation and temporary accommodation sufficient to give them time to make their own arrangements, after which no further duty is owed.

c)   Applicants who are homeless but have no priority need are only entitled to advice and assistance directed to finding accommodation.

2.1.6   Challenging housing authority decisions about homelessness

Though Part III of the Housing Act imposes duties on local authorities in relation to the homeless, authorities have considerable discretion in how those duties are interpreted and administered. As a result the ability of an applicant to challenge the decisions made by the authority is crucial. A major omission of the Act is the absence of any rights of appeal for the applicant so that any challenge to the authority has to be made through an application for judicial review. This complex legal process is available, subject to a requirement of leave (permission to bring the case), in the Divisional Court of the Queen's Bench Division of the High Court. Such a challenge can only be made on the basis that the authority exercised its discretionary powers unlawfully eg by not considering some important fact. Judicial review is legally very complex and only provides remedies at the discretion of the court. A House of Lords decision in 1986[1] has made it clear that judicial review should not be used to compensate for the lack of effective rights of appeal and that applications will only be entertained in exceptional circumstances.

2.2 SECURITY OF TENURE

For a large number of people living in rented accommodation the security, or otherwise, of their tenure in that accommodation is often a matter of considerable concern. Security of tenure is an issue which goes to the heart of housing law and its complexity is such that only a very basic outline can be provided in a book of this nature. Social work clients who are unsure of their housing tenure rights or who receive a notice to quit their accommodation or who think they face eviction should seek specialist advice as soon as possible.

2.2.1 Tenancies and licences

The vast majority of those who are living in accommodation as a tenant have established rights of tenure and can only be lawfully evicted by a court order.

Licensees have only a permission to occupy accommodation and therefore have no security of tenure though a court order will be required to obtain the eviction of most licensees.

It is important therefore to be able to identify whether someone is occupying accommodation as a tenant or as a licensee. The title given to any 'accommodation agreement' is not conclusive as to its true nature and the indications that an agreement constitutes a tenancy are the payment of rent and the right of exclusive possession.

2.2.2 Private tenants

a) Where the tenant moved in *before 15.1.89* and:

— they have exclusive possession of at least one room;

[1] *Puhlhofer v London Borough of Hillingdon* [1986] 1 All ER 467.

— there is no resident landlord;

— no meals or substantial services are provided by the landlord;

then there is likely to be a *fully protected tenancy (a regulated tenancy)* with the result that:

— the landlord must establish grounds for possession set out in the Rent Act 1977;

— the tenant cannot be evicted without a court order;

— the tenant may apply for a fair rent to be established.

A number of tenancies which began before 15.1.89 are not fully protected by the Rent Act 1977. These include tenancies where:

— the rateable value is very high;

— where the rent is very low;

— the rent includes a payment for 'board';

— where the rent includes payment for a substantial amount of personal services for the tenant;

— the letting is to a student by an educational institution;

— there is a holiday letting.

b) Where the tenant moved in *on or after 15.1.89* and:

— the tenant has exclusive possession of at least one room;

— there is no resident landlord;

then the tenancy will be covered by the Housing Act 1988 and must be either an *assured tenancy* or an *assured shorthold tenancy*.

i. *Assured tenancy:*

— possession will only be possible through a court order;

— the tenant will pay a market rent;

ii. *Assured shorthold tenancy:*

— the tenant's right to remain in the property will be determined by the length of the tenancy agreement (minimum of six months);

— possession will be granted by a court order;

— the tenant will pay a market rent.

2.2.3 Housing association tenants

a)   Tenants who moved in *prior to 15.1.89* have a *secure tenancy* with the result that:

— they can only be evicted by a court order on proof of grounds;

— a fair rent will be registered;

— the tenant will enjoy a number of rights known as the 'Tenant's Charter'; including the right to buy (except where the association is a charitable housing association), the right to take in lodgers and the right, in certain circumstances, to carry out repairs.

b)   Tenants who moved in *on or after 15.1.89* will have an *assured tenancy* with the result that:

— eviction will only be possible through a court order;

— there is no entitlement to a fair rent;

— there is no right to buy.

2.2.4 Council tenants

Council tenants have a *secure tenancy* with the result that:

— eviction will only be possible through a court order;

— the rent will be fixed by the council;

— the tenant will enjoy the rights of the 'Tenant's Charter' including the right to buy.

Tenants who think that their security is in any way threatened, eg by receipt of a notice to quit, must get immediate specialist advice.

A list of housing aid centres and law centres, who will be able to provide the necessary help appears in the Housing Rights Guide published by SHAC (see the addresses and materials sections at the end of the chapter).

2.3   PROTECTION FROM EVICTION

The eviction of tenants by a landlord without the necessary legal powers is a crime. Harassment is committed by landlords who try to get tenants out directly or indirectly by threats or violence or by withdrawing services such as water and gas. Both harassment and unlawful eviction are criminal offences under the Protection from Eviction Act 1977, as amended by the Housing Act 1988, and may also be the basis for a civil action. Once civil proceedings have begun a tenant may be able to obtain an interim injunction preventing the landlord continuing the harassment or stopping any attempt to evict the tenant. This interim injunction may be confirmed as permanent at a full hearing and a tenant who has been harassed or illegally evicted may be entitled to substantial damages.

A criminal prosecution for illegal eviction or harassment may be brought by a local authority tenancy relations officer. A successful prosecution can result in a fine and the court can make a criminal compensation award to the victim.

2.4   LICENSEES

The majority of licensees come within the provisions of the Protection from Eviction Act 1977 with the result that a landlord wishing to evict them must serve a written notice and obtain a court order before evicting them.

2.5   HOUSING REPAIRS

The condition of many rented flats and houses is very poor, sometimes to the extent that it affects the health of those living in such accommodation. Responsibilities concerning the fabric and repair of rented accommodation are regulated by statute and by the terms of the lease under which the property is occupied. The legal aspect of housing repairs is again very complex and specialist help should be sought. The environmental health department of a local authority may take on the task of enforcing repairs on behalf of private tenants. Independent advice will be available from law centres, housing aid centres, housing advice centres and citizens' advice bureaux.

2.5.1 Statutory responsibilities of landlords under section 11 of the Landlord and Tenant Act 1985

Where a tenancy, which is not for a fixed term of more than 7 years, has been granted after 24.10.61, section 11 of the Landlord and Tenant Act 1985 implies into that tenancy agreement an obligation on the landlord to keep in repair the structure and exterior of the accommodation, basins, sinks, baths and other sanitary installations in the dwelling; and installations for heating water and space heating.

Tenants can enforce these duties against a landlord who has not done the repairs, after reasonable notice, by an action in the county court for an order that the repairs are done and for appropriate damages.

Tenants can also ask the local authority environmental health department to inspect the property and take action against the landlord.

2.5.2 Local authority responsibilities

Local authority environmental health officers have wide powers under the Housing Act 1985 and the Environmental Protection Act 1990 to enforce the principle that private tenants should not be forced to live in accommodation that is likely to affect the health and safety of tenants or that is unfit for human habitation.

The Environmental Protection Act 1990 provides that where a local authority is satisfied that there is a statutory nuisance it must serve an abatement notice on the person responsible. In relation to premises a statutory nuisance is defined as 'any premises in such a state as to be prejudicial to health or a nuisance' (section 79). SHAC's *Housing Rights Guide* identifies examples: dampness, leaking roof, broken bannisters, rotten floorboards, piles of rubbish, dangerous wiring, falling slates and rotten window frames. The abatement notice will specify the necessary repairs and a time within which they must be completed. If the order is not complied with the local authority may apply to the magistrates' court for an order against the landlord which may be enforced by a fine and compensation order where appropriate. In the event of continuing default the necessary repairs can be undertaken by the local authority with the cost recovered from the landlord. Expedited orders are available under the Act where urgent repairs are needed. Criticism of these powers centres on i) the delay which is often involved; ii) the reluctance of some authorities to take action; and iii) the fact that the Act may tackle only the manifestation of a problem which may return in time.

Tenants can take a landlord to court themselves under section 82 of the Act where the level of disrepair constitutes a statutory nuisance.

The Housing Act 1985 provides local authorities with wide powers to deal with disrepair. If a property is found to be unfit then the authority can order that appropriate repairs be carried out or that it be closed thereby preventing anyone from living in it.

Unfitness is defined by reference to standards of repair, stability, freedom from damp, internal arrangement, natural lighting and ventilation, water supply, drainage, sanitary provision, facilities for the preparation and cooking of food, and the disposal of waste water.

If the accommodation can be brought up to the required standard of repair at reasonable expense then the environmental health officer can serve a repair notice which can be enforced by court action if necessary. Improvement notices may also be served which require the landlord to install certain amenities and improve the property to a particular standard. If this is not possible then the accommodation must no longer be used for human habitation; it must be closed and the occupier must be rehoused.

If the property is not unfit, but in substantial disrepair or in bad enough condition to interfere with the comfort of the tenant, then the authority can serve a notice on the landlord under section 190 of the Housing Act 1985 giving details of the repairs needed and a time in which the work must be completed. If the landlord fails to do the work the local authority can do the work themselves and claim the cost from the landlord.

Council tenants have essentially the same rights in relation to repairs as private tenants under the Landlord and Tenant Act 1985 and section 82 of the Environmental Protection Act 1990. However, because councils cannot serve 'repair notices' on themselves tenants cannot use legislation which would in effect require environmental health officers to serve notices on their own authority. This excludes the provisons of the Housing Act 1985 and the Environmental Protection Act 1990 discussed above though an informal system of notification exists under which environmental health officers called in by council tenants will notify housing departments of repairs which would have led to notices being issued under the Act against a private landlord.

Council tenants have the right to do minor repairs themselves and to seek reimbursement from the authority.

Housing association tenants have all the same rights in respect of repairs as private tenants. They also have a right to repair and to seek payment from the association.

2.6 HOUSING BENEFIT

2.6.1 Principles

Housing benefit is a means tested benefit which provides help with rent for those with low incomes. It is administered by local authorities. The law concerning housing benefit is contained in the Social Security Act 1986 and in regulations made under the Act, principally the Housing Benefit (General) Regulations 1987.

It is possible to distinguish between 'passported housing benefit' which is available for income support claimants, and 'means tested housing benefit' which is available to those who do not receive income support and therefore need to have their means assessed for housing benefit purposes.

2.6.2 Elements of housing benefit

Housing benefit is made up of distinct elements:

— rent rebate for council tenants;

— a rent allowance for housing association and private tenants.

2.6.3 Rates

Passported housing benefit is normally paid to income support/ housing benefit claimants at 100% of their 'eligible' rent.

Means tested housing benefit will be paid to housing benefit claimants on a sliding scale based on a comparison between their income and their 'applicable amount' for housing benefit purposes.

2.6.4 Payment

Housing benefit is paid in a variety of ways. Council tenants will receive it by way of a deduction in their rent so if housing benefit is paid at 100% then council tenants will not pay any rent. Private tenants will receive their housing benefit directly from the local authority or it may be paid to the landlord direct.

2.6.5 Assessment and calculation

The important elements of the housing benefit calculation are the applicable amount, income (if not on income support), eligible rent and deductions for non-dependants living in the claimant's home.

Applicable amount

The applicable amount of a housing benefit claimant is calculated by reference to personal allowances, which reflect the family composition of the claimant, together with any premiums to which the claimant, partner and dependants are entitled. All the appropriate amounts are included in 'scale rates' which are uprated each year.

Income

In most respects the calculation of income is the same as is done for income support so that it is aggregated and includes earned income, other income and capital. The capital cut off is, however, set at £16,000 so that any claimant with capital of under £16,000 may be entitled to housing benefit though capital over £3000 will be taken to produce a tariff weekly income of £1 for every unit of £250 over the £3000.

Eligible housing costs

Housing costs which are met through the housing benefit scheme are rent, and some service charges in very limited circumstances.

A number of housing costs are NOT eligible for housing benefit; these include:

— water rates;

— business rates;

— mortgage interest and the interest on home improvement loans;

— payments under a co-ownership scheme;

— charges for fuel or meals.

Housing benefit assessment is thus normally based on the actual amount of rent due. Regulations provide that the assessment can be based on a lower figure if the rent is unreasonably high compared to rent for suitable alternative accommodation or the accommodation is unreasonably large for the people living in it. If a local authority decide to employ this 'rent stop' the assessment of housing benefit will be based on a rent figure the authority consider appropriate.

Non-dependants deductions

Regulations provide a scale of deductions to be made to a claimant's housing benefit in respect of certain non-dependants who live in the same household.

2.6.6 Challenging a housing benefit decision

Applications for housing benefit are made to the claimant's local authority and the decision on a claim must be notified to the claimant in writing. A full statement detailing how a particular housing benefit decision has been reached must be provided by the authority on request.

Claimants can require the authority to review their housing benefit decision and on completion of the reconsideration a written decision with reasons must be provided.

The claimant has the right to a second review, or 'appeal', to be heard by a review board made up of local authority councillors acting independently of the authority. The claimant has the right to be heard by the review board and may be represented though legal aid is not available. The board must provide a written decision.

There are no further appeal procedures but the decision of the review board may be challenged through an application for judicial review.

3 SOCIAL WORK LAW AND PRACTICE: some issues for discussion

3.1 OTHER ASPECTS OF HOUSING FOR PARTICULAR SOCIAL WORK CLIENTS

Though housing is an issue in which social workers do not have direct statutory powers or duties there are nevertheless areas of practice which are circumscribed by statutory duties which involve housing matters.

Even without reference to specialised housing or homelessness legislation many field social workers working with clients who are ill, have a physical disability or learning difficulty, will find significant aspects of their practice concerned with housing. Thus any attempt to provide a definition of 'housing rights' for social work would have to include the access of clients to Part III accommodation and the availability of alterations and adaptions to clients' homes provided for by the Chronically Sick and

Disabled Persons Act. The community care provisions of the National Health Service and Community Care Act 1990 relating to assessment and care service provision for clients who are disabled may also be relevant.

Section 21 of the National Assistance Act 1948 allows, and where the Secretary of State so directs requires, local authorities to arrange for the provision of (Part III) residential accommodation for 'persons who by reason of age, illness, disability or any other circumstances are in need of care and attention which is not otherwise available to them'.

Section 29 of the National Assistance Act 1948 establishes an enabling power for local authorities to promote the welfare of people who are disabled. Pursuant to that power the Chronically Sick and Disabled Persons Act 1970 provides by section 2(1)(e) for 'the provision of assistance for that person in arranging for the carrying out of any works of adaptation in his home or the provision of any additional facilities designed to secure his greater safety, comfort or convenience'.

It should also be remembered that the Social Fund provides community care grants and it may be possible to persuade a social fund officer that a grant should be paid to a client on income support for furniture, minor structural repairs and maintenance costs, redecoration and refurbishment and other similar expenses where such a grant is connected with establishing the client in the community or preventing them having to enter institutional care.

3.2   ENFORCING 'HOUSING RIGHTS'

It should be clear that any discussion of 'housing rights' is a particularly broad discussion and in this book it also includes material covered in other chapters.

Talking in terms of 'rights' is problematic in a number of respects. Housing law is complex and it is unlikely that many clients will be able to enforce their 'housing rights' without specialist advice and assistance. Few field social workers will have such an expertise and it is likely therefore that clients will have to be referred to one of the (fortunately) many specialist housing aid or housing advice centres. Such expertise is also available from law centres and from a number of solicitors who specialise in housing law; though advice and assistance from a solicitor will have to be paid for. Currently the green form scheme provides the necessary access for those who do not have the resources to pay private legal fees though the legal aid board has indicated that it may at some time in the future withdraw welfare rights and housing rights advice from the green form scheme and contract for the provision of such legal advice and assistance with appropriate advice agencies and solicitors.

Access to specialist advice and even to the courts cannot guarantee the adequate attainment of all 'housing rights'. There is a chronic shortage of adequate accommodation; as a 'scarce resource' housing has to be rationed. In the private sector this rationing is achieved by the housing market in the sense that the availability and cost of accommodation for sale and for rent largely determines the supply of accommodation. In the public sector the availability and cost of local authority and housing association accommodation achieves an equivalent rationing. Housing benefit modifies the rationing effect of cost but does nothing to increase the supply of a scarce resource.

Those who are prevented from securing accommodation by this process of rationing are often forced to seek help from local authorities under the homelessness provisions of the Housing Act 1985. In many ways the discretionary powers of local authorities under the Act over issues such as priority need and intentional homelessness allow authorities to lessen their responsibilities under the Act should they wish to do so. Even where an applicant is accepted as being a person who is homeless unintentionally and having a priority need most housing authorities do not have a stock of empty dwellings available to accommodate successful applicants. Many authorities will discharge their responsibilities by paying for bed and breakfast accommodation often on a long term basis.

In such a scenario local authority field social workers will often find themselves acting as crisis managers for people who are homeless and as an advocate and negotiator with the housing authority on behalf of such clients. Their responsibilities may not end with the provision of accommodation. Clients defined as having a priority need in relation to accommodation are also likely to have 'social work' needs. As an example families with young children forced to live in bed and breakfast accommodation will require whatever support and help can be offered under Part III and Schedule 2 of the Children Act 1989 so as to support and promote the care and upbringing of the children by their family.

People with a mental disorder who are homeless will often require social work support for their vulnerability exists in respect of both housing and social work needs. The policy of closing a number of long stay psychiatric hospitals has meant that significant numbers of patients with a mental disorder have been discharged into the community without adequate after-care and support. This is despite the National Health Service and Community Care Act 1990 and the provisions of section 117 of the Mental Health Act which provides for statutory after-care to be provided by the local social services authority together with the district health authority for discharged patients who have been detained for treatment under section 3 or under a hospital order and those transferred to hospital from prison. Many of those being discharged under the current policy of community care do not receive appropriate after-care nor do they have their community care needs appropriately assessed or provided for.

Many such ex-patients become homeless and either end up in bed and breakfast accommodation or sleeping rough. Social workers may have duties to such people under section 29 of the National Assistance Act, section 2 of the Chronically Sick and Disabled Persons Act 1970 and the National Health Service and Community Care Act 1990 but enforcement is problematic if not impossible and the financial resources for community care are inadequate. So although the housing needs of such clients may be 'satisfied' in the sense that the vulnerable should be entitled to housing under the homelessness legislation, appropriate accommodation and other support is often not available so that their 'social work' needs are not provided for.

4 CASE STUDIES

These case studies are primarily concerned with housing rights though they raise a number of other issues concerning social work practice. Responses can be limited to the housing issues but a broader consideration of how social work might respond to the circumstances faced by these clients will provide a more comprehensive and realistic discussion.

1.   Sharon is 19 and is living with her mother and stepfather in a small house. She does not get on with them and has violent arguments with her stepfather who hits her. She is pregnant and wants a flat of her own.

She has approached the social services department for help.

What help can be offered to her?

Is she entitled to accommodation from the housing authority?

2.   Hassan has been living in a bedsit in a house belonging to his landlord Derek for a year. Derek lives in a flat on the bottom floor of the house. The house is in a serious state of disrepair; the roof leaks, there is condensation everywhere and the wiring is dangerous. Hassan told Derek about the problems some months ago but nothing has been done. Last week he told Derek that he was going to complain to the council about the state of the house and his bedsit. Derek was abusive and yesterday Hassan received a letter from Derek which included the following threat:

If you don't get out of the house by the end of the week my brother will lock you out. He has a nasty temper.

Hassan is a client of yours and wants to know what his position is concerning the threat, his security of tenure and the repairs to his bedsit.

3.   Rena and Vassili are a married couple. Rena is pregnant. Before they got married they both lived in single rooms in bedsit accommodation. Vassili left his room after a row with his landlord over the rent. He moved in with Rena, but her room was so cramped that they left and moved in with her parents in the neighbouring town. They do not get on with her parents and would like to move into council accommodation in Hackney, the part of East London Vassili was brought up in as a child.

Advise them on the best course of action regarding their accommodation and explain their legal rights (if any) to obtain accommodation in Hackney.

4.   Alf has been a voluntary patient at a psychiatric hospital for the last five years. He was discharged three weeks ago when the hospital was closed. Though accommodation had been arranged for him he has been living rough since he left hospital. He says he went to have a look at the place but didn't like the look of it. He is clearly very depressed and withdrawn and his physical health is not good. He has a very bad cough and his clothes are dirty and damp.

Alf has been picked up by the police as he was taking a milk bottle from a front step. The police have rung the social services department and asked you, as the duty social worker, to 'take him on or we will have to charge him!'

What can you do?

5.   Suzy is 17 and has been living in London for a month since she arrived from Glasgow. She has been referred to you by the police after they raided a squat in a drugs raid. Suzy, who is very depressed and upset, tells you that she has been living in the squat and raising money by working as a prostitute and occasionally selling drugs for someone else who also lived in the squat. It transpires that she left home in Glasgow when she had a violent row with her boyfriend with whom she was sharing a bedsit.

Advise her on her entitlement, if any, to housing assistance.

5   ACTIVITIES

1.   Social workers should be aware of the policies and services provided by their local authority for people who are homeless. This information may be readily available to field social workers but may require social work students to investigate the situation.

2.   It is interesting to identify how the channel of communication between social services departments and housing authorities works. How, for example, does a social worker deal with a client who has local authority accommodation which is in need of urgent repair? What do you do if the repairs are not done?

3. Does the housing authority have a homeless persons unit? Are there any social workers attached to it? If so, how are cases and clients divided between them and social services?

4. It is important to know where independent specialist advice and assistance is available. Is there a law centre in your area? Which local solicitors will do housing rights work under the legal aid scheme? Is there a housing advice/aid centre in your area?

5. Build up a set of good reference materials including the Housing Booklets published by the Department of the Environment.

6. Get an up to date edition of the *Housing Rights Guide* which is published annually by SHAC.

7. Get hold of a copy of the *Department of Social Security Guide to Housing Benefit* from their leaflets section (address in chapter on social security).

8. Become familiar with the way in which your local authority handles enquiries and problems concerning housing benefit. If a client wants to have a review of the decision or take an appeal is there anyone who can give appropriate advice and assistance?

6 ADDRESSES

CHAR (Housing Campaign for Single People),
5–15 Cromer Street,
London WC1H 8LS.
Phone 071 833 2071.

Child Poverty Action Group Ltd (Publications),
1–5 Bath Street,
London EC1V 9PY.
Phone 071 253 3406.

Department of the Environment,
PO Box 135,
Bradford,
W. Yorks BD9 4HU.

SHAC (London Housing Aid Centre),
189A Old Brompton Road,
London SW5 OAR.
Phone 071 373 7276

Shelter (National Campaign
for the Homeless),
88 Old Street,
London EC1V 9HU.
Phone 071 253 0202.

Shelter Wales,
57 Walter Road,
Swansea SA1 5PZ.
Phone 0792 469400.

7 MATERIALS

7.1 HOUSING RIGHTS MATERIALS FOR BASIC SOCIAL WORK PRACTICE

Department of the Environment Housing Booklets:

No 1   *The Tenants' Charter.*
No 2   *Right to Repair.*
No 19   *Assured Tenancies: Lettings under the Housing Act 1988.*
No 20   *Repairs.*
No 21   *'He wants me out'. Protection against harassment and illegal eviction.*
No 24   *Notice That You Must Leave.*
No 25   *Regulated Tenancies.*
No 26   *The Rights and Duties of Landlords and Tenants of Houses.*
No 27   *The Management of Flats.*
No 29   *Guide for the Tenants of Housing Associations.*

'Guide to Housing Benefit' Department of Social Security.

'Housing Rights Guide' (Published annually) SHAC.

SHAC Leaflets: 'The Housing Act and You';
i.   *Housing Association Tenants*;
ii.   *Private Tenants*.

Shelter Factsheets on Homelessness and Disrepair. Shelter.

Shelter Practice Notes:

— *Unfitness.*

— *Overcrowding.*

7.2   FURTHER READING

McKenny J., Thompson L. *Rights Guide for Home Owners* (9th edn 1992–93) SHAC and Child Poverty Action Group.

Arden, A. *Homeless Persons* (3rd edn, 1988) Legal Action Group.

Arden, A. *Manual of Housing Law* (1989) Sweet and Maxwell.

Luba, J. *Repairs: Tenants Rights* (1990) Legal Action Group.

Index